Compared to the voluminous writings on female sex workers, much less is known about their clients. Filling this gap, *Why Men Buy Sex* is nothing short of ground-breaking. Birch's book is a comprehensive study of male clients in Australia – documenting their demographic background, the services they buy, the reasons why they buy sex, and how they feel about it. Using both survey questionnaires with a large number of clients, as well as in-depth interviews with a subsample of them, the book shows that they do not fit conventional stereotypes, that they have a wide variety of motives and experiences, and that many of them develop long-term relationships with the women they encounter.

Ronald Weitzer, *Professor of Sociology,*
George Washington University, USA

Providing more much-needed detailed analysis about men who purchase sex from women, this book offers a contemporary overview of the existing literature, as well as showcasing a significant mixed method study on men who procure sex in New South Wales. Offering new ways of theorising motivations through quantitative modelling, in the context of creeping criminalisation, this volume provides an important contribution to knowledge and debate on this subject.

Teela Sanders, *Reader in Sociology, School of Sociology & Social Policy,*
University of Leeds, UK

Why Men Buy Sex

Sex work has been a contentious issue in a variety of ways throughout history – socially, morally, ethically, religiously and politically. Traditionally noted as one of the oldest professions in the world, sex work has commonly been demonised and is often viewed as a social disgrace. While sex work involves both providers of sexual services, most commonly women, and purchasers of sexual services, most commonly men, providers have attracted the most social commentary. Recent research shows that a limited number of studies have been conducted since 1990 concerning men who procure sexual services. This book aims to help reset this balance.

In this book, Philip Birch examines the procurement of female sexual services with a focus on the personal and social aspects of men who procure such exchanges and offers insight into the demographics amongst men who purchase sexual services, alongside an analysis of the reasons why they purchase sex. This book brings together existing literature with analyses of new data to develop a multi-factor model reflecting men's procurement of sexual services and demonstrates the complexities surrounding the procuration of these sexual services in exchange for money.

The book considers what contribution the understanding of the personal and social aspects of men who procure sexual services has on re-theorising the purchasing of sex in the twenty-first century and will be of interest to academics and students involved in the study of criminology, criminal justice, social policy, law, sociology, sexuality and gender studies.

Philip Birch, BSocSci (Hons); PG Cert (HEP); PG Cert (SSRM); PG Dip (SocSci.); MSc; PhD, is a criminologist and lecturer in Policing, Criminal and Community Justice at UWS, Australia. He has held posts at UNSW, Australia and the University of Huddersfield, UK. Prior to entering academia Philip worked as a criminologist in the field, holding posts in the UK prison service, as well as in the crime and disorder field, which involved managing a specialist crime unit. Philip researches the areas of aggression and the management and treatment of offenders, as well as sex work.

Philip is the editor in chief of the *Journal of Criminological Research, Policy and Practice* (JCRPP) and currently sits on the editorial board of the *Journal of Aggression, Conflict and Peace Research* (Emerald Publishing).

Routledge studies in crime and society

Why Men Buy Sex

Examining sex worker clients

Philip Birch

Routledge
Taylor & Francis Group

LONDON AND NEW YORK

First published 2015
by Routledge
2 Park Square, Milton Park, Abingdon, Oxfordshire OX14 4RN

and by Routledge
711 Third Avenue, New York, NY 10017

First issued in paperback 2016

Routledge is an imprint of the Taylor & Francis Group, an informa business

British Library Cataloguing in Publication Data
A catalogue record for this book is available from the British Library

Library of Congress Cataloging-in-Publication Data
Birch, Philip (Criminologist)
Why men buy sex: examining sex worker clients / Philip Birch. – First Edition.
    pages cm. – (Routledge studies in crime and society; 17)
    1. Prostitutes' customers. 2. Prostitutes. 3. Men–Sexual behavior.
    I. Title.
    HQ118.B57 2015
    306.70811–dc23   2014036288

ISBN 13: 978-1-138-28852-2 (pbk)
ISBN 13: 978-0-415-73848-4 (hbk)

Typeset in Times New Roman
by Wearset Ltd, Boldon, Tyne and Wear

This book is dedicated to (Professor) Jane L. Ireland and (Dr) Carol A. Ireland. Since first meeting you both in 1993 not only have you become my long time research collaborators and colleagues, but you have become my family. You have played, and continue to do so, a significant role in the development and direction of my career. Thank you for all you have done, and continue to do for me!

Contents

Figures

Tables

Acknowledgements

I would first like to thank the men who procure sexual services in New South Wales (NSW), Australia for taking part in this study. Without their involvement, contribution and enthusiasm for this research, this volume would not have been possible. I would also like to thank the female sex workers, clergy, medics and the women's collective groups in NSW who gave up their time to participate. The data obtained from these groups added richness and depth to the body of data provided by the male clients. The participation of all these groups is unique in this field of research. I would also like to thank SWOP (the Sydney based Sex Worker Project), who kindly reviewed the data collection tools used in the study and supported the recruitment of participants. Thanks also to Sage, who kindly gave me permission to reproduce a short extract from one of their journals in Chapter 3. Permission has also been granted from the World Health Organization (WHO) and Springer (both in Chapter 7).

Acknowledgements are also paid to colleagues who have contributed helpful comments, advice and guidance in relation to this work: Dr Desmond McDonnell, Professor Richard Hugman, Professor Jane Ireland and Professor Eileen Baldry.

Abbreviations

ABS	Australian Bureau of Statistics
ACT	Australian Capital Territory
ANZSOC	Australian and New Zealand Standard Offence Classification
GLM	Good Lives Model
MAPSS	Multi-factor analysis choice model for the procurement of sexual services
NSW	New South Wales
NWIA	National Wellness Institute of Australia
PERMA	Positive emotion, engagement, relationships, meaning and accomplishment
REA	Rapid evidence assessment
SAPSS	Single factor analysis choice model for the procurement of sexual services
UN	United Nations

Part I

Theorising sex work and the procurement of sexual services

Introduction

Sex work has been a contentious matter over time in a variety of ways – socially, morally, ethically, religiously and politically. Noted as one of the oldest professions in the world (Matthews, 2008), sex work involves providers of sexual services, most commonly women, and purchasers of sexual services, most commonly men: providers have attracted the most social commentary. This book will examine this lesser explored aspect of sex work, the procurement of sexual services by male purchasers. It is acknowledged that sex work encompasses many aspects, such as male sex work as well as cultural differences in relation to the procurement of sexual services. It has been and is associated in certain circumstances with abhorrent and criminal acts, such as child prostitution, people trafficking and smuggling, sexual coercion and organised crime. This volume, though, will focus on the procurement of sexual services from heterosexual female providers by male purchasers within a de-criminalised Western cultural context, with a view to understanding and making sense of some men's reasons for purchasing sex. The term 'sex worker' and 'sex work' rather than 'prostitute' and 'prostitution' will be employed in this volume by the author as a means of reflecting the focus of this book: a focus on voluntary, non-coerced exchanges of sexual services.

Sex work has been constructed variously as deviant and immoral, or as a normative function with a market value. Brooks Gordon (2006) documents that in the main, throughout 'Western' history a man's access to the provision of female sexual services was advocated as 'his' right, whereas 'she' (who sold her sexual services) attracted stigma and was a social disgrace. Documentation throughout history, for example in the medieval times, with particular reference to sex work in Europe, highlights the role of the Church and medical science in how the sex work industry was governed and subsequently perceived by society. Brooks Gordon (2006) documents how the Church redefined the sex work industry, from a business requiring payment to one of promiscuity. This provides a background to the way sex work is still considered to be an immoral act by some contemporary social groups. Brooks Gordon argues that religious teachings of the Church, in particular the Roman Catholic Church during the medieval times and beyond, supported by medical science, encouraged a man not to engage in sex with 'his' wife for non-procreational sex as this was said to be immoral and also dangerous as it often resulted in pregnancy leading to an increased chance of death during childbirth (Brooks Gordon, 2006). To redress this and to prevent rape and sodomy, men were encouraged to satisfy their sexual urges by using sex workers. More contemporaneously, modern feminist views, with particular reference to radical feminists such as Sheila Jeffreys (1997), have constructed sex work as patriarchal objectifying, sexual domination and violence towards women by men. This has long been reflected in some jurisdictions such as Sweden, the United Kingdom and most states of the United States of America where the purchasing of sex has been criminalised. So attitudes towards female sex work in Euro-Western cultures have been associated over recent centuries with deviancy, creating stigma, and in most parts of the world criminalisation.

However, not all historical documentation of sex work problematises it. Perkins (1991), for example, discusses the courtesan, a woman who was well educated and at the top of the social strata in society. Since around the mid-twentieth century, sex work has been reconceptualised by some to be a legitimate profession when willingly entered into and freely exited from. This has been the case for scholars such as Teela Sanders, Jane Pitcher, Hilary Kinnell and Ron Weitzer, to name but a few. Clients of sex workers too, are seen to be making a legitimate and valid choice in their procurement, rather than being perceived as passive agents who cannot control 'their' sexual urges. Debates regarding sex work raised by researchers, some of whom, like Roberta Pekins, have been sex workers, illustrate that most research and writing produced on this social practice are by those who are not directly involved in it. This may be why a misleading picture of this social practice is perpetuated.

Understanding why men purchase sex

Men who purchase sex, along with the sex worker who sells sex, are the main actors in the procurement of sexual service, yet understanding why men pay for sex has been poorly explored and theorised (Weitzer, 2005, 2009; Brooks Gordon, 2006). Commonly, sex work research has focussed on those who sell sexual services, with a small amount of attention paid towards those who purchase such services. As Weitzer acknowledges, those who procure sexual services are 'traditionally ignored' (2005: 224). Addressing this gap in the research will provide a more informed understanding of the practice of sex work.

Scholars such as Weitzer (2005; 2009) have criticised the lack of rigour in theoretical developments concerning sex work. Weitzer has argued that advancements have been politically motivated and based on overly descriptive research (Weitzer, 2005: 214–215). He proposes that developments in sex work research should use middle range theories applied to empirical data in order to examine and understand the variety of components that make up sex work, from supply to demand to pimp to the sauna receptionist. Weitzer critiques the standards of research used in order to establish the current knowledge base that surrounds the different aspects of the sex work industry, claiming that there are few primary research studies conducted where significant sample sizes have been used. This finding is echoed by Wilcox *et al.* (2009), who conducted a Rapid Evidence Assessment (REA) on men's procurement of sexual services. The REA was an examination of studies in the English language concerned with men's procurement of sexual services since 1990. Some 220 studies were identified and assessed, and from this 179 studies were verified as reliable and valid in terms of set criteria: research design, methodology/methods and analytical approach and demonstration of findings. Nevertheless, there was an over reliance on qualitative research methods, indicating a lack of quantitative research design, and a lack of mixed methods research drawing from quantitative and qualitative methodologies. The REA revealed, first, support for Weitzer's 2005 claim that procurers of sexual services are poorly researched, and second, that scholars, along with policy makers and legislators, attempting to categorise men and their behaviour are doing so with evidence from limited data sets.

This volume aims in part to address some of these shortcomings and to establish a new framework and direction for research on this topic area.

Current theorising on men who procure sexual services: a brief introduction

Recently, Monto and McRee (2005) coined the terms *'everyman perspective'* and *'peculiar man perspective'* as a means of categorising what they saw as the ways in which men who purchase sex were perceived. The *'everyman perspective'* suggests that some clients of sex workers are no different from any other man, whilst the *'peculiar man perspective'* implies that some clients of sex workers have some unique qualities, such as being psychologically deficient, socially inadequate or sexually deviant. This conceptualisation of men who procure sexual services reflects and reinforces the binary conceptualisation of the sex work industry as deviant/immoral or as normative with a market value. This volume will use Monto and McRee's typology of men who procure sexual services when considering sex work as deviant and sex work as normative in order to frame these discussions.

Since the 1960s, social scientists have attempted to offer an understanding of men's procurement of sexual services by applying theoretical positions to explain this social practice. In this volume, the procurement of sexual services is referred to as a social practice. It is appropriate to apply this term for a number of reasons: the procurement of sexual services has been in existence for millennia and as the work in this volume will outline, in both the work of others and from within the empirical research underpinning this volume, this 'social practice' is a regular feature of these men's social lives and is a common practice. Theories of the 'individual' and the 'social' have been applied, and have, on the whole, been used to explain male procurement of sex as a negative social practice, supporting Monto and McRee's 'peculiar man perspective'. Even research in the 1980s, for example by McLeod (1982), which focused on men's procurement of a sexual service as a commodity, implied the purchasing and selling of sex as deviant. It was not until the new millennium that men's procurement of sexual services began to be considered as normative and to display a 'normative value'. This normative perspective is illustrated by the work of Sanders (2008a) and more recently by that of Milrod and Weitzer (2012). In these works, men's emotional and intimacy needs are evidenced as reasons for the procurement of sexual services. It is important to note here, that research seldom acknowledges women as purchasers of sexual services, or men as purchasers of sex with men. Weitzer uses these omissions to argue that the current understanding of this social practice is poor, and he uses *essentialist* and *normalisation* approaches to understanding the practices of the sex work industry. He argues that while such approaches may offer some understanding of the female supplier/male consumer transaction, it is not helpful in understanding other forms of this practice, for example between transgender supplier/consumer. However, although these social phenomena are even less understood than that of male purchasers of female sexual services as indicated earlier, they will not be explored in this volume.

Four frameworks used by scholars and commentators to understand men's involvement in this social practice – deviancy, power relations, normative value and exchange – are examined in the first part of this volume. Theories of *deviancy*, including pathology, and theories of '*power relations*', with particular reference to the influence of radical feminism, religion, the Church and the law in understanding men's procurement of sexual services as deviant and/or immoral are examined. In contrast, theories of *normative value and commodity*, considering behavioural and sexual scripts and how these guide behaviour can be used to understand sex work as legitimate and acceptable behaviour. These sit alongside theories of *exchange* that consider both social and sexual exchange and how humans are motivated by the purchasing of commodities. Whilst considering the theoretical perspectives of 'theories of normative value and commodity', to explain why men procure sexual services, a brief survey of feminism's pro sex work perspective will be undertaken; this strand of feminism supports and advocates sex work as a valid choice of occupation.

Each of the frameworks are examined and critiqued as a means of 'making sense of men's procurement of sexual services'. The approach and process adopted within this book begins to address what Weitzer claims is lacking in the discourse around the different elements of sex work concerning the poor theorising on the sex work industry as well as acknowledging how the 'meaning [customers] attached to paid encounters' is overlooked (2005: 225).

Aim of the study underpinning this volume

Based on a sample of a self-identified cohort of men who procure sexual services in NSW, Australia, the main aim of the empirical research that underpins this volume is to:

> Examine the procurement of female sexual services with a focus on the personal and social characteristics, reasons and experiences of men who procure such services.

The research aim is addressed by the following research questions, which are the focus of Part II of this volume:

1   Are there common demographics amongst a cohort of men who purchase sexual services in NSW and if so what are they?
2   What are the reasons men give for purchasing sexual services in NSW?
3   What services do men purchase within the sex work industry in NSW?
4   In relation to men who purchase sex, what are the views of particular groups in society with an interest in the sex work industry?
5   What contributions do these new understandings of the personal and social aspects of men who procure sexual services make to re-theorising this social practice in the twenty-first century?

Drawing on a mixed method approach to social research, this study was conducted in two phases. Phase one investigated the personal and social characteristics of men who procure sexual services, along with exploring their reasons for engaging in this behaviour, utilising a quantitative method, a questionnaire. The second phase of the research used in-depth interviews to examine the reasons men give for their procurement of sexual services. This second phase of data collection was extended to two other cohorts: female sex workers who were asked why they thought the men who procured their services did so, and specific groups in society: the clergy, health professionals and women's collective groups in NSW who were asked their views of men who procure sexual services from women. The findings from the two phases are brought together in order to examine why men procure sexual services. This provides a new understanding of the transaction of sexual services between female providers and male purchasers, in a non-coercive and regulated context, contributing to the debate regarding the morality and utility of this social practice and assisting to build theory in this field of study.

This study advances the under-theorised and under-examined area of why men purchase sex in the twenty-first century. It does this in a number of ways.

First, whilst sex work theorising can be traced to early written records in the Roman era (Brookes-Gordon, 2006: 2) the focus of such theorising has been on the female provider. Theorising of men's procurement of sexual services is relatively new, with Charles Winick in the 1960s the first social scientist to develop such a discourse. Understanding the procurement of sexual services from the client's perspective is still a relatively new area of study.

Second, the theorising that has been done since the 1960s has primarily viewed men's behaviour in purchasing sex, as deviant and pathological. Such behaviour could be argued to have been understood through a medical model over time. Some theorising has viewed men's procurement of sexual services as an economic issue, that is, men who purchased sex were doing so in the same way as they bought any other commodity. Very recently men's procurement of sex has been viewed through the lens of emotions and intimacy (Sanders, 2008a, 2008b; Milrod and Weitzer, 2012). A common feature of the small but growing body of literature examining men's procurement of sexual services, however, is the use of the single factorial explanation for this behaviour; that is men's procurement of sexual services is being explained using an 'either–or' approach, a binary method. Men purchase sex because they are deviant, or pathological, or purchasers of a commodity or because they are emotionally deprived. Current theorising on the procurement of sexual services is summarised in this volume though the creation of the SAPSS model (single factor analysis choice model for the procurement of sexual services). This volume explores the existing literature and analyses the data gathered, evidencing a multi-factorial understanding and explanation of men's procurement of sexual services and showing the complexities surrounding men's purchasing of sex. This complexity is shown through the development of the MAPSS model (multi-factor analysis choice model for the procurement of sexual services) based on the data gathered during this current research.

Third, the REA conducted by Wilcox *et al.* (2009) evidenced the limited number of quantitative studies conducted on men who procure sexual services. These quantitative studies were criticised for the limited numbers in the study samples, which in turn prevented robust statistical analysis. The data analysed in this book is from a sample of 309 men who purchase sexual services, making this one of the largest studies to date on a cohort of men who purchase sex.

The organisation of this book

The volume is divided into two parts and has eight chapters excluding the two introductory chapters of Parts I and II. Chapter 1 – 'Deconstructing sexuality and understanding the procurement of sex' draws upon key theories from disciplinary domains such as biology, psychology and sociology. Theorists such as Freud, Kinsey and Ellis have all contributed to the debate on sexual identity and behaviours; therefore this chapter plays a significant role in theoretically contextualising this volume. Within Chapter 1, 'sex' is understood to be more than a natural desire, with the social and cultural contexts playing an important role in how 'sex' is performed. This provides insight into why a social practice such as sex work takes place. The deconstruction of 'sex' is also considered in relation to gender. Chapter 1 sets the scene for why sex can be and has been understood as deviant/immoral or as playing a normative function in society and in an individual's (sexual) identity.

Chapter 2 'Understanding sex work 1: deviant and immoral', examines sex work through the theoretical lens of deviancy and institutional power relations, namely perspectives from theorists in law and radical feminism. This chapter outlines how deviancy is defined and considers the procurement of sexual services as an act of deviancy. Consideration is given to the stigma associated with those involved in the sex work industry and how this promotes deviancy by the breeching of social norms evident in mores and the law. The criminal, religious, moral, political and legislative guidance and control that are argued to reduce and prevent such an activity from occurring are discussed, as are patriarchal relations favouring men's hyper-masculine promiscuous behaviours and the objectification of women. It is also acknowledged in this chapter that aspects of the sex work industry are abhorrent and are crimes against women (and men) who are trafficked and coerced into sex work. This chapter concludes that through a process of definition, men who procure sexual services are socially constructed as deviant.

Chapter 3 – 'Understanding sex work 2: normative values and commodity', considers sex work through the theoretical lens of power relations from a gender oppression perspective, namely pro sex work feminists, normative values and behaviour and economic models. Such theoretical framings of this social practice lend themselves to viewing the procurement of sexual services as part of the market economy in which sex work is a valuable service to society, as well as arguing for freedom of choice for those involved in sex work. Examining sex work and the procurement of sexual services through these theoretical lenses suggests that the provision and purchasing of sex is linked to a number of pro-social issues, including sex as socially functional and to the buying (and selling) of sex as a right. An aspect of purchasing sex as a pro-social activity is made through the argument in this chapter that some men who experience low self-esteem and poor social skills, and who lack skills to pursue intimacy address these personal issues through their engagement in the sex work industry. The purchasing of sexual services may be the only consensual way these men can fulfil their sexual needs and attend to their emotional well being. This chapter concludes by bringing together the key theoretical perspectives presented in Chapters 2 and 3 and introduces the reader to the SAPSS model. The SAPSS model is the first step, based on existing literature and evidence, towards 'making sense' of men's procurement of sexual services. This chapter concludes Part I of this volume and the theorising of sex work and the procurement of sexual services.

Part II of this book centres on rethinking sex work through the examination of the procurement of sexual services and introduces the reader to the empirical research that underpins this book. Beginning with Chapter 4, entitled 'Contextualising the cohort: the personal and social characteristics of men who procure sexual services', this chapter is the first of three empirically based chapters and discusses the findings, primarily from the first phase data collection in which 309 men in NSW, Australia were surveyed. From the data, an understanding of the demographic background of the sample is identified, including an age profile, ethnic background, occupational status and marital status of the men. Further data analysis provides information on the sexual satisfaction of those men who are married or living in a de facto relationship, and the men's disclosure of their purchasing of sex. This chapter also draws on some of the qualitative data from the male interviews in which a deeper understanding of some of these variables is sought from the personal experiences and lives of some men who procure sexual services. Finally the chapter concludes by revealing what these men believe the public perception is of them and their behaviour.

Chapter 5 presents further data from the study, derived from the 309 questionnaires, entitled 'The 5WH of men's procurement of sexual services'. The chapter initially presents findings based on the men's histories of purchasing sexual services, as well as some logistics surrounding their procurement, including age at the time of first procurement, where sex was purchased, the time of week and day of procurement, as well as the services procured. This part of the chapter is organised around the mnemonic of '5WH' – the five '*whats*' of men's procurement of sexual services. The components of the mnemonic are five key questions that are central when considering men's procurement of sexual services. The mnemonic also plays an important role in relation to the final aspect of this findings chapter, where men's reasons for procuring sexual services are identified using a cluster analysis. The analysis undertaken reveals five clusters (types) of men in the study who procure sexual services and their reasons.

The final 'results' chapter, Chapter 6 – 'Examining why men procure sexual services' draws upon the 36 interviews. The thematic analysis of the men's interview data builds on the variables considered in Chapter 5, with reasons for men's procurement of sexual services emerging. This chapter allows for a consideration of the differences between reasons that influence the first time men procure sexual services, onset reasons, and the reasons that influence men's continuation in procuring sexual services. This brings to the fore differences amongst the men in their reasons for first time procurement compared with why they continue to procure. Through this analysis a layer of complexity to understanding the procurement of sexual services is uncovered, in that the reasons men procure sexual services are multi-faceted and evolve between the time a man first procures sexual services and when a man returns to procure. This chapter illuminates the differences between those who are actively involved in the social practice and those who are not. With the conclusion of this final findings chapter, the book is able to consider new ways of making sense of men's procurement of sexual services. In light of the data presented, a re-theorising of this social practice is considered in Chapter 7.

Chapter 7, entitled 'Making sense of men's procurement of sexual services: a new understanding of this social phenomenon', is a detailed discussion of the current study's findings in the light of existing knowledge in order to re-theorise why men procure sexual services. The chapter critically reflects on existing knowledge and questions its strength in applicability for understanding this social practice. This chapter also considers research that has examined why humans have sex outside of the sex work industry to assess if there is symmetry between why humans have sex within the sex work industry. Chapter 7 introduces the theoretical lens of 'well being', within a framework of positive psychology, as a perspective more in keeping with the findings to understand this social practice. In conclusion, a definition of well being specifically applicable to those who procure sexual services is presented, and based on data presented in this volume and the discussions that have taken place in Chapter 7, a revision and enhancement of the SAPSS model presented in Chapter 3 take place. As a result of this revision the creation of a new model entitled the MAPSS model is presented. The revised model reflects not only the data presented in this study but the new way of understanding men who procure sexual services presented in the chapter.

Finally, Chapter 8 – 'Conclusion, recommendations and implications for further study' summarises the main points of the empirical research of this volume including the development of the '5WH' mnemonic; the recognition of differences between reasons men give for procuring sexual services for the first time and reasons for their continued engagement; the MAPSS model and a definition of well being for the procurement of sexual services, all of which have emerged from the findings. Chapter 8 recognises the limitations of the empirical research underpinning this volume, and recommends further and new directions in research concerning the procurement of sexual services.

Conclusion

This introductory chapter of Part I of this volume has offered a brief synopsis of the book, drawing out the importance of the work through the aim and research questions of the empirical research underpinning this work, along with a brief description of the chapters. The following chapter, Chapter 1 will consider the concepts of sex and gender, and offer a deconstruction of 'sex' in order to contextualise the behaviours exhibited by men who procure sexual services.

1 Deconstructing sexuality and understanding the procurement of sex

As Millet (1970) explained:

> Coitus can scarcely be said to take place in a vacuum, although of itself it appears a biological and physical activity, it is sat so deeply within the larger context of human affairs that is serves as a charged microcosm of the variety of attitudes and values to which culture subscribes.
>
> (p. 23)

Millet's quote is an important starting point for this volume, because in order to contextualise and gain insight into the procurement of sexual services, consideration needs to be given to the term 'sex' and what it means. Sex can be understood through biological explanations such as natural urges and drivers, but as Kimmel and Plante (2004) note, sex is as much to do with how people interact with each other in a social context as with biology, and is informed by cultural assumptions. So men's procurement of sex, whatever that may mean for each individual, may be as much if not more influenced by social values, norms and other desires as just by a desire to engage in the physical act of intercourse. As Gagnon and Simon (1970) suggests, 'people become sexual in the same way they become everything else. Without much reflection they pick up directions from their social environment' (Gagnon and Simon, 1970: 2). Sexual behaviour can be argued to be a product of the interactions of our biological constitution and what we learn from our cultures. In other words, in part, people are socialised into sex and as gender is also constructed through socialisation processes (Shepherd, 2009: 8), 'gender' and 'sex' are intimately related but are not the same and must be distinguished. 'Gender' is a fluid term denoting a continuum ranging from feminine to masculine and is a socially and culturally constructed phenomenon (Garza-Mercer *et al.*, 2006: 109), reflected in sayings such as 'boys don't cry' or 'that is not very lady-like'. 'Sex' refers to the 'biological and physiological characteristics that differentiate males from females, e.g. sex chromosomes, hormone levels, testes, ovaries' (Kauth, 2007: 15).

How can understandings of sex and gender assist in understanding men's procurement of sexual services? A beginning might be made by considering the writings on sex by one of the most influential social theorists of the twentieth century, Sigmund Freud. Freud is a key figure in the developmental and psycho-analytical psychology arena, recognised for his three principle essays on sexuality (1962), which, despite being written in a more conservative era, are still influential and relevant to the study of the psychology of human sexuality in the twenty-first century (Chodorow, 2000). Freud's notion of sexuality is individualistic in nature, viewing sexuality as 'affection, love and physical pleasure' (White *et al.*, 2010: 221). It is argued though that Freud's understanding of sexuality is limited and contributes to criticisms of the Freudian model (Marcus, 1975). Marcus (1975) outlines the criticisms angled at Freud and his work, which include the fact he fails to consider the full extent of sexuality and what it involves. Freud's understanding of sexuality lies within the origins and developments of sexuality as an internal and biologically driven force, overlooking the important influence of social context. Freud's consideration of sexuality in this way has led to narrow interpretations of what constitutes sexuality. Freud's work makes the claim that 'normal' sex is simply the act of (vaginal) sexual intercourse between a man and women. This position supports negative views on particular expressions of sexuality, such as homosexuality and sex work.

Freud was a pioneer in the field of childhood sexuality and in exploring the development of the libidinal drive. His theory proposed that individuals progress through a series of psychosexual stages, beginning in infancy, in order to develop and successfully reach sexual maturity (White *et al.*, 2010). These stages reflect the child's ever evolving quest for sexual and physical pleasure, with, at each stage, the individual's libido focused on a particular part of the body, or erogenous zone (Demir, 2012). During each stage the child is faced with challenges such as poor engagement and socialisation practices with others. If these challenges arise and are not resolved, Freud theorised that the individual may develop a fixation with a particular erogenous zone of pleasure, which also represents a broader psychological and psychosocial issue (White *et al.*, 2010). Ultimately, Freud's study of the sexual development of children attempted to 'trace the play of influences which govern the evolution of infantile sexuality till its outcome in perversion, neurosis or normal sexual life' (Freud, 1962: 38).

In his renowned essays on sexuality Freud (1962) theorises on these sexual developmental stages. Freud's first essay considers sexual deviations, where he outlines his views on the perversions that plague some individuals and lead to deviation from normal sexual and personality development (Marcus, 1975). As noted above, 'normal sex' was seen by Freud to be vaginal intercourse between a man and a woman, with any other act deviating from this position being classified as 'abnormal'. Freud outlined many abnormal acts, such as the use of the anus, sexual fetishisms and bondage and discipline sexual acts. He simply summarised all abnormal sex to be a result of an individual projecting their libido onto any object not deemed appropriate for sex. 'Infantile sexuality' is the second deliberation Freud makes on sexuality. This essay includes his view of masturbation and other aspects of the sexual discovery and developmental process beginning in infancy (Chodorow, 2000). In this penultimate essay Freud outlines the four stages of development in sexuality during infancy. These stages are the oral stage, anal stage, phallic stage and latency stage, and as outlined in Freud's work (1962) a number of problems can arise during this period, lasting up to the age of six. Such problems range from penis envy, to an aggressive drive developing in an infant due to breast-feeding, along with a failure of the super ego to repress sexual desires of the phallic stage. These problems contribute to abnormalities in sex and the expression of such in adulthood, for example, as Freud saw it, the purchasing and selling of sex.

In Freud's final essay, 'transformations of puberty', which could be argued as his most influential of the three essays, he discusses the final stage of genital primacy; the conflicts, fixations and deviations in the course of development that lead to abnormal perversions; the various erogenous zones, pleasure principle and libido theory (Marcus, 1975). For Freud it was this stage in life when 'normal' sexual behaviour starts to manifest, subject to no problems arising from the previous stages of one's sexual development. Behaviours that fall outside the definition of 'normal' sexual behaviour such as fetishisms or having sex for non-procreational purposes are a product of abnormalities in the psychosexual development of a child. Once behaviours have been established, it becomes a permanent fixture in the person's psychological constitution. As Garza-Mercer *et al.* stated, Freud viewed sex for reasons other than procreation as 'pathological and perverse, although the pleasure principle explained the pursuit of sexual pleasure and desire for immediate gratification' (2006: 112). The application of Freud's work to understanding sex work, and, more importantly for this volume, the procurers of sexual services, considers clients of sex workers as perverse individuals who suffer poor psychological traits that are a product of disruptions in sexual development during childhood. This position resonates with one of the typologies that Monto and McRee (2005) offer as a means for understanding men who procure sexual services – the 'peculiar' man.

Freud proposed there were three classes of persons: those with perversions, the neurotics, and normal sexual individuals. Marcus (1975: 30) discussed these classes and also stated that Freud believed perversions are habitually present in the sexuality of normal individuals. These though do not in turn label them as neurotic; for 'the sexual life of healthy adults is rarely without perverse constituents in it' (1975: 30) and 'normal' people have been known to perform repulsive and socially stigmatised sexual acts. However, as Malinowski (1979) observed, it is when these perverse fixations replace the normal sexual aims that the individual then crosses over to the pathological dimension of sexuality, a position with which sex work is commonly associated. Freud's theories on sexual deviancy and pathology were extended by theorists such as Charles Winick, who wrote about the sex work industry as deviant. These issues are addressed and considered in depth in the next chapter, Chapter 2.

In summary Freud's view of perversions expressed through one's sexuality is a result of unresolved conflict at particular stages of childhood development. This conflict can be instigated by different experiences such as abuse and childhood loss. In sum, this theorising on sexuality has led some scholars to apply such a discourse to sex work, leading to the view that sex work is deviant and perverse and a result of unresolved childhood sexual conflicts and development. Freud's approach to sexuality and the approach by those who have used his work to explain sex work have not only demonised sex work but also more broadly have underplayed other theoretical understandings of sexuality, for example that proposed by evolutionary psychology, the importance of environment and its impact on how sexuality is played out and expressed.

Evolutionary psychology and sex

Evolutionary psychological theories offer a different way of understanding the development of sexuality from Freud, therefore providing another perspective by which to interpret and understand men's procurement of sexual services. Evolutionary psychological explanations focus primarily on the 'ultimate (reproductive) causes of traits' (Kauth, 2007: 11). This therefore offers an understanding and insight into the evolved sexual psychology of the overall general population, rather than a more individualistic understanding as offered by scholars such as Freud (Buss and Schmitt, 1993). The evolutionary psychological perspective on sexuality examines proximate factors, such as 'genes, hormones, environmental toxins, disease, personality, early childhood social experiences, stress, trauma [and] family dynamics' (Kauth, 2007: 11), and focuses on the impact more individualistic and environmental factors have on an individuals' sexual development. These proximate factors such as family dynamics are argued to be crucial in understanding which internal psychological processes influence individuals to behave in sexually motivated ways and participate in certain sexual acts, such as engaging in commercial sex (Kinsey *et al.*, 1948; White *et al.*, 2010).

> The relationship between proximate and ultimate causal factors is that evolutionary theories of human sexuality represent the background, while proximate theories are the foreground. For a clear picture of human sexuality, both ultimate and proximate explanations are necessary and require integration.
>
> (Kauth, 2007: 11)

Evolutionists proclaim that 'humans are preoccupied with sexuality because we are hardwired to do so' (Garza-Mercer *et al.*, 2006: 112). This means it is in our inherent nature to act on our sexual desires and urges in interplay with our surrounding environment (Buss and Schmitt, 1993). This approach states that the human species has evolved over time and acquired adaptive traits that seek to solve the problems related to survival and reproductive successes that have affected our ancestors in the past (Buss and Schmitt, 1993; Sefcek *et al.*, 2007). The natural selection theory, originally proposed by Darwin, was later extended to form the sexual selection theory. The sexual selection theory focuses on the physical adaptations and psychological differences between the two sexes that influence mating preferences and behaviour in a way that gives them an advantage over competing others (Pinker and Bloom, 1992). Incorporating both natural selection and sexual selection theories, the study of sexuality in a psychological frame is argued by proponents to provide an effective approach to understanding and explaining human sexuality as it has evolved over time to adapt to the current conditions faced in contemporary society (Kauth, 2007: 3). It also is said to allow for and explain matters such as high divorce rates in some societies, as, in a rapidly evolving society where people are living longer, men's and women's needs may change. These needs may not be met through one marriage or by having just one sexual partner over one's life course. Therefore, engaging in a social practice such as the procurement of sexual services can be argued to be an integral part of the psychological constitution of human beings, based on the sexual selection theory

Most evolutionary psychological theories focus on reproductive sex as a means for survival and sexual selection; however Garza-Mercer *et al.* (2006: 111) argues it is sexual pleasure, not procreation, that ultimately drives human sexuality. This can be illustrated by the fact that non-reproductive sex is evident not only among the human species but other mammals as well, such as bonobo chimpanzees. Some argue that humans have evolved to a point where there is a clear separation between sex for reproduction and sex merely for pleasure (Graaf and Rademakers, 2006). This may offer an insight as to why people procure sex, although this does not mean such a practice of sex for pleasure is acceptable to all. At various times, Christian churches, for example have frowned upon having sex with your wife/husband for non-procreational purposes (Brooks Gordon, 2006).

Evolutionary psychologists such as Kauth (2007) and Sefcek *et al.* (2007) suggest that sexual and physical pleasure are intrinsic components of human sexuality. Pleasurable sensations can be obtained by various sexual acts, often not including traditional vaginal intercourse but rather stimulation of other erogenous zones (Kauth, 2007: 7; Sefcek *et al.*, 2007). Both men and women seek out quality physical pleasure however, 'when sexual pleasure comes under the scrutiny of social regulations and cultural restrictions its expression and experience is altered, modified, regulated, and even criminalized' (Garza-Mercer *et al.*, 2006: 114). Sex with a wife or husband for pleasure may now be acceptable in most contemporary societies, and in fact has been in ancient societies as evidenced in writings, drawings and carvings from ancient Greece, Rome and India. However, in many societies, for example in China, it is generally socially unacceptable to have sex outside marriage (Zheng *et al.*, 2011). It is the combination of sex for pleasure and sex outside marriage that seems to create the stigmatised nature of the sex work industry and the regulation and criminalisation of it, which exists across the globe. Sex work has been exposed to social regulation of various forms, since written records began (Brooks Gordon, 2006).

Kinsey *et al.* (1948) in the foundational Kinsey reports, released in the United States of America, argued that there is a multitude of sexual behaviours capable of pleasuring men and women that do not serve the purpose of procreation. These sexual behaviours include, but are not limited to: masturbation, oral sex, anal sex, and sex-play with adult toys (Garza-Mercer *et al.*, 2006: 111). This is further illustrated by the fact that individuals who are infertile, post-menopausal or even prepubescent are all capable of experiencing sexual desires and sexual play for pleasure (Graaf and Rademakers, 2006). Thus it has been suggested that 'for most of us, sexual pleasure, not procreation, influences how our sexuality is understood, experienced, and realized' (Garza-Mercer *et al.*, 2006: 122). So, in summary, it is acknowledged by scholars that sexual behaviours are not always intended for procreational purposes, but for pleasure purposes. Sexual pleasure is an end in itself and is sought by both men and women. It is this understanding of 'sexuality' that is most closely associated with the purchasing of sexual services.

Understanding the influence of culture on sex

The individualistic and psychological understandings of sex, summarised above, are challenged by the work of scholars such as Vance (1991) and Kimmell and Plante (2004), who consider the impact of social and cultural contexts on sex. For example, Vance (1991) considers the cultural-influence model, which redresses what are seen to be the shortfalls of some psychological explanations of sexuality said to underplay the social and cultural context of sexuality. The cultural-influence model views sexuality as biologically determined yet gender specific. Learning is important in shaping sexual behaviours and attitudes, and culture is viewed as encouraging or discouraging the expression of sexuality, sexual attitudes and identity. Cultural-influence models recognise variations in cultural attitudes, such as the difference amongst some cultures that accept homosexuality and those cultures that do not. This difference can also be found within the sex work industry, where some cultures accept this practice whilst others do not. The cultural-influence model recognises that such variations encourage or restrict behaviour.

A cultural-influence analysis using international prevalence data of men's procurement of sexual services provides information on the encouragement or restriction of this social activity by culture. The National Sexual Attitudes and Lifestyle Survey (NATSAL, 2001) conducted in the United Kingdom reported approximately 4 per cent of men paying for sex in the previous five years, with 1 per cent claiming to do have done so in the previous 12 months. However, over the previous decade or so, the United Kingdom has introduced a number of laws criminalising those who are involved in the sex work industry. The 1985 Criminal Justice Act introduced the criminal act of kerb crawling, while in 1998 the Crime and Disorder Act introduced Anti-Social Behaviour orders, which have been used to target those in the sex work industry (Kinnell, 2008). These findings may suggest a number of things: men may be reluctant to admit to purchasing sex, even if the survey is anonymous, so this may be an under-counting, and/ or there may be fewer sex workers offering sexual services, and/or fewer men purchasing sex due to fear of persecution. In stark comparison, research in Thailand, where sex work is not criminalised and there is greater cultural acceptance of sex work, up to 74 per cent of men report paying for sex (Wilcox *et al.*, 2009).

Based on such data, Brooks Gordon and Gelsthorpe (2003b) suggest that it is unclear whether these trends reflect the actual number of men who procure sexual services or the social attitudes towards the purchasing of sex within these countries. What can be concluded is that the difference amongst these prevalence studies may reflect variations of cultural attitudes concerning the sex work industry.

Using a different approach to consider the cultural impact of attitudes to sex and the purchasing of sex, Waskul and Plante (2010) consider sexuality from a symbolic interactionist perspective. This is a sociological perspective, which considers social interactions and processes at a micro level in order to understand their subjective meaning (Taylor *et al.*, 1996). This approach suggests that sexual behaviour should be placed in the context of meaning, and argues that biological theories ignore the social aspect of sexuality. In fact they argue that sexuality is social, and that the meanings of sexual behaviour are more important than the sexual acts. This theorisation is important to this study, as, it may suggest that the wider reasons, not just the sexual urge, of men who procure sexual services are central and that such knowledge may lead to new understandings of this sexual behaviour.

Gecas and Libby (1976: 33) apply symbolic interactionist principles to sexuality and sexual identity, as they claim that viewing sexuality in biological or essentialist terms misses 'its distinctively human aspect'. They suggest that there are four identifiable symbolic codes that regulate sexuality in a society, including traditional codes (based largely on religion involving sin and guilt); romantic codes (where love, particularly in the context of marriage, is essential for sexual behaviour); recreational codes (emphasising pleasure and de-emphasising institutional implications of sexuality); and utilitarian codes (where sexuality is used to gain some other end, such as money or status). They assert that people may follow many different codes, or scripts, such as a religious script developed within the family, a recreational script developed within peer groups and a sexual script developed within an intimate relationship. These scripts, including sexual scripts, can be best understood in the context of normative behaviours. Sexual scripts may be one useful way to understand men's procurement of sexual services and in fact some contemporary writings on men who purchase sex reflect this. Sanders (2008a) for example introduces the concepts of emotions and intimacy into her work on why men purchase sexual services, claiming that some men purchase sex in order to address loneliness and feelings of being socially inadequate. This work begins to move and extend the discussion into the normative function that sex work may have in some men's lives and suggests the possibility of a range of conceptions of sex work and why men purchase sex.

Similarly, extending the cultural consideration of sexuality, Longmore (1998) considers sexuality from the symbolic interactionist approach, stating that although biological perspectives may provide evidence that we are sexual, they do not explain how we are sexual. Longmore (1998) identifies two streams of symbolic interactionism: situational and structural. These allow a consideration of 'how' as humans we are sexual. The situational approach focuses on how individuals define situations, how individuals create meaning, and how individuals define themselves, where sexual behaviour may seem irrational to outside observers. Therefore, if applied to the purchasing of sexual services, those who are actively engaged in the behaviour will define the situation in a rational way compared to those who do not procure sexual services; to this latter group such behaviour will be understood as irrational. The structural approach in comparison focuses on role assignment determined by an individual's position in the social structure. This approach highlights the influence of peers and family on sexual attitudes and behaviours, where individuals may be influenced by competing or negative views. By bringing together the two strands of symbolic interactionism – creating and defining a situation (the situation) and the influence of others on attitudes and behaviours (the structural) – an insight is offered into why some men may keep the procurement of sexual services a secret from family members and friends.

Masculinity and understanding men who procure sexual services

A further cultural or normative perspective, which may facilitate the understanding of sexual behaviour, can be found in revisiting the term 'gender'.

Some theorists such as Courtenay (2000) argue that men may think and act in the way that they do because of existing concepts of femininity and masculinity. Such concepts are not only open to vast interpretation, but they become complex as they can be culturally interpreted. This can result in pressure from society to conform to the concept definitions (Courtenay, 2000). These behaviours include: 'the denial of weakness or vulnerability, emotional and physical control, the appearance of being strong and robust, dismissal of any need for help, a ceaseless interest in sex, the display of aggressive behaviour and physical dominance' (Courtenay, 2000: 1389).

This position can be linked to the 'Expectation States Theory', which aims to 'explain how status beliefs operate to sustain social hierarchies' (Shields, 2008: 65). In Expectation States Theory, 'positive emotions emerge in situations when an individual behaves according to the expectations associated with their status, while negative emotions emerge when performance expectations associated with their status are violated' (Stets and Asencio, 2008: 1055). One of the central aspects of this theory is the premise that status beliefs are widely shared cultural beliefs that express the status relationship between one social group and another within a given society (Ridgeway and Bourge, 2004). Gender (a socially constructed way of being a girl or boy, a man or woman) functions as a background identity for all people in their respective societies and therefore impacts on background status beliefs that are always present in social interactions (Shields, 2008). The notion of gender and of identity therefore need to be understood within the context of sexuality, because how we understand what it is to be a boy or a girl impacts on identity. This process has been shaped by status beliefs, that is, what society expects, as this influences what is deemed acceptable or not.

From this premise the various theoretical frameworks used to understand why men procure sexual services can be viewed as reflections of different 'status beliefs' from within society. For example, men's procurement of sexual services has been described and explained in common parlance, over time as men just being men. Mansson (2004) states that men's procurement of sexual services is driven by their natural sexual behaviour (a biological origin), but he also views its social origin as an integral part of the behaviour. Masculinity theory has developed out of the social construction of gender paradigm, with Allwood (1998), for example, stating that the term encompasses and reflects a range of meanings. It can reflect the discourse surrounding the power relations between the sexes, as well as the relationship between men and women both socially and culturally.

Masculinity, in the view of some theorists, has become the 'shortest way to refer to how men act, think, believe and appear' (Hearn and Pringle, 2006: 7). 'Masculinity' focuses of the socialisation of men in society (Pleck *et al.*, 1993), which theorists argue, has promoted over the past century 'male' qualities such as being independent and being an achiever. Seidler (1994) outlines two ways of understanding masculinity: one through a lens of biology (objective) and the other through the lens of social construction (impartial). These two ways of understanding masculinity reflect how men experience the social world – the objective; and how society and culture understand men's experiences of the social world – the impartial. When juxtaposed, the 'objective' and 'impartial' positions can conflict and can result in a variety of challenges when defining and performing masculinity. For example, there is tension between men's experiences and how society expects men to act (Seidler, 1994: 116). Social expectations 'tell' men how to behave rather than allowing individual experiences to take priority. The implication of this can be that men may negate aspects of their lives, such as denial of weaknesses or the non-expression of emotions and feelings. Such conceptualisations of masculinity can be criticised for overlooking characteristics that may be more associated with women, such as the expression of emotions. Being a man means 'not being like a woman' (Kimmell, 1994: 126). Experience of emotions, feeling powerless and not being in control are not associated with being a man. Good *et al.* (1994) understand this as an instrumental versus a rational distinction between men and women. This reflects the hegemonic ideal of masculinity, which involves being successful, rational and powerful. Hegemonic masculinity has been defined by Connell as: 'The configuration of gender practice, which embodies the currently accepted answer to the problem of legitimacy of patriarchy, which guarantees (or is taken to guarantee) the dominant position of men and the subordination of women' (1995: 77). When the conceptualisation of masculinity is applied to behaviours such as the procurement of sex work it offers an insight into the characterisation of this social practice as an act of power and domination. This position has dominated writings by factions of feminism such as radical and Marxist feminists.

Masculinity theory offers an insight into 'maleness', that is, what it is to be a man as well as what constitutes male behaviour. The masculinity literature identifies the normative characteristics of what it is to be a man – muscular, brave and in control – however, when the terms of masculinity and 'man' are considered across time, cultures and other social contexts, the complexities of masculinity and 'maleness' are evident (Mosse, 1998). It is only within situations where an 'excess of masculinity' is expressed that consideration is given to it (Reeser, 2010: 1), for example when the boxer is waiting to start his fight or when a man is controlling a woman. Connell (2005) identifies how masculinity is sustained through cultural and institutional practices that allow a hierarchy in masculinity to be established. So certain 'male' practices in various cultures can be played out through domination and subordination such as the dominance of heterosexual men over homosexual men; or played out through marginalisation such as the exclusion of black men in favour of white men or working class men in favour of middle class men. Out of these cultural practices, normative definitions of what masculinity is and what it is to be a man (for example always fearless, always in control) have developed. This line of argument concludes that many men, shaped by such male cultural norms, engage in practices that exhibit their maleness. The procurement of sexual services is one such practice. If this is how men demonstrate their maleness, it is not surprising that many feminists, in particular radical feminists, abhor the practice of men purchasing sex. Feminist theorising has had a role in the construction of male identity (Seidler, 1994; Hearn and Pringle, 2006), which in part has problematised all men and masculinity as a form of violence towards women (Seidler, 1994). For example, Carole Pateman (1988) claims that men's procurement of sexual services is a reflection of a hyper-masculine heterosexuality, as well as being one of the means by which men control women. What such extreme views suggest is that all men are the same. This is a common category mistake, one that is also levelled against the sex work industry, and those who procure sexual services. Theorists such as Seidler argue this categorisation of men 'encourages men to hide their feelings'. They are left to resolve the 'experience [of] tension between what they need for themselves and what culture defines as their need' (1994: 108 and 116). This often results in men being understood solely through a prism of patriarchy, control and authority. Such a homogenising view regarding what constitutes masculinity is challenged by various scholars (Seidler, 1994; Hearn and Pringle, 2006), who are redefining it as being more flexible, arguing that masculinity should encompass the various experiences and feelings that men actually have, not what socially constructed forms dictate they should have.

Furthermore, there may be a false logic in the conclusion that the purchasing of all female sexual services by men is a manifestation of that patriarchal power. Holter (2000) argues that the relationship between the provider and purchaser of sexual services in some contexts is misunderstood and is inaccurately used to portray men's purchasing of sexual services as a continuation of patriarchal domination. Prieur and Taksdal (1993) drawing on their empirical research, suggest that some men who purchase sex lack power in their social and everyday lives, which contributes to their need and wish to procure sex. Holter (2000) suggests that in some cases the issue of gender and power is more evident amongst men of lower status than amongst higher status men. Therefore, more men from lower socio-economic classes would be expected to purchase sex than from higher socio-economic classes. But evidence fails to support this position and even demonstrates the opposite. For example, in studies by Faugier and Cranfield (1995), Elliot and McGaw (2002) and Ewasiw *et al.* (2006), the occupational status of sex worker clients reflect a range of occupational categories, though evidence tends to a skew towards those from higher socio-economic classes. For example, occupations from the social stratification class band A – doctors, lawyers, university lectures and bankers – were found to be the most common purchasers of sex. So, the use of traditional definitions of masculinity may not be a useful theoretical lens to use when attempting to understand the procurement of sexual services.

Conclusion

Biological, psychological and cultural theories of sexuality and sexual expression have been summarised in this chapter to provide, in part, useful approaches to understanding why some men, in twenty-first-century NSW, Australia, purchase sex. Many elements, including gender, sexual orientation, sexual behaviours, sexual attitudes and sexual identity (White *et al.*, 2010), and disciplinary areas such as psychology and sociology have been canvassed. Sexuality can be understood through evolutionary and developmental psychological theories, as well as culturally focused ones. This array of theoretical positions in understanding sexuality illustrates the complicated nature of sexuality, expressions of sex and the place of sexual practices in a society. Freud argued that expressions of sexuality can be performed in a 'normal' way or a 'perverse' way, with the latter form of expression leading to sexually deviant behaviours. It is this 'perverse' execution of sexuality that some theorists have used to understand the phenomenon of sex work and those involved (Winick, 1962).

This chapter also considered alternative understandings of sexuality by considering evolutionary theories that acknowledge the role of sexual pleasure, and recognise that the act of sex is not always performed for procreational purposes. This in itself challenges the attribution of 'perverse' sexual behaviour that some social groupings and scholars have used to demonise sexual behaviour outside marriage and for pleasure rather than procreation. However, biological and psychological approaches underplay how societal attitudes and beliefs shape individuals and societies. Culturally inclusive theories, such as symbolic interactionism, recognise that societal attitudes and beliefs shape individual ideas and acceptance around the performance of 'sexuality'. As a result, such culturally inclusive theories offer an alternative understanding as to what constitutes acceptable and unacceptable behaviour.

Using these theoretical frameworks to understand why men procure sexual services reflects the complex and multi-faceted nature of sexuality and sexual performance. The literature on and views about the procurement of sexual services have tended to be simplistic, portraying the sex industry and the purchase of sex in a single factorial way, such as deviancy/gender oppression versus a more liberal, normative position (Weitzer, 2005). This volume challenges this simplistic, single factorial understanding of why men procure sexual services, and will explore the purchasing of sex through a number of perspectives in order to mount this challenge.

This volume continues by considering in some detail the theoretical frameworks used to understand the practice of procuring sexual services. In order to do this, the following two chapters consider the procurement of sexual services by men through two lenses; the first through the theoretical lens of deviancy and immorality, and the second through a normative framework, which encompasses the 'market' value of sex work. These chapters provide a critical analysis of how men's procurement of sexual services is popularly and currently understood.

2 Understanding sex work 1
Deviant and immoral

The apparent breaching of socially accepted norms by sex workers (constructed as prostitutes) and men who purchase sex has been constructed as deviant for over 40 years in the modern era. The work of scholars such as Winick (1962) and, more contemporaneously, Monto and McRee (2005) construct men who purchase sex in a binary manner. One side of this dichotomous representation is the 'peculiar man', which portrays a man who purchases sexual services as one who is distinctively different from the general population of men. The other side is the 'everyman' portrayal, which views customers of sex workers as no different from the men in the general population. This latter portrayal of men who procure sexual services will be discussed further in Chapter 3. Within this chapter, consideration is given to how some theoretical frameworks have provided an understanding of men's procurement of sexual services from the 'peculiar man' perspective of Monto and McRee's 2005 typology. This is achieved by considering the act of procurement as deviant, immoral and pathological. The following chapter will therefore, first, consider what deviance is and how this is used to define human behaviour, ranging from the breaching of a social norm to the violation of a criminal code. Relevant sociological theories such as Howard Becker's labelling theory (1963) will be applied to the discussion in order to illustrate how some theorists and social commentators have labelled men's procurement of sexual services as 'peculiar'. Aspects of feminism are also considered in relation to the proposition that men's involvement in the sex work industry in this way supports the 'peculiar' man typology. This chapter then concludes by considering the legislative frameworks, which are applied to the sex work industry both within and outside of Australia, but with a particular focus on NSW, Australia – the geographical location in which the research for this book took place. The consideration of the law in this way highlights how men are criminalised in some parts of the world but not in others for procuring sexual services, exemplifying how the typology of the 'peculiar' man is applied to men who engage in this act in a criminalising context.

Deviance and its origins

Social norms are viewed as the shared beliefs and goals of a society that allow for the maintenance of social order (Giddens, 2005). Therefore, the breaching of social norms is seen as detrimental to the social fabric of society, and the breach of such can have a variety of consequences depending on its severity (Sumner, 1994). Social norms can be conceptualised into three categories according to Sumner (1994): folk laws, mores and laws. Folk laws apply to everyday behaviours, such as sending a Christmas card at Christmas. Sumner points out for example, that if you send the card in July people may consider you strange, but that this would not be seen as a severe breach of social norms. Mores, relate to socio-cultural behaviours, morals and ethics, for example the acceptance or not of the purchasing of sexual services. Actions that breach some mores, such as infidelity and the purchasing of sexual services can be viewed as severe and can have serious punitive consequences. Violation of such codes of behaviour, like that of the former Italian Prime Minister, Silvio Berlusconi, with his alleged inappropriate conduct with a 17-year-old sex worker, could lead to permanent damage to one's reputation and have a negative material impact, such as dismissal from employment.

While the above breaches of social norms are informal and attract informal sanctions, the final category to be considered is that of the law. Sumner identifies 'laws' as the third typology in which social norms can be breached. Here, the sanctions are of a formal nature, they are rules legislated by government, and sanctions can include the loss of liberty. Both mores and laws have been used over time and place to control sex work, in particular to punish prostitutes, and to a lesser extent to prevent men from purchasing sex. As sex workers breach social norms to a severe extent in some societies, they are by definition deviant, and from time to time men who purchase sex are seen as deviant by association. Here can be seen slippage between mores and laws, with mores becoming enshrined in law. For example where sex work and purchasing sex, once seen as breaching mores, is now elevated to criminal behaviour, or where sex work that was a crime is de-criminalised and moved to the level of mores.

Deviancy can be defined as behaviour that is 'bizarre, unexpected, predatory and/or self destructive' (Humphreys, 2006: xiii). Since the emergence of the concept in the 1950s, deviancy has been criticised by many. This has been, in particular, the case in relation to sex work. It is claimed that the term deviancy is no longer applicable in an era of 'social control' (Roach Anleu, 2006: 2) as it is claimed that terms such as normalisation, governance and regulation, which reflect a nuanced and more sophisticated approach to the maintenance of social norms, are now used rather than deviancy. However, Roach Anleu goes on to clarify that deviancy is not related solely to such terms. The term deviancy covers a wider range of activities and behaviours, from rules of etiquette to breaches of law (Roach Anleu, 2006: 2). What the term deviancy encapsulates is a break away, a deviating from the social norms of a society. Deviancy is created through interaction; within the social world this interaction is between human beings. It is through everyday routine that social norms are displayed or breached, creating deviancy; therefore, deviancy can be argued to be a part of everyday routine. This proposition supports the interactionist's understanding of deviancy, where actions and behaviours of an individual or group (the interaction) are either accepted or rejected (deemed deviant). So the portrayal of men as deviant for purchasing sex for example, labels them as pathological and sick (Stroller, 1975. This position can be further illustrated by considering the work of Lemert (1951), a pioneer in the area of deviancy studies, who considered societal reaction towards an individual's behaviour as having enough merit to label behaviour deviant. Lemert was one of the first scholars to reflect upon how society can construct who is to be labelled 'good' and who is to be labelled 'bad'. This position was extended in the work of Becker (1963), an interactionist who also examined deviancy, documenting deviant behaviour as more than just about the act or behaviour someone commits; he saw it as more to do with how others apply rules and sanctions to the behaviour.

Labelling theory (Becker, 1963) offers an interactionist's understanding of how societal reaction has impacted in a negative manner on sex work. In order to identify an action as deviant, Becker provided a three step process. First, a behaviour or action needs to be defined: for example a man purchasing sex from a sex worker. Second those involved in that behaviour, the 'actors', need to be labelled: labels such as deviant, sick, pathological, perverse (Winick, 1962; Stroller, 1975; Jeffreys, 1997). Third, those involved in both the labelling and those labelled respond to that label: for example the behaviour or action is stopped by the individual or group; or the behaviour or action is driven underground; or the behaviour is criminalised through legislation. There is a history of sex work being driven 'underground' when criminalised. For example, the sex work industry in the United Kingdom was labelled criminal and driven underground during the 1950s, with those providing sex being imprisoned for their newly defined 'illegal' behaviour (Kinnell, 2008). A response to this criminalisation by sex workers in the United Kingdom at the time was to move their place of work to less visible locations, locations such as waste lands and industrial areas, making the sex workers more vulnerable to violence and exploitation (Kinnell, 2008). Many sex work activists and writers claimed this fostered an environment that led to violent attacks on and murders of sex workers by the 'Yorkshire Ripper' and other similar violence in the 1970s and 1980s (Kinnell, 2008).

The labelling of sex work has taken many forms, as have the responses to such labelling. Sex work has been documented to be, and labelled as, a violation against women, yet it has been promoted as legitimate work (Brooks Gordon, 2006). Heidensohn (1968) defines the event of societal reactions towards others' actions and behaviours that break social mores as the 'process of definitions by means of deviancy and the labelling of deviants by means of a complexity of feedbacks and reinforcements' (p. 168). Of course this same process applies to behaviour that is socially acceptable. In other words, behaviour and actions are socially constructed in different cultures and at different times as deviant, acceptable or something in between. This though, is not an instant process, and the commissioning of the label 'deviant' onto an individual and/or group is something that takes place over a sustained period and is a result of interaction between the rule breaker(s) and the community (Rosenblum, 1975). This is evident when considering the historical development of sex work, where at various times sex work was seen as acceptable in terms of both selling and purchasing, but at other times as not acceptable, with those involved in sex work being re-defined as unacceptable. For example, the Church during the fifteenth and sixteenth century re-defined sex work, which it had sanctioned previously, as immoral due to changing values and sex work's perceived relationship with 'promiscuity' (Brooks Gordon, 2006). However the quality of modern sex work research, which has informed positions advocated by institutions such as Christian churches, has been questioned for its reliability and validity (Weitzer, 1999; Wilcox *et al.*, 2009). As illustrated by Wilcox *et al.* (2009) there has been a lack of robust, scientific, evidenced based research concerning the sex work industry, with particular reference to the clients of sex workers. Therefore, this suggests that the defining and re-defining of sex work over time has been primarily informed by social mores and values of 'the day'. These mores and values could, nevertheless, be argued to be the least reflective of what the general population thinks about sex work and their clients. For example, it has been shown that the American population has become more tolerant of sex work over the years (Cao and Maguire, 2013). The definition of sex work and the view and treatment of those who are involved in such a social practice are subjective; they are social constructions offered by powerful and influential groups in society.

In the modern and postmodern eras, criminal sanctions have been imposed on sex work, redefining it as 'criminal' in many parts of the world. In contrast, during ancient Roman times access to sex workers had been advocated as the right of a man (Brooks Gordon, 2006), displaying the patriarchal attitude of the era. This illustration of the redefinition of sex work, exemplifies Phillips and Smith's (2003) view that a large proportion of deviancy can be classified as incivility or disrespectful behaviour or immoral acts. Deviancy can fall into juxtapositions of 'deviancy–crime' or 'deviancy–crime free'. Sex work and its many components have fallen into both domains at different times over history. These definitional and labelling shifts can be attributed to changes over time in a society's moral tone, and cultural, political and religious development. The social construction of deviancy (Humphrey, 2006) suggests that it is within the scope of culture that customs, beliefs and acceptable standards of living and behaviours are validated – the very elements used to measure whether behaviour is accepted or rejected. Over time and through periods of social change, these customs, beliefs and standards of living and behaviours evolve. Sometimes, as noted above, this has resulted in social practices that were once viewed as acceptable being demonised or the reverse.

In relation to sex work, this process has been evident, as outlined by Brooks Gordon's (2006) historical account of the sex work industry. Nevertheless, the procurement of sexual services, although mostly signified as deviant has been variously tolerated and even accepted positively in some cultures across the globe and over time. NSW, Australia for example, has developed some of the most liberal laws concerning sex work in the world (Egger and Harcourt, 1993), as discussed further in this chapter.

However, these developments and changes in laws concerning sex work or similar issues, for example legalising homosexuality, can be used to label some jurisdictions as 'loose' in terms of their customs, beliefs and standards of living and behaviours. The adoption of such positions in law, policy and practice are liberal in nature. One way of illustrating how such differences in views and laws concerning what is acceptable and unacceptable develop and change over time, is by examining what customs, beliefs and behaviours societies value. This is known as society's 'valuation' of particular actions and behaviours (Lemert, 1951). This approach posits that, when making a decision as to which action to take and which behaviours to exhibit, individuals weigh up the value consequences of the choice. They consider factors that have a positive impact, as well as assessing what sacrifices might need to be made. As long as choices are made that add value rather than lessen value (sacrifices) the behaviour becomes normalised (Lemert, 1951). Alternatively, if the value is less, the behaviour is constructed as deviant. Lemert's position therefore suggests that the impact of sex work is that it lessens social values due to its violation of society's expectations surrounding intimate relations, so it is a form of deviance. This position assumes a number of 'givens', such as that all human beings are capable of making rational decisions and have choices all of the time. But this is clearly not the case as some people have poor cognitive processing that can lead to irrational decisions and poor social skills (Huesmann, 1998), and people may have very limited choices due to their personal and geographical circumstances. So choosing to purchase sex at a particular time may be the most rational, acceptable and valuable action for a particular individual as it may have a positive effect on that person.

Two further aspects of deviancy that can be argued through Lemert's position are: sex work is concerned with practices of unusual and excessive desires, and so is deviant; and that women sex workers amass advantages that they may not necessarily be worthy of within a patriarchal society, such as more money and power over men and that this is deviant (Lemert, 1951). Countering these views, Rosenblum (1975) argued that Lemert's view has more to do with the fact that sex work is an occupation in which female sexuality dominates over the male sexuality. This perspicacity lends itself to the conclusion that men's procurement of sexual services is deviant because the norm is patriarchal and society does not accept female sexuality as dominant. This perhaps reveals more about Lemert's patriarchal ideology than about the deviancy of sex work, that is, that sex work where the woman chooses freely to sell sex and to accept or not accept a client (not coercive or trafficked sex work), is deviant in relation to patriarchy.

In summary, sexuality has been considered through deviancy studies as the exploitation of sexuality for gain, whether that be selling or purchasing, and is argued to be a deviant act as it comes at the cost of societal norms, values and expectations. Sexuality is a central theme in the debate about sex work (Brookes Gordon, 2006) and the practices engaged in through sex work have allowed those who sell sexual services, as well as those who are purchasing sexual services, to be labelled deviant. This is a reflection of such practices being viewed as non-reflective of sexual social norms such as monogamous relationships, thus positioning sex work as deviant. The following section extends this discussion by explicitly considering society's influence on the perception of the sex work industry.

Society's influence on the sex work industry

Over time and across different cultures sex work has been accepted as a social practice. In contrast it has also become a vilified practice, which has later regained its accepted status through laws. This shift from acceptance, to non-acceptance, and in some instances back again, has been influenced by groups such as the Church, the media, medical science, feminism and the law. These social groups have all contributed to the modern debate on sex work, reflected in the array of polices, laws and public health practices. Brooks Gordon (2006) documents the manner in which the Church and medical science, for example, during the medieval times, played an increasingly powerful role in the way in which sex work was perceived and ultimately governed. Religious teachings in the fifteenth and sixteenth centuries, supported men's procurement of sexual services as men's uncontrollable urges needed to be released in a pro-social manner (Brooks Gordon, 2006). Male masturbation was seen, by the Church, as self-destructive and abusive to the body, but sex with one's wife for non-pro-creational sex was also frowned upon, so to prevent an increase in rape and sodomy, men were encouraged to control their sexual urges by purchasing sex (Brooks Gordon, 2006).

Brooks Gordon goes on though to record how the Church then redefined the sex work industry from a 'business' for which sex workers were paid, to being an unacceptable promiscuous activity, and therefore morally abhorrent. 'Medical science' in history has contributed to this discourse by stating that men had a weaker sex drive in comparison to their female counterparts, and could not control their sexual urges. As a result men, most conveniently, could not be blamed for their 'immoral' promiscuous behaviour.

But not all historical documentation of the sex work industry problematises it or promotes a negative view of this social practice. Perkins (1991) documents the place of sanctioned prostitution in many cultures, for example the courtesan who was well educated, often quite wealthy, able to choose her clients, and at the top of the social strata in various societies across the ages. Ideological approaches to prostitution, along with attitudes towards this practice, have varied over time and a number have been mentioned briefly. However, contemporaneously the theorising of sex work can be firmly located within the scope of the law and feminism. Before exploring these aspects, consideration is given to aspects of contemporary theorising of sex work that reflect the typology of the 'peculiar' man.

Applying deviancy and immorality to contemporary understanding of men's procurement of sexual services

One approach that has been used to explain men's purchasing of sex has been that they are mentally ill. Using empirical work with men, Winick (1962) concluded that men who purchased sex were psychologically disturbed. He was influenced by the work of Lombroso, who researched and wrote in Italy in the second half of the eighteenth century and who believed that criminals were inherently criminal and displayed certain anti-social and aberrant characteristics, which explained why they behaved in a socially unacceptable manner. Lombroso, who applied a form of 'Darwinism' to the study of criminality, using post-mortems with prisoners, concluded that offenders were biologically different to non-offenders. He labelled criminals atavistic, biological throwbacks. Through his work, Lombroso further theorised that offenders are degenerative due to their pathological conditions; they are individuals who cannot control their behaviour. Much of Winick's work portrayed men in this way too, prefiguring to some extent the 'peculiar man' position outlined by Monto and McRee. Lombroso's theory was also used by Sheldon (1947), who argued body type corresponds with, even predicts, a person's criminal profile. Sheldon documented three body types with characteristics associated with each, as outlined in Table 2.1.

These characteristics can be applied to men who purchase sexual services. For example, McLeod's (1982) work would suggest that men who procured sex had an endomorph body type (self-indulgent) or a mesomorph body type (impulsive) because sex was a commodity to them. Men were purchasing sex because they could not control (and therefore were acting impulsively) their self-indulgent natures, which in this case manifest in innate sexual urges.

This proposition of biological deficiencies explaining men's behaviour, removes agency so individuals cannot be held to account for their behaviour. Winick applied this theory to men who procure sexual services, concluding that such men must be blameless for their actions. In this approach therefore, the use of the label 'deviant' for men who procure sexual services is inappropriate. As documented by Weitzer (2005), who provides contemporary evidence supporting the position, labelling men who procure sexual services as deviant distorts reality. He documents that some police personnel in the United States of America have described men who purchase sexual services as pillars of society, and who, due to their high social and occupation status, would suffer serious negative consequences if their procurement of sexual services was criminalised. The criminalisation of such men leads to long term difficulties for them, due to, for example, the termination of employment and divorce. In this theoretical approach, these men could be seen as suffering unfairly as they cannot control their sexual urges and behaviour. In contrast, the women who sell sex and who

Table 2.1 Sheldon (1947) deviant body types and characteristics

Body type	Characteristics associated with body type
Endomorph	Self indulgent
Mesomorph	Impulsive and aggressive
Ectomorph	Introverted and sensitive

have been labelled deviant through biological explanations offered by scholars such as Lombroso, have not been so fortunate in having their behaviour accepted as uncontrollable and are viewed as responsible for their behaviour. This could be viewed as sex workers being treated unfairly, leading to their behaviour being viewed as unchangeable and non-manageable and to sex workers being exposed to legal intervention controlling their behaviour. This is exemplified in the United Kingdom in the early to mid-1900s when sex work was made illegal (Kinnell, 2008).

Following Winick, the biological framework for understanding men's procurement of sex was extended by the work of Stroller. In 1975, Stroller, claimed men who purchased sexual services were perverse; they were in search of unusual sexual practices within unhealthy regular timeframes, thus they were, by definition, deviant. Stroller stated that this could be explained through Sigmund Freud's Oedipus complex, correlating with his views on sexuality. For example, Stroller suggests that men, who procure such services, live out a fantasy of hatred towards their fathers, and of sleeping with their mothers through their sexual experience with a sex worker. Stroller's theory reflected Freud's position that inappropriate behaviour is a reflection of repressed sexual expression. According to Freud (1923) such behaviour indicates the under development of the id, ego and superego, based on poor socialisation, leading to an individual not being able to control their behaviour. This then is, by definition deviant behaviour. In his work, Freud specifically referred to prostitution, claiming that those involved in sex work fail to reach sexual maturation, a result of the failure of the development of the super ego resulting in irresponsible and impulsive behaviour.

A major limitation of Freud's work, and thus Stroller's work, which has been used to support a number of contemporary positions on men who procure sexual services, is that it is methodologically flawed. These flaws include the inability to scientifically test the functions and existence of the id, ego and superego – concepts that some social science researchers would see as un-testable and therefore invalid due to concepts being beyond the physical world (Smith, 2002).

It is through the theoretical framework of deviancy and its application that corrective programmes operated by the criminal justice system in certain parts of the world address men's procurement of sexual services. Developed in the United States of America, 'John' schools are an intervention administered by corrective services, where men who are arrested for soliciting, mainly kerb crawling as one would expect if soliciting is the main source of evidence for prosecution, are placed in a 'rehabilitative' programme in order to prevent further 're-offending' (i.e. further purchasing of sexual services). Such intervention heavily draws on cognitive behavioural models to inform the content of their programmes and is a pertinent way to illustrate how men's behaviour has been constructed as deviant and to 'need correcting'.

In summary the theoretical frameworks of deviancy and immorality may have some strength in explaining men's procurement of sexual services, as the purchasing of sex can be classified as deviant due to the breaching of social norms.

These norms include the norm of monogamy, as the purchasing of sex by married men de-values the marriage promise between heterosexual couples. In Western cultures marriage requires being faithful, sexual intercourse is constructed as being a special act between a loving couple, and the act of purchasing sex is seen as devaluing this. These breaches can be considered 'crime free' deviancy. However, with the introduction of laws that criminalise sex work, men who procure sexual services become criminals – they have breached the law. The common thread tying this together is the social construction, including through the law, of social norms.

A major limitation in the work surrounding the sex work industry, and more pertinently regarding men who procure sexual services, is the lack of scientifically robust research supporting the claim that men who procure sexual services are pathological and 'sick'. The work of Winick (1962) and Stroller (1975) can be argued to be methodologically flawed in the same way as that of Lombroso (2007) and Freud (1962), as their research lacked control groups, and there is an inability to empirically test their work. It has been noted already that most approaches to understanding sex work have been constructed by those not involved in the practice and that there has been little robust research focusing on the purchasers of sexual services (see the work of Wilcox *et al.*, 2009). Despite this, assertions are made about providers and purchasers of sex, usually based on moral or ideological positions, not on verifiable evidence. These assertions have impacted negatively on the perception of sex work by the general public and have influenced policy debates and legislation internationally. One group that has been prominent in sex work debates in the postmodern era is the feminist movement, although it is acknowledged that there are many feminisms. It is not suggested here that there is a unified feminist movement. The following section considers a radical, and in part Marxist, feminist's perspective on the deviancy and immorality of men's procurement of sexual services. It then moves on to examine legislative developments and how they have been shaped by and have shaped social views of the purchasing of sex.

Feminism, sex work, deviancy and immorality

The role feminism has played in influencing policy, law and public debate concerning sex work over the past century, has been significant, with the impact being understood through two schools of thought: a 'prostitution as harm' approach and a libertarian approach. Radical feminists, along with some Marxist feminists, have generally taken a 'sex work as harm' approach, as the selling of sex is argued to be a mechanism for sustaining male dominance over women. As Barry (1995) argues, sex work is dehumanising and a means of objectifying women. This ideological framework sees prostitution as the epitome of female oppression by men and, regardless of the circumstance the prostitute is a victim: 'rape, battery, sexual harassment, sexual abuse of children, prostitution and pornography emphasise and actualise the distinct power of men over women in society' (MacKinnon, 1990: 127).

Weitzer suggests that for radical feminists prostitution is the very definition of male domination over, exploitation of and violence against, women (2005: 34). Radical feminists suggest that there can be no such thing as voluntary or willing participation in prostitution, as consent is not possible for women in the framework of male domination socially, sexually and economically. Therefore, all men purchasing sexual services from female sex workers are committing violence against women. For example, Farley *et al.* (1998) state that women who sell sex are not only experiencing violence but that this is a violation of all women's human rights.

The idea of sex as violence can also be seen in MacKinnon's work (1990) where all heterosexual sex work is demeaning and an act of violence. Pateman (1988) further argues that when a woman engages in prostitution she is selling herself in a very different and much more quantifiable way than is required by any other profession. This view is supported by other feminist theorists, who argue that when a woman contracts herself out for sexual use she severs the integrity of body and self to her psychological detriment (Barry, 1995; Jeffreys, 1997).

From an essentialist viewpoint, feminist groups argue that the commodification of sex as an act is intrinsically wrong. Pateman (1988) suggests that 'womanhood ... is confirmed in sexual activity, and when a prostitute contracts out the use of her body she is thus selling herself in a very real sense' (p. 207). This essentialist view holds that the sex market has inherent qualities of promoting 'inferior forms of personhood' (Radin, 1987), thus devaluing the women involved by placing them in a situation of domination and as mere commodities.

This feminist perspective, which is traditionally unsupportive of sex work, can be traced to the late nineteenth century with the emergence of first wave feminist ideals. In line with this was a moral panic about 'white slavery' through prostitution, a clear link back to the concept of deviancy and its links to social mores. Countries across the globe moved to outlaw the trafficking of women in 1904, culminating in the UN International Convention for the Suppression of the Traffic in Persons (1949) that prohibited not only trafficking but prostitution in all forms regardless of consent (Outshoorn, 2005: 142). As noted by Sullivan, this initial feminist approach towards prostitution, tied to ideas of white slavery, has been referred to as a 'feminist human rights approach' as it was argued that prostitution was 'incompatible with the dignity and worth of the human person' (2001: 168–169).

The disapproval of prostitution by radical feminists is apparent in the vocabulary employed. Jeffreys uses terms such as 'prostituted women', 'sex slaves' and 'survivors' (1997: 30) with, in some circumstances, good reason. However, this position fails to acknowledge sanctioned sex work as Perkins (1991), for example, documents. This can be illustrated by the fact that there is an International Sex Workers Union, which seeks to protect the working conditions of sex workers, with many of these workers not classifying themselves as victims (see International Sex Workers Union website, online, available at: www.iusw. org). So although radical feminists have universalised sex work as violence, this is an ideological position and does not necessarily accord with all the everyday activity and experience of those involved in sex work.

However, it is not only radical feminists who argue against all forms of sex work. Prostitution, using a Marxist perspective, is 'the cornerstone of all sexual exploitation' and the class conditions of patriarchal societies are 'fully revealed in prostitution' (Barry, 1995: 9–24). Barry argues that class domination 'is so pervasive that it actually invokes consent, collusion or some form of cooperation from the oppressed' (1995: 23–24) and as such any 'consent' to engaging in sex work is ultimately false as it is simply a reaction to the ingrained male domination of society. Recent qualitative research has described the way in which working in prostitution leads to even greater dependency on men, through economic exploitation, greater levels of poverty, homelessness and violence (Phoenix, 2000, Kinnell, 2006). This dependency is argued to be a two-way phenomenon. When taken to its logical conclusion though, this means all patriarchal arrangements, including marriage, are violence against women. So there is a question in this analysis as to whether marriage is the ultimate form of sanctioned sexual exploitation, as women's sexual availability is not even valued in monetary terms and rape and sexual violence in marriage is more common than in sex work. If official crime data and prevalence studies globally are to be relied upon; 'prevalence estimates of rape victimisation range between 6 and 59 per cent of women having experienced sexual abuse from their husbands or boyfriends in their lifetime' (Dartnall and Jewkes, 2002: 3)

Contemporary research though suggests that is it not only the women who sell sexual services who are dependent on the men who purchase sex, but also the men who purchase sex who are dependent emotionally on the women who sell it. For example, the work of Sanders (2008a) examines how men base their procurement of sexual services on conventional sexual scripts. Men, who purchase such services, engage with female workers as they do their wife, girlfriend, or a partner. Scholars such as Sanders (2008a, 2008b), Milrod and Weitzer (2012) add a new dimension to understanding why men purchase sexual services, that of emotional needs, which are addressed by such a procurement and offering a critique, in part, of the 'prostitution as harm' approach. This critique is discussed in detail in the following chapter, Chapter 3.

In summary, the radical feminist approach towards prostitution advocates an abolitionist policy to end all forms of women in sex work. Finstad and Hoigard (1992) conclude that prostitution is an 'abomination', 'brutal oppression' and as such must be opposed. As noted by Kesler (2002) this stance on prostitution, namely that all women who are engaged in sex work (prostitutes) need to be saved, is largely unsupported by those sex workers who voluntarily engage in prostitution as they feel it is antagonistic to their way of life. It is noted in the work of Alexander and Delacoste that 'many prostitutes feel that they are feminists as they "identify with feminist values such as independence, financial autonomy, sexual self-determination, personal strength, and female bonding"' (1987: 307). Ironically, the 'all sex work is violence against women' position sustains the very stereotypes that radical feminists want to overcome. By portraying all women involved in sex work as victims, radical feminists remove agency from women. This is not to deny that some women are forced into prostitution (as some are into marriage), are enslaved (as some are in marriage) and are treated violently (as some are in marriage) and that all such treatment is and should be treated as criminal. It is also based on a Western view of sexuality, which ignores cultural context as noted by Kempadoo (1999), who recognised that in African and Caribbean countries:

> where one can speak of a continuum of sexual relations from monogamy to multiple sex partners and where sex may be considered as a valuable asset for a women to trade with are ignored in favour of specific western ideologies and moralities regarding sexual relations.
>
> (p. 12)

Furthermore, there is limited recognition by radical feminists regarding the emotional intimacy reportedly involved in some procurement of sexual services and the function some sex workers play in such a transaction, such as being a 'counsellor'. In the Australian context there is limited work on this subject matter, bar the influential work of Roberta Perkins (1991).

Law criminalising sex work

It has been argued by Bottomley and Parker (1997) that the law has power to create meaning and make sense of the social world. This therefore applies to the social meaning of sex work. Law though, is itself based in a particular ideological paradigm depending on the society's cultural and political framing. The ideological context of the law in countries such as Australia, the United States and the United Kingdom has been argued to be a liberal one (Bottomley and Parker, 1997). Liberalism has a number of elements, including liberty, individualism, equality, justice, rights and rationality, but these do not always marry well (Bottomley and Parker, 1997) with the law. It is argued by some critical theorists, that fundamentally the law is the exercise of power as well as the 'prize of the powerful' (Bottomley and Parker, 1997) with the majority of people excluded from exercising this power. Those who have this power are in a position to define and re-define social norms and thus, by default, categorise certain actions and behaviours as deviant. For example, within a patriarchal society most laws that concern the sex work industry have focused on criminalising the women who sell sexual services (Kinnell, 2008). The second wave of feminism used its influence to enact changes in the law, which have in some jurisdictions criminalised men who purchase sex. There are postmodern laws that criminalise the sex work industry by criminalising men in a variety of different ways for procuring sexual services, such as for kerb crawling as noted earlier in the discussion of 'John's' programs. But the law's relationship with power is multi-dimensional in nature, in that the law legitimates power, is a source of power as well as acting as a product of power (Pfohl, 1994). In relation to sex work, it can be argued that the law constructs what are appropriate and inappropriate perceptions of sexuality, thus setting clear parameters of what it is to be a woman and what it is to be a man in whichever society particular laws governing sexual behaviour hold. Laws and changes in law over time governing the sex work industry, provide windows into the diverse conceptualisations of and shifts in morality towards this social practice (Brooks *et al.*, 2003a; McKeganey and Barnard, 1996).

The way in which sex work is characterised within the legislative framework in a country impacts on, not only the sex worker, but also on all of those involved in the industry, from brothel owner to purchaser. A 2009 review of legislation of prostitution in 100 countries revealed that 50 countries had legalised prostitution, ten had limited legality and in 40 countries prostitution was illegal (ProCon, 2009). But legislation covers a range of prostitution practices, from street based sex work to pimping and brothel ownership, and even when legal in one aspect, another aspect of sex work may be illegal.[1] Furthermore, legislation concerning the sex work industry can be separated into two distinct areas: one that addresses the supply of prostitution, that is laws that concern prostitutes and the supply of sex; and laws aimed at clients. Internationally the majority of legislation concerning sex work is focused on the 'supply' aspect, with sex workers and their practices governed by law. The governing of the supply aspect of prostitution is not limited to the actual act of providing sexual services; it extends to brothel ownership and management, instances of pimping (or third party involvement/facilitation) and instances of trafficking and people smuggling for the purposes of prostitution. Legislation that criminalises all forms of the provision of sexual services, places a meaning on sex work that denotes this social practice as bad, deviant, and immoral.

Until recently though, the client has been absent largely from sex work legislation; however, that has begun to change. Legislative changes in Sweden and the United States, to name just two jurisdictions, have framed men as the 'problem' in this social practice. Where once the sex worker was the deviant and evil person, all sex work clients are deemed as deviant and criminal, following the work of theorists such as Winick (1962) and Stroller (1975) and of radical feminist theorists such as Jeffreys (1997).

Australian law and sex work

There are various legislative approaches across Australia concerning the sex work industry, which demonstrate a mixed approach to dealing with both the supply and demand side of sex work. NSW has decriminalised prostitution (albeit with restrictions on the location of soliciting for street based sex work), Queensland, Victoria, Australian Capital Territory (ACT) and the Northern Territory legislation still holds that 'street-based prostitution is prohibited [while] other venues and labour forms are licensed by strict regulatory frameworks' (Ditmore, 2006). Most forms of prostitution are illegal in South Australia, Western Australia and Tasmania, although prosecutions are 'generally targeted at street-based sex work' (Ditmore, 2006). Despite many of the states prohibiting what is legal in NSW, each has, at some point, attempted to liberalise its laws. Some time ago Roberta Perkins commented: 'Legislators of this century [twentieth] have continued to fail to realise that prostitutes are not a special breed of women with compulsions to indulge in criminal behaviour' (Perkins, 1991).

Table 2.2 summarises the legal frameworks applied to the sex work industry across Australia. As well as regulating directly the work of sex workers, these laws impact on the way clients are thought of and treated.

Table 2.2 illustrates the complex nature of sex work law in Australia due to this issue being addressed at state level. But, a common feature of Australian law is how it focuses primarily on those who provide sexual services, the seller, rather than on those who procure sexual services, the buyer. However, the fact should not be overlooked that although Australian sex work law focuses on the sex worker, it has a direct impact on the procurer of sex from sex workers and how, when and if they engage with the sex work industry. The various laws across Australia, will therefore impact on the clients of sex workers in a variety of ways.

Understanding the NSW context

Within this volume, based on the empirical research considered in Chapters 4 to 6, an exploration of sex work clients' reasons for, and experiences of procuring sexual services in NSW is offered, so a more detailed context for sex work in NSW is necessary. The current approach to sex work legislation in NSW is that of decriminalisation.[2] The act of exchanging money for sexual services was decriminalised throughout the state in 1995 (Disorderly Houses Amendment Act, 1995), with the sex work industry managed by policies established in three domains:

* WorkCover NSW,
* NSW Health,
* Local governments.

WorkCover NSW ensures the establishments where prostitutes operate are compliant with occupational health and safety requirements, and NSW Health protects the health of the workers and their clients. Pinto *et al.* (1990) suggest that the decriminalisation of the sex work industry will benefit the health of workers, as they can obtain a health check without the fear of being arrested. In regard to sexually transmitted infections in NSW, female sex workers have one of the lowest prevalence rates amongst all groups in society, and in fact, there has never been a recorded case of HIV transmission involving a female sex worker in Australia (Sex Workers Outreach Project, 2007). The traditional stereotype that sex workers transmit STIs and other related diseases (Earle and Sharp, 2007) may still, at times, be attached to the sex work industry in NSW. However, the legalisation surrounding prostitution in NSW and its decriminalisation can be correlated with an increase in sexual health checks for those in the sex work

Table 2.2 Summary of sex work law, Australia (excluding NSW)*

State	Act of legislation	Brief outline
QLD	Prostitution Act (Amended 2011)	The two forms of legal sex work in QLD are: Working privately and on own – it is an offence to work in pairs. Sexual services can be conducted in a licensed brothel.
VIC	Prostitution Control Act 1994	Brothel work must be licensed, and is limited to six rooms. Sex work is regulated by the local councils.
ACT	Prostitution Act 1992	There are strict criminal controls in relation to the geographic location where sex work can happen. Brothels, studios and agencies must be registered with the Registrar of Brothels and Escort Agencies. Private work is not an offence if it is out of the sex worker's own home.
NT	Prostitution Regulation Act 2004	Brothels are illegal. Soliciting and street work is illegal. Escort agencies require a licence and each escort requires a police certificate.
TAS	Sex Industry Offences Act 2005	A self-employed sex worker is legal in Tasmania – in groups of two or less workers. Street based sex work is illegal. It is illegal to keep and manage a brothel and receive payments for sexual services. Clients are not criminalised for procuring from self-employed sex workers.
SA	Summary Offences Act (1953) and Criminal Law Consolidation Act (1935–1976)	Street based sex work is illegal. Sex work in a sex worker's private home is illegal; however, it is not if conducted within the client's home. It is illegal to keep and manage a brothel and receive payments for sexual services.
WA	Prostitution Bill (2011)	Illegal for private workers to work from residential areas. Licensing system for all sex workers, owners and managers of sex work premises. Street based sex work is illegal. Registration of all sex workers and sex industry business owners and managers will be held by the government, with access for the police to the register. Heavy penalties and in some cases prison sentences for not complying.

Note
* Some information sourced through the Scarlett Alliance website (online, available at: www.scar-lettalliance.org.au).

industry (Kilvington *et al.*, 2001). In fact, many support programmes for sex workers are funded by public health money. Research by Fox *et al.* (2006: 321) shows that 98 per cent of sex workers from well regulated Sydney brothels use condoms consistently. On the other hand, the same research states that only 78 per cent of sex workers from poorly regulated or illegal brothels use condoms consistently. The contrast is due to the availability of condoms in the workplace and support from brothel owners for health promotion initiatives (Fox *et al.*, 2006: 322).

The decriminalisation of prostitution in NSW is embedded in a range of laws, the most recent of which is the Brothels Legislation Amendment Act 2007 (NSW), under which local governments in NSW have the authority to identify and close down any 'unauthorised' brothels. However, under this legislation a brothel closure order cannot be issued against a premises with only one sex worker (Sex Workers Outreach Project, 2007). NSW is also the only Australian state or territory that allows street prostitution, as long as it is not within a certain distance of churches, schools, hospitals or other such institutions (Weitzer, 2009).

Positive outcomes of this decriminalised context are widely promoted by prostitutes' collectives in all states of Australia, because in NSW sex workers' choice of employment no longer results in arrest or a criminal record and such arrangements contribute to sex workers' personal safety. This in turn contributes to the reduction of criminal proceedings and enhancement of personal safety for clients. Australian sex workers believe that decriminalisation is 'the most workable, realistic and compassionate option' (Pinto *et al.*, 1990). However, the lack of anti-discrimination legislation in regard to the profession in NSW is a major concern for sex workers (Sex Workers Outreach Project, 2007). Overall, the policy adopted by the NSW government in regard to the sex work industry could be considered a liberal approach compared to both the international legislative frameworks and those of other Australian states and territories.

Despite the lack of criminality in NSW with regard to the exchange of money for sexual services, policies and the operational aspects of the sex work industry are still met with substantial hostility. The Coalition against Trafficking in Women clearly states on its website that the sex work industry 'exploits women, regardless of women's consent' (Weitzer, 2009). There is absolutely no question that human trafficking and people smuggling of any kind, and in this case women and children for the purposes of (coerced) prostitution, is abhorrent and criminal, but not all women in the sex work industry have been trafficked/people smuggled or have been forced into prostitution. In particular locations where the sex work industry is decriminalised and/or regulated, trafficking and people smuggling for the purposes of prostitution is more likely to be reduced (Harcourt *et al.*, 2005: 125).

So the claim by the anti-trafficking coalition, that all sex work is exploitative, implying that all women in the industry are trafficked (or have been involved in people smuggling) in some way deserves close attention and debate. The claim appears to be an ideological one, not one based on evidence. Such a claim also has a negative impact on how the clients of sex workers are perceived – by default they are the cause of women's exploitation in this context because they provide the demand for sex work.

Conclusion

In conclusion, sex work and the procurement of sexual services have been constructed and understood in a variety of ways, but most often as deviant and immoral. Historically it is evident how social institutions such as the Church and medical profession, as well the criminal justice system (in some parts of the world), have placed the social actors involved in sex work into the context of a specific time. For example, making allowances for men to purchase sex due to their 'inability to control' sexual urges, or blaming women for the disgrace that being a prostitute brought onto themselves and their families (Brooks Gordon, 2006). This perception of sex work as deviant and immoral has been conveyed through theoretical writings concerning the sex work industry as well as through laws. Early theorists such as Winick used their work as a platform to demonise men who procured sexual services, thus complementing the social values and norms of that time. This construction of men, who procure sexual services as deviant, has continued in more contemporary writings and through the theoretical framework of radical feminism. Radical feminists have argued that all sex work is exploitation and a violation of women, is oppressive and reflects the patriarchal society in which we live. The laws surrounding the sex work industry have further supported the deviancy perspective of sex work, evidenced in many parts of the world. Even in a state such as NSW, Australia, where the decriminalisation of sex work has taken place, laws still facilitate the deviant and immoral view of sex work. This is reflected in the lack of application of anti-discrimination laws and labour rights to those involved in this social practice despite these being afforded to all other workers and businesses.

These responses to sex work over time convey a clear message of what sex work is: sex work is a form of deviancy and those who provide it and those who purchase sex are deviant, because sex work breaches social norms that have been formally and informally encoded in a society's mores and laws. This is what Heidensohn (1968) defines as the 'process of definition', with sex work and those who are involved in it having been defined as deviant. Nevertheless, it is arguable that this is only one perspective to consider when making sense of men's procurement of sexual services.

Chapter 3 now focuses on alternative understandings and constructions of sex work and of those who purchase sex. Alternative writings have used theories of normative values, behaviour and function in order to understand sex work and those who are involved in it. Sex work in some contexts has been viewed by some as a behaviour that in various ways serves needs in society and of human beings on a personal level, as well as sex work adding value to the market economy. These perspectives are now considered.

Notes

1 In Germany, whilst sex work and thus the purchasing of sex is legal, street based sex work is illegal in some cities such as Munich, yet legal in others such as Berlin and Hamburg.
2 This includes street based sex work, however there are restrictions for where street based sex work can take place, see 1988 Summary Offences Act.

3 Understanding sex work 2

Normative values and commodity

As outlined in Chapter 2, Monto and McRee (2005) identified two competing typologies for understanding men who procure sexual services. These typologies, which are reflected in contemporary theorising about such men, depict a man who is 'peculiar' (discussed in the previous chapter), while the alternative typology depicts a man who procures sexual services as no different to any man in society. The alternative discourse to the 'peculiar' man typology of men who procure sexual services is the 'everyman' perspective (Monto and McRee, 2005: 505). Within this discourse of the 'everyman' perspective customers of sex workers are viewed as being like any other man in the community, offering an opposing view to the deviant and immoral character the 'peculiar' man perspective offers for understanding men who procure sexual services. The 'everyman' perspective by Monto and McRee (2005) offers a more pro-social understanding concerning men who engage in the act of procurement. Based on this pro-social typology, this chapter will consider the normative value (as opposed to the deviant approach discussed in the last chapter), that has been associated with men's procurement of sexual services, and which includes the consideration of sex, in these circumstances, as a commodity. Those scholars and social commentators who adopt such an approach to understanding men's procurement of sexual services in essence agree that the purchasing of sexual services is a valuable practice in society. There are three theoretical lenses through which these scholars and social commentators pursue this argument:

1   Sex work as 'work' and its commodification;
2   Theories of social exchange;
3   Emotions and experiences of intimacy.

This chapter will consider each of these theoretical frameworks in turn. This will enable a consideration of a pro-social position concerning sex work and those who purchase sex.

Sex work as 'work'

In stark contrast to the radical feminist's position on sex work, some liberal feminist writing portrays sex work as a form of work and, by inference, as a commodity. Women who sell this commodity are seen in the same way as any small business person who has a commodity to sell. Such a position reflects the work of scholars such as Sanders (2005) and Sanders *et al.* (2009). Sex work is understood as a commercial activity in which the exchange is seen in the same way as any other exchange of a commodity in the marketplace. Over the last four decades the idea that 'sex work' is a valid, freely chosen profession has been supported by a range of postmodern theorists and second wave feminists (here after termed 'sex work feminists'). Sex work feminists are represented by scholars such as Teela Sanders, Rosie Campbell, Belinda Brooks Gordon, Jane Pitcher, Roberta Perkins, Hilary Kinnell and Wendy Chapkis. This approach seeks to 'maintain a crucial moral distinction between prostitutes as sex workers and prostitution as a practice and institution' (Overall, 1992: 708), suggesting that the terms prostitution and prostitute carry negative connotations linked to societal taboos. The very language of this theoretical approach and the set of beliefs that surround its position seek the normalisation of sex work. This normalisation is sought by using the terms 'sex work' rather than 'prostitution' and 'sex worker' rather than 'prostitute' or 'prostituted woman'. By extension this has the potential to have a positive impact on how the clients of sex workers are viewed. Carrying this position further, Bindman and Doezema (1997) argue, given the liberalisation of society, for a rejection of the idea of a distinct group of women who are engaged in sex work. Rather, they suggest, there is a continuum of ways of engaging in sexual practices, both socially and psychologically, of which sex work is but one.

Further to the idea of the normalisation of sex work, is the active pursuit of the lessening of the gender divide by giving female sex workers better protection of their civil and labour rights through legitimation of sex work as normal work. This changes gender power relations in sex work and helps to combat the persistent representation of sex workers as abnormal women, bereft of morals. Sex work feminists also attempt to distance themselves from the understanding of sex workers as victims. They do so by noting that '(radical feminist) researchers have difficulty in understanding rational, not to mention positive, reasons for choosing sex work and find it easier to think of prostitutes as victims' (Vanwesenbeeck, 2001: 259). Nevertheless, sex work feminists do recognise that some women are forced into sex work, are victimised, and that this criminal behaviour by those who traffic, coerce and pay low wages, occurs in the same way that exploitation of workers may occur in many industries. This can be illustrated through the example that wages below the minimum wage are paid to foreign workers by some big mining companies (Caldwell, 2012). But this does not apply to many sex workers in a legalised, regulated context (Sanders and Campbell, 2007) in the same way as it does not apply to many workers in other industries.

Sex work feminists argue that their theoretical approach towards sex work advances both the rights of the willing sex workers as well as the rights to the protection of the law of those who are forced into the profession, such as trafficked prostitutes and sex slaves. For example, Bernstein (2001) suggests that this is achieved by ensuring that the willing sex worker has adequate labour and civil rights protection. This would then act as a means of exposing those who traffic or force women into prostitution due to various regulatory measures governing sex work, just like any other regulated work. The crucial point here is that sex work feminists argue that sex work must be recognised as legitimate work. This distinction is important as ensuring the difference between willing sex workers and forced sex workers can contribute to differentiating between men involved in purchasing sex from willing sex workers, compared to others who exploit poorly regulated and coerced female sex workers. This would include pimps and drug dealers as well as some men who pay for sex as a means of abusing women.

In this push for a clear distinction between willing sex work and forced prostitution, sex work feminists such as Sanders *et al.* (2009) argue from a policy perspective, that when all movement of sex workers across country borders is defined as trafficking (as set out in the United Nations Protocol to prevent, supress and punish trafficking in persons)[1] incidents of voluntary migration are disregarded (UN, 1999). On this note sex work feminists also suggest that within the focus on prostitution in current trafficking laws there is a clear genderisation, as most prostitutes are female (Vanwesenbeeck, 2001). This, they claim could lead to the repression of female movement across borders. Furthermore, it is suggested that to have this gender specific focus within trafficking policy, disregards men and boys being trafficked and subsequently leads to a lack of recognition of this in policy. This can also be argued from the perspective of people smuggling. It is for these reasons that sex work feminists advocate a clear distinction between voluntary migration for the purposes of being a sex worker and the criminal act of trafficking (and people smuggling) individuals for the purpose of prostitution. In contradiction to this nuanced understanding of trafficked/people smuggled sex workers and willing sex worker migration, the Global Alliance Against Trafficked Women[2] suggests that in terms of policy concerning trafficking and people smuggling, prostitution need not be mentioned at all as it is assumed in the following definition of trafficking:

> all acts involved in the recruitment and/or transportation of a women within and across national borders for work or services by means of violence or threat of violence, abuse of authority or dominant position, debt-bondage, deception or other forms of coercion.
>
> (GAATW, 2001)

However within this distinction of forced prostitute and sex worker, sex work feminists often brush over the various factors that can cause a sex worker to 'choose' prostitution as a career. As Anderson and O'Connell Davidson suggest, many women who elect to enter sex work do so as a means of escaping poverty, stating 'it is dull economic compulsion that drives many of them into sex work' (2002: 94) rather than take slave-like factory and assembly line work. This suggests that the reasons for some women taking up sex work do not arise from deviant behaviour or violence against women, but from some women's poor access to reasonably paid work in the market economy. This highlights the continuing inequality of income for women compared with men across most of the globe. It also supports the view that sex work can be understood in some circumstances as just another form of work, in particular for women who may only be able to attract low paid work. Those in retail or manufacturing industries, for example, may, rationally, view sex work as a better paid labour option.

In terms of freedom of consent to engage in sex work, sex work feminists such as Sullivan (2001) recognise Foucault's concept of no 'essential freedom'. This is unimpeded by modes of control, but instead it is argued that freedom is a practice enacted as a resistance to power and ingrained concepts of acceptability. Using this concept, engagement in sex work is a pursuit of freedom by challenging the norms of society and what it deems acceptable roles for women. This pursuit of freedom can be extended to the clients of sex workers, in that their engagement with a sex worker is connected to their pursuit of freedom.

This theoretical approach to sex work of 'sex as work' is not only advocated by 'sex work feminists', but is also popular with radical liberals such as Marques (2010: 320–332). Radical liberalism holds that there should be free choice in all aspects of life, not hindered by government or religious intervention. It is within this approach that radical liberals advocate that engagement in sex work or the purchasing of sexual services should be an individual decision as it is an expression of freedom of sexuality. Equally, individuals should have the choice to not purchase sex and to have sex in a monogamous marriage relationship. Some caution needs to be applied to this position, as with any promotion of 'freedom of choice' it should be recognised that not everyone has 'free choice'. This can be referenced in particular to sexual expression due to a range of individual, social and structural disadvantages. Take for example a 24-year-old person with intellectual disability, whose chronological age suggests a person who has access to a number of rights and privileges, for example driving a car, voting and finding and having a sexual relationship. However, the intellectual disability may prevent them from accessing these rights and privileges; they may not have the social skills to go on a date or initiate and sustain a relationship. Purchasing sex may be a reasonable, in fact the only, choice for a person in this position. There is, for example, formal and legitimate support from government and disability organisations for people with disability to purchase sex, as can be seen on the Touching Base website (online, available at: www.touchingbase.org/) and the Scarlet Road sex worker group. This example challenges the common negative images that many have of men who purchase sex, such as sexually perverted or sexually insatiable men who objectify women.

Sex work feminists such as Garcia-Rodrigo (2009) criticise the abolitionist approach towards prostitution because they believe that it fails to account for the many women who would be adversely affected by the loss of their only form of income. Garcia-Rodrigo (2009) suggests that this is a violation of their freedom to work. Sex work feminists also question the validity of the abolitionist approach and many of the 'prostitution as exploitation' arguments, proposing that much of the discussion and debate is without reference to or consultation with those who are actually engaged in the profession and as such is a product of bias and assumed knowledge. Margo St James, an ex-prostitute who founded the sex worker advocacy group COYOTE (Call Off Your Old Tired Ethics), suggests that any theoretical approach towards prostitution and its regulation should be generated 'from the inside out' (1987: 85) in order to reduce issues of further stigmatisation. From this ideal, Weitzer argues that many radical feminist literatures on the negatives of prostitution ignore counter evidence, use anecdotal evidence and use the most disadvantaged sector of the sex industry as their empirical research samples (2005: 34).

In summary, there are some feminists – sex work feminists – who advocate the normative value and function of sex work. Sex work, they argue, empowers people, for example by offering individual freedom and choice to those who sell sex. This empowerment can encompass people feeling they have a commodity that is worth selling and they choose to do so within an economic market. Such market needs are met through a range of products being purchased, such as a sex act. The position of sex work feminists is challenged on a number of levels, most notably on the position that sex work is a form of deviancy that breaches social norms. The work of sex work feminists suggests that this can be overcome by valuing and recognising sex work as legitimate work. With this recognition of sex work being legitimate work, by default sex workers would be exposed to labour rights, more effective civil rights and other forms of protection. Ultimately, understandings of prostitution are subjective. There is acknowledgement amongst various groups opposed to sex work, and as outlined by Califia (1994: 245) that even if full gender equality was achieved prostitution would always exist as 'there will always be people who don't have the charm or social skill to woo a partner', and as such sex work serves a valuable social purpose. This is highlighted in international research, where loneliness and stress have been cited as reasons for men's procurement of sexual services (Kennedy *et al.*, 2004). The position argued by sex work feminists, that sex work is legitimate work in which a commodity is being sold and bought, is supported through other theoretical frameworks. Theories, such as social exchange theory provide an account of how this can occur within human relations, regardless of their nature, conventional or not.

Theories of social exchange and the purchasing of sexual services

Some research on men who procure sexual services claims that men demonstrate a self-focused and commodified approach to purchasing sex that is not part of an intimate relationship (McLeod, 1982; Blanchard, 1994; McKeganey and Barnard, 1996). Therefore social exchange theory can be used as a theoretical framework to understand men's procurement of sexual services. Social exchange theory is most commonly associated with economics and how the individual interacts with the market, as outlined by Homons in 1961 (Gergen *et al.*, 1980).

However, subsequent to the development of this theory in the 1960s, sociologists, anthropologists and social psychologists have applied its principles to social actors interacting with other social actors. Gergen *et al.* propose that social exchange theory is concerned with the analysis of: 'a series of transactions in which rewards and costs (in the form of behaviour) are produced to others in exchange for behaviours that may be "consumed" by self' (1980: viii).

Social exchange theory is a 'social psychological and sociological perspective that explains social change and stability as a process of negotiated exchanges between parties' (Lawler and Thye, 1999: 218). It assumes that self-interested individuals transact with other self-interested individuals to accomplish distinct goals that they cannot achieve alone. Lawler and Thye state, 'two or more actors, each of who has something of value to the other, decide whether to exchange and in what amount. This can be in the form of love and relationship or a business deal' (1999: 224), and the social positions the actors play are fundamental causes of emotions and feelings.

Considering the exchange theory in relation to interpersonal relationships Levinger and Huesmann (1980) suggest that continued interaction on this level is determined by the outcome of the first interaction, and if there are to be anymore these will be based on reciprocity. It is reciprocity that eventually leads to an interdependent relationship. These elements throughout the exchange ensure a relationship is sustained. Many clients of sex workers are identified, both by themselves and the workers, as 'regular' clients. Sanders (2008b) defines a regular client as one who is a consistent user of a market within the sex industry and visits a small select number of sex workers. It is further claimed that a small volume of men are responsible for a large volume of sex work usage (Brooks Gordon, 2006). This suggests that within the transaction of a sexual service both parties are engaged in behaviours that lead to the other party receiving something that can be consumed, for example money, emotional intimacy, a sex act, and involves reciprocity and interdependency.

Supporting this interpretation of some sex work interactions, the 11-point process proposed by Levinger and Huesmann that people who are engaged in an interpersonal relationship pass through (1980), can be used to describe the context and setting in which sex work takes place. While based on a conventional relationship, this model can be mapped onto the engagement of those involved in the provision and procurement of sexual services. This questions the perceived non-conventional status of the sex worker–client relationship. Those 11 points include requesting a meeting, disclosing of information about self, engaging in sexual acts, harmony within the exchange, planned future meetings and permanence in arrangement. All 11 points are features of the procurement of a sexual service that involves both rewards and costs for all actors engaged in the interaction.

Rewards and costs, in terms of actions of the actor, can be labelled in two ways: behavioural or relational (Levinger and Huesmann, 1980: 175). Behavioural rewards are defined as an instant reward the actor receives, e.g. a sexual act, the feeling of proximity, money; whilst relational rewards are centred on the 'state of the relationship', such as the longevity, which is important for both parties in the transaction of sexual services. Levinger and Huesmann (1980) argue that social exchange theory allows us to understand the inter-action between a couple within an interpersonal relationship by considering the *state of interaction*, that is the range of transactions engaged in such as talking and counselling and sexual interactions, as well as *level of involvement* (that is how often the couple interact). If high payoffs are experienced by both parties then a sustained level of involvement is achieved, providing a rationale for why men purchase sexual services over a sustained period of time. For example, Plumridge *et al.* (1997) in a New Zealand study found the length of time men procure sexual services was most commonly once a month with this pattern of behaviour taking place between a period of 1–20 years for those sampled. While behavioural rewards are based on instant gratification, rela-tional rewards are something deeper that are experienced by both parties to sustain the relationship. This suggests this type of sex work transaction has a normative function.

Social exchange theory, as illustrated by Sprecher (1998), may also be helpful in examining gender and sexuality within a sexual relationship. While this work specifically focuses on conventional relationships it clearly has applicability to the understanding of the transaction of sexual services within the sex work industry. Exchange theory stipulates three assumptions. First, it assumes that social behaviour is a series of exchange(s) in which individuals maximise rewards and minimise costs and when individuals receive rewards from others, they feel obligated to return the reward (Sprecher, 1998). Second, individuals assess the degree of perceived balance in the relationship between a partner's input and outcomes, with those individuals who are in inequitable relationships becoming more dissatisfied and facing greater sexual dissatisfaction than those who are in a more equal relationship (Sprecher, 1998). Third, it is identified that the communication for onset to sexual activity and negotiation for sex in a cou-ple's early stages of a relationship is crucial and disagreements by partners can lead to conflict, e.g. in a heterosexual relationship he may not be ready for sex but she is and vice versa (Sprecher, 1998). While there may never be verbal communication within a relationship about wanting to have sex, exchanges or trades such as gifts are presented more by those who want sex (Sprecher, 1998). Social exchange thus helps to explain why individuals seek sexual gratification outside marriage or long term conventional relationships. If there is a lack of ful-filment of the three assumptions outlined by Sprecher within more conventional relationships, then a partner may seek sexual services elsewhere. Therefore, if, for example, a male partner does not receive maximum rewards and minimum costs from within his relationship, he may acquire them from elsewhere, e.g. from within the sex work industry. Social exchange theory can also be demon-strated as applicable to the sex worker–client relationship through reports of sex workers themselves, where they claim they receive gifts from clients who they see on a regular basis (Sanders, 2008a). The application of social exchange theory and sex work is explored further below.

Applying social exchange to sex work

Heterosexual communities can be considered as marketplaces according to Baumeister and Vohs (2004), where men and women seek sex from each other in exchange for other resources. For example, Wilcox *et al.* document a range of resources men obtain from procuring sexual services, including 'sexual gratification', 'a girlfriend experience' and 'status from peers' (2009: 6). Baumeister and Vohs consider exchange theory to be cultural. Exchanges of resources for other resources differ over time and place, depending on the social norms and cultural assumptions that impact on the different social roles that males and females play, for example as purchasers and sellers of sex. They argue that social exchange theory is a good predictor of behaviour, as choices about sexual interactions are shaped by analysing costs and benefits. People will only proceed if they stand to gain more than they lose, for example financial gain from the sex worker's perspective and a girlfriend experience from a male client's perspective.

This is further exemplified through Baumeister and Vohs' (2004) application of social exchange theory to sex work, where a rationale is offered for why the majority of sex workers are female, and the majority of clients are male. They hold that female sexuality is valued more highly than male sexuality reflecting the patriarchal nature of most societies. Men also appear to be willing to pay for sex for a number of reasons, such as thinking that paying for sex is a more straightforward and a less hypocritical version of courtship or marriage, while some research suggests men view sex workers as a low cost alternative to traditional sexual relationships (Wilcox *et al.*, 2009).

Links between social exchange theory, sex work and masculinity have been considered by Marttila (2003). Marttila frames these concepts in terms of consumerism and applies them to sexuality, specifically to men who purchase sex. She highlights the common hegemonic definition of masculinity in Western cultures (considered in Chapter 1), but argues that masculinity and identity must be considered in the plural, with multiple masculine identities between individuals as well as within individual men. Therefore, men can hold a range of identities, where, for example, most sex worker clients in her study were married, and many also had children. However, Marttila found that a common reason for men purchasing sex was to demonstrate masculinity. This is argued to be a reflection of the normative function that sex work has in society – that of men demonstrating their 'maleness'. The 'performance' of heterosexuality was a prominent factor, suggesting that masculinity is continually questioned within society and thus has to be performed constantly, because 'men want to be granted their manhood from other men' (Kimmel, 1994: 129). While evidence suggests that men do not tell many people about their procurement of sexual services (McKeganey, 2006), men tend to be aware of other men's purchasing of sexual services, as exemplified by the percentage of men who procure sexual services due to peer pressure (Wilcox *et al.*, 2009).

Furthermore, Marttila notes that cultural assumptions surrounding consumerism and masculinity have resulted in some societies viewing sex work as a conscious consumer choice. She suggests that this is why men may now consider purchasing sex as a signifier of their masculinity, as not only does having sex with a woman 'make you a man', but as consumers, men who can afford this luxury are also able to assert their masculine status of wealth and success.

The theory of social exchange contributes to the debate on sex work as being a normative function in society. Viewing the purchasing and selling of sex through social exchange theory places such an exchange within the context of an interpersonal relationship offering rewards to both parties involved in the exchange, whether that be a financial gain or an emotional gain. Social exchange theory provides a way of understanding the emotional benefits that a social exchange has on actors involved. Applied to the study of sex work, the theory provides an avenue by which to explore the importance of emotions and intimacy. It is the emotions and intimacy aspect of the procurement of sexual services that this chapter now considers in order to explore further the normative value and function that sex work may have in society.

Emotions, intimacy and the procurement of sexual services

In recent years there has been an attempt to understand the procurement of sexual services through exploring emotional intimacy. Emotions are defined in a multitude of ways. One of the most commonly used definitions refers to emotions as 'a relatively short-lived positive or negative evaluation state that has neurological and cognitive elements' (Lawler and Thye, 1999: 217). Typically emotions and intimacy have been understood through neurobiological and cognitive theorising, although there is a growing body of literature on emotions that have been framed by sociological determination and definition. Solomon (1978) for example recognised an emotion as:

> a network of conceptual and perceptual structures in which the objects and people in our world, others' action and our own are given significance. An emotion [is] a system of judgements, which in turn is a sub-system to the whole of our ways of viewing the world.
>
> (p. 187)

Bandes (2009) describes emotions as 'display rules or expression norms' in society that act as regulation for acceptable behaviour. According to Bandes emotions provide:

> scripts for socially appropriate enactment of emotion' amongst males and females ... emotions drive us to care about the outcome of our decision-making,... motivate us to take action, or refrain from taking action. The neurobiological processes are shaped, refined, and communicated in a social and cultural context.
>
> (Bandes, 2009: 7)

These quotes demonstrate general agreement on what emotions are. The literature suggests similarities across cultures and time on primary emotions such as surprise, fear, disgust, sadness and joy. These primary emotions lead to secondary emotions, which are more sociologically framed: for example the feeling of anger is a secondary emotion after an initial feeling of fear (a primary emotion) (Turner and Stets, 2006)

Shields *et al.* (2006) describe the gendered nature of emotions that lend themselves to stereotypes that 'pertain to ideas of appropriateness and legitimacy' (p. 64). Simply put, who is allowed to have what emotion and when is culturally determined. This becomes particularly important in intimate situations, as it is suggested that there are many levels of emotion that Western society conditions men to feel 'wrong' about. Men are socially conditioned to place more emphasis on physical intimacy, for example a physical sexual act rather than displaying the emotional intimacy coinciding with such physical acts such as tenderness. Some argue that beliefs about emotion occupy a central place in our understanding of what it means to be a man or a woman. West and Zimmerman (1987) propose that emotions are a result of men and women doing gender. They suggest that gender is not something one has, but rather, something which one does and, in line with the generally held sociological view, that gender roles are learned. However, due to notions of what masculine and feminine are, and how these can change over time, place and various contexts – gender modifies, which means people can play different roles in different situations.

In terms of men and emotions, as Seidler (1994) has noted: 'Traditionally, men have relied upon women to provide them with an account and understanding of what they are experiencing in their emotional lives' (1994: 109). It is therefore not surprising that men may negate their responsibilities in conventional relationships when it is only women who perform key aspects of maintaining a romantic relationship. Furthermore, if men are able to, and are encouraged to engage in the expressing of emotions during their encounter with a sex worker, it is important to recognise sex work as an acceptable practice.

Traditionally 'real' men have not identified themselves as having emotional needs, primarily through the construction of masculinity and femininity (discussed earlier in Chapter 1). This has resulted in the construction of the male identity (Seidler, 1994: 108), which involves men not showing their emotions.

It can be argued that social pressures to appear masculine may influence younger men to visit a sex worker in the first instance. Seidler (2007) proposes that 'young men often disdain their own vulnerability of emotions fearing that these can threaten their male identities' (p. 81). This sociologically produced disdain can result in pressure placed on young men, which influences them to place importance on physical heterosexual intimacy as a means of displaying feelings and emotions, commonly identified as being female qualities. Therefore, the visiting of sex workers by men can be seen as a mechanism for displaying such feelings and emotions. In this way of thinking about emotions and sex, men's procurement of sexual services can be understood to have a normative function in that the act allows men to display their emotions and engage in the feeling of intimacy that traditionally are not associated with being a man.

Theories of intimacy

Intimacy has been described as involving mutual trust and acceptance that lends itself to an affectionate bond being established between two people (Sullivan, 1953). Such a definition presents intimacy as the search for emotional closeness, self-validation and support, and it is through the satisfaction of these needs that the individual acquires the capacity for intimacy. Intimacy also reflects the quality of a relationship rather than just an individual's capacity for engaging in a relationship (Thériault, 1998). Therefore, there is a clear link between intimacy and emotions. Research into intimacy would suggest that closeness is experienced if emotions are shared amongst those involved (Collins and Feeny, 2004).

Thinking sociologically, intimacy has a social basis (Gaia, 2002; Hook *et al.*, 2003) it represents the avoidance of loneliness; and people seek relationships, whether conventional or purchased, in order to establish a sense of intimacy. But in modern social life there are some who regard intimacy as oppressive, with its apparent demand for constant emotional closeness (Jamieson, 1998). This sense of oppression may reflect gender differences. Gaia (2002) for example has suggested that women tend to talk more often about intimate topics, whereas the daily interactions of men are significantly less intimate than those of women. Women, therefore, are more likely to be placed into the category of 'high-intimacy' (Gaia, 2002: 162) when compared with men. Nevertheless, whatever the explanations for gender differences regarding intimacy are, the focus of this book is on why men purchase sex and therefore, in this case, on the potential for the drive and need for intimacy to play a role in men's purchasing of sex.

Douglas (1977) argues that women generally appear to believe that intimacy means love, affection and the expression of warm feelings, while men believe it to mean sexual behaviour and physical closeness. However, recent research into intimacy and emotions, which focuses on how men process emotional cues and information, may throw a different light on men's views of intimacy and why some men purchase sex. Focusing on the emotions of male customers allows an exploration of factors that drive diverse groups of men of different backgrounds and cultures, to purchase sexual services. Sanders (2008a, 2008b) explored the narratives of heterosexual men who procure sexual services and the tensions between their desires for emotional and sexual intimacy and between emotional and sexual immersion and their fear of emotional vulnerability.

In relation to client–sex worker relations, Bernstein (2001) suggests commercial sexual demand varies between male customers depending on their attitudinal disposition. This is supported by other research on sex worker clients, with, for example, Jordan (1997) supporting this notion based on qualitative in-depth interviews with male clients of sex workers. A major theme emerging in Jordan's analysis was the purchasing of sex to solve emotional problems. This is in keeping with previous research examining reasons why men purchase sex. Such research reported 'socio-emotional problems', as measured by emotional and physical dissatisfaction, such as feeling neglected and being unsatisfied sexually (Sullivan and Simon, 1998).

The Internet, intimacy and sex work

The notion that providing sexual services facilitates men in dealing with emotional difficulties could be explained, in part, by the argument that commercialised sex services provide male clients with a 'fantasy world of subservience that corrects the real power deficits that they may experience in everyday life' (Bernstein, 2001: 398). Within globalised consumer cultures and the means by which these are communicated contemporaneously, gendered and sexed images are projected. As a result, young men may feel they are 'trapped into constantly having to compare themselves with these images' (Seidler, 2007: 20). The effects of rapidly developing communications on gender and sexuality including intimate relationships are inextricably connected to the procurement of sexual services in the early twenty-first century. For example, Internet dating has promoted the idea that an individual will have a greater chance of finding their soul mate through the virtual realm (Earle and Sharp, 2008). There is much debate as to whether genuine emotions and intimacy are developed when a relationship is conducted online (Scott *et al.*, 2006; Sternberg, 1997). Online intimacy is explored in depth by Scott *et al.* (2006), who claim a number of possibilities for intimacy development including that it may be a result of an individual's *ability* to establish an emotional connection with someone, rather than by what mode of communication is used (2006: 759). However Scott *et al.* also suggest that intimacy may be more influenced by the mode of communication used in the relationship than by a person's relational capacity or skills (2006: 760). Therefore, greater intimacy may be felt between individuals who have close and confidential communications using both verbal and non-verbal channels. The results of the research by Scott *et al.* (2006) found significantly lower levels of intimacy in those who used online dating compared to the higher levels of intimacy reported by those who established relationships using more conventional means. These findings are strengthened by other work suggesting that individuals who struggle with intimacy in their face-to-face relationships may turn to online relationships as an alternative (Earle and Sharp, 2008). Based on the research of Scott *et al.* (2006) and Earle and Sharp (2008), it has been inferred that men who purchase sexual services online are less likely to desire a social interaction based on intimacy. Such research has further suggested that these individuals possess personality traits that make it harder for them to establish intimacy and emotional attachments when they engage in a face-to-face relationship. From the research into online sex work, men who engage in procuring this type of sex work can be viewed as individuals who may lack emotional stability. They may also be considered socially incapable and engage in online commercial sex to fill a physical or emotional void within their lives (Chapkis, 1997).

Although this volume is exploring face-to-face procurement of sex work, not the procurement of sexual services online, if emotional and intimacy deficits or lack of skill are reasons for men's procurement of online sexual services, it is of some importance to understand how these deficits originate because this may add to the argument that sex work has a normative function. One means of exploring this further is through the concept of behavioural scripts.

Behavioural scripts and their links to intimate relationships

As considered above, emotions and levels of intimacy are displayed through behaviour. However, behaviour, it is argued by Huesmann (1998), is based on behavioural scripts; scripts are guides for social action. Within the field of social psychology a 'script' is better known as a schema concerned with an event. A schema is a 'cognitive structure that represents knowledge about a concept or type of stimulus' (Fiske and Taylor, 1991: 8). It is a cognitive process that allows an understanding of a particular situation, like paying a bill in a restaurant, or engaging in behaviour that is associated with courtship. Scripts ensure we behave appropriately in given situations in a particular culture, and if a person lacks the relevant scripts for a particular event then they are prone to interpret the situation and the people involved in the situation incorrectly. When humans are considering how to behave in a particular circumstance, scripts are very important aspects of decision making (Ireland, 2008). Seal and Ehrhardt (2003) explore these scripts in sexual interactions, depicting men as having a general desire for physical closeness through a sexual act early in courtship. Females on the other hand, tend to construct sexual intimacy in terms of love and romance (Seal and Ehrhardt, 2003). They go on to argue that sexual intimacy can be understood through two discourses: 'sex as love and romance' and 'sex as conquest' (Seal and Ehrhardt, 2003). How these types of intimacy are played out can be encouraged or hindered by the behavioural scripts a person relies on to inform such behaviour.

Within a sexual context, behavioural scripts can be termed sexual scripts. Sexual scripts play a particularly important role in the recognition and display of emotions among men and women. A sexual script is 'a set of shared conventions based on mutual dependency that sets out the boundaries and roles that determine control, power, initiation, pleasure and so forth' (Sanders, 2008a: 401). Society depicts men as needing sex, whilst a female who acts in the same way is often described in derogatory terms. In many societies it is commonly thought that sexual scripts for men are those that script the male as seeking physical, and not emotional closeness. However, research by Sanders (2008a) considering the sexual scripts of men who procure sexual services suggests that men can display behaviour based on sexual scripts of emotional closeness.

Sexual scripts and the procurement of sexual services

Sanders (2008a) applies the framework of sexual scripts to the procurement of sexual services, using her research with a sample of 28 regular clients with

whom she conducted in-depth interviews. She was exploring the men's relationships with sex workers compared to relationships of a more 'conventional'
nature. Sanders claimed: 'there are similarities in the acting out of the sexual
scripts and in the process of sexual engagement and emotional desires, satisfaction and vulnerability between men in conventional and commercial sexual relationships' (p. 401).

Sanders' work suggests that there is a misunderstanding in some theoretical
writings on men who procure sexual services and in the way their behaviour is
understood as there is a failure to acknowledge that the patterns of engagement
are similar to those associated with conventional courtship. She draws a distinction between what motivates men to purchase sex and the role motivations play
in the interaction. Sanders (2008a) suggests that regular clients are attempting to
establish the same elements that contribute to a long term relationship, for
example seeing just one sex worker is important for some clients, as the monogamy they experience through this action is a desired goal. However, this is not
the case with non-regular clients or repeat users who tend to go to more than one
sex market and use multiple sex workers. She documents six overarching conventional behaviours, related to courtship behaviour that men who purchase sex
regularly engage in:

1   Communication – regular clients like to have in-depth conversations in
     which they want to share their likes and dislikes, life histories and develop a
     level of communication that is linked to a high level of intimacy within a
     relationship;
2   Courtship rituals – regular clients seek sex workers who are prepared to
     engage in activities such as being taken to dinner, which clients see as just
     as important as the sexual act being paid for;
3   Sexual familiarity – regular clients are wanting the 'girlfriend experience' in
     which seeing the same worker is important as it lends itself to establish
     emotional intimacy through such regularity;
4   The want for mutual satisfaction – regular clients want to believe that the
     sex worker has had as much of a rewarding experience as they have. While
     Sanders quotes Weinburg *et al.* (1999) regarding the fact that sex workers
     do not find the experience as rewarding as the clients, the exchange theory,
     as discussed above, would argue there must be some level of mutuality
     otherwise the transaction would not continue;
5   Emotional connections – regular clients over a sustained period of time
     engage in communication and sexual acts with the same sex workers, which
     allow them to feel as though a friendship has been established, based on a
     level of trust that has been achieved through the longevity of their trans-
     action. Through this, clients feel there is an emotional connection between
     themselves and the sex worker (Sanders, 2008a: 405).[3]

Sanders (2008a) argues that normative behaviours are acted out in the procurement of some sexual services; normative behaviours that would be used by a

husband interacting with his wife. Sanders advocates that sexual activities are only one element of commercial sex. Such evidence indicates that male clients may need to establish a sense of emotional attachment and intimacy through a sex worker, as they cannot obtain these through any other medium. Based on Sanders work it could be argued that men who procure sex following these types of scripts may in fact be attending to their psycho-social well being, in the same way as other men may attend to their psycho-social well being through meditation and other related practices associated with a positive way of life. People who fail to attend to their psycho-social well being, for example through lack of an intimate relationship, experience more stress-related symptoms, are more likely to develop illness, have slower recovery from illness and have a high probability of relapse/recurrence or illness. They also have higher mortality and accident rates, show depressed immunological functioning, and are more at risk of depression (Hook *et al.*, 2003: 463). Therefore, if the procurement of voluntary sexual services has a normative function in the lives of men who engage in the procurement of sexual services, the demonising and in some instances the criminalising of those men could be argued as having a detrimental effect on their health and well being.

Sex work as a normative function of society?

The above theoretical considerations and research findings provide alternative ways of understanding and interpreting men's procurement of sexual services to those considered in Chapter 2. The research and theoretical positions exploring sexual services in this chapter suggest that some sex workers and those who procure sex are engaging in a market economy. It is also argued that the sex industry provides a valuable service to men who are unable to express and experience emotional intimacy in the conventional way. Therefore one conclusion could be that men's procurement of sexual services, in most cases, is one of choice. Whilst the act is in response to a range of instinctual behaviours and structural economic forces that suggests that men's purchasing of sexual services fulfils a normative function.

The literature has also opened up an exploration of sexual scripts in relation to the procurement of sex. Understanding the purchasing of sex through the use of the concepts of behaviour scripts and subsequent sexual scripts, suggests that men's execution of emotions and intimacy may be misunderstood. The importance that the procurement of sexual services has on men's lives may have been underestimated. This may be aligned to Shields *et al.*'s (2006) second level of emotions, that is, the level of emotions that is socially constructed and that informs society how women and men should behave. Work conducted by scholars such as Sanders (2008a) has pointed to the involvement and exchange of emotions and intimacy between sex workers and their clients as a clear indication of the normative function sex work may play within society.

Making sense of men's procurement of sexual services: introducing the SAPSS model

The procurement of sexual services interpreted in the various ways examined so far, that is, as a normative function, and as deviance and immorality, can be modelled by drawing together the theoretical strands. Doing so visually displays how the various positions try to make sense of men's procurement of sexual services. This model, the single factor analysis choice model for the procurement of sexual service (SAPSS) model, is displayed in Figure 3.1.

The SAPSS model illustrates the knowledge base currently used to understand why men purchase sexual services, providing three 'choice routes', but which can be understood under two conceptualisations, deviant/immoral or normative. The model recognises and reflects how the current theorising on the procurement of sexual services, based on the two conceptualisations, is separate, distinct and binary in its understanding of this social practice.

The first choice route illustrates the understanding of men's procurement of sexual services through deviancy, as discussed in Chapter 2. By understanding the procurement of sexual services through this choice route, the immorality created by the operations of the sex work industry is seen as the output. Positioning sex work as immoral ultimately leads to the stigmatisation of workers and

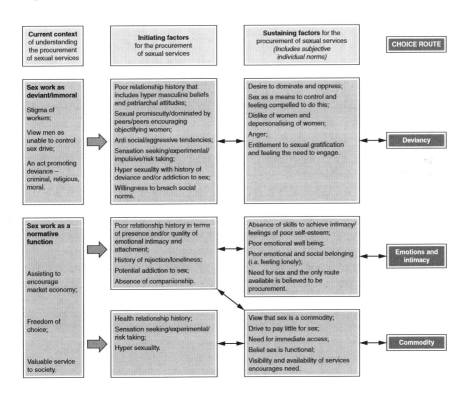

Figure 3.1 The SAPSS model.

places men as passive agents who are fulfilling an uncontrollable (sexual) urge. The purchasing of sex is seen as a deviant act from a range of perspectives, criminal, moral and religious. Within the choice route of deviance, men are portrayed as having anti-social and dysfunctional tendencies. This behaviour derives from patriarchal beliefs leading to hyper-masculine behaviour with aggressive tendencies. Within this choice route, men's procurement of sexual services is a reflection of impulsivity and represents a group within society who are aggressive risk takers. This explanation of the purchasing of sex, therefore, positions the male purchaser as fulfilling a need to dominate women, and rewards them with sexual gratification to which they believe they have a right.

Consideration of this 'immoral' understanding suggests a number of criticisms, such as the ignoring of female purchasers and male providers. Such a position overlooks the many choices that providers and purchasers of sexual services make when engaging in the sex work industry. Understanding men's procurement of sexual services through a theory of deviance can also over simplify explanations as to why men purchase sex. This is in part addressed by the normative conceptualisation with two choice routes outlined in the SAPSS model, one being the 'emotions and intimacy' choice route and the other the 'commodity' choice route. These remaining choice routes illustrate a normative function that the procurement of sexual services can play in the lives of those concerned, such as addressing the need for intimacy, engaging in a free market economy and individual freedom.

The choice route of 'emotions and intimacy' represents men's procurement as a result of poor attachments in previous relationships or lack of ability to attract an intimate partner. This choice route represents men who have faced a history of rejection and experienced an absence of companionship. This in turn has led men to a vulnerable state with reference to their well being and social belonging. But these men still need and have a desire for sex, and the procurement of such is the only option available. It also addresses the masculinity positioning of men, who through the social construction of emotions and feelings are perceived as not 'manly' if they act out sexual intimacy. Some choose sex work as the place to do this.

Finally, understanding the procurement of sexual services through a choice route of 'commodity', can imply that men who procure sexual services experience hyper levels of sexuality coupled with risk taking and sensation seeking. This choice route suggests purchasing sex is functional and that men need immediate access to sex. Nevertheless, what the normative function choice routes of emotions and intimacy and of commodification, outlined in the model above, fail to address is the deviant features that some men who procure sexual services may have. The deviant features of procuring sexual services can involve a range of issues such as the breaching of social norms, illustrated by those men who are married, yet still procure sexual services.

The SAPSS model draws together in a schematic way, for the first time, ways in which men's procurement of sex has been constructed and made sense of over time. The SAPSS model represents the theoretical perspectives that have been used to understand men's procurement of sexual services. Men are: deviant; or emotionally lonely; or perceive sex as a product that can be bought. These have provided an understanding of men's procurement of sexual services to date with a tendency for proponents of each approach to use that to the exclusion of the others. However, there has been little scientifically reliable and valid research documenting the linkages and correlations between the various choice routes men take in order to make sense of their procurement. By investigating the personal and social characteristics of a cohort of men based in NSW, Australia who procure sexual services, this book will address, in part, such a gap. Through the exploration of the reasons men give for procuring such services, based on the analysis of surveys and interviews from the sample in this study, connections amongst these choice routes can be made. This empirical research will seek to re-theorise and extend an understanding of men's procurement of sexual services.

Conclusion

This chapter has considered the procurement of sexual services within a normative framework. Scholars such as pro sex work feminists who draw a distinction between voluntary sex work and coerced prostitution promote the normalisation of this social practice. Scholars such as Sanders, Campbell and Kinnell for example view sex work as a form of work. By considering sex work in this way, the selling and procuring of these services can be understood through a prism of empowerment for both sex workers and their clients. The notion that sex work is empowering for those involved in this social practice challenges the deviant narratives that some scholars such as Jeffreys (1997) use to make sense of sex work.

The commodification of sex work was further considered in this chapter using theories such as social exchange theory. The procuring of sexual services and its value in society is extended through this discourse and symbolises the normative function that the procurement of sexual services plays in the lives of some men. This position is further explored through the consideration of how engaging in this social practice supports men in attending to their emotions and intimacy needs. Through the work of scholars such as Sanders (2008a), it is recognised that the act of procurement follows a similar pattern to that more commonly associated with conventional relationships.

In order to bring the theory chapters in this volume to a conclusion, the final section of this chapter introduced the SAPSS model. The SAPSS has been created and presented in this chapter to document visually the binary conceptualisation of the procurement of sexual services. The conceptualisation of deviant/immoral and normative function highlighted in the model reflects the theorising that is currently used to make sense of this social practice.

This chapter brings Part I of this volume to a close, in which sex work and the procurement of sexual services has been theorised. The second part of this work focuses on examining why men purchase sexual services, based on empirical research conducted in NSW, Australia.

Notes

1 Trafficking is: the recruitment, transportation, transfer, harbouring or receipt of persons, by means of the threat or use of force or other forms of coercion, of abduction, of fraud, of deception, of the abuse of power or of a position of vulnerability or of giving or receiving payments or benefits to achieve the consent of a person having control over another person, for the purpose of exploitation. Exploitation shall include, at a minimum, the exploitation of the prostitution of others or other forms of sexual exploitation, forced labour or services, slavery or practices similar to slavery, servitude or the removal or organs (UN, 1999, 2).

2 A feminist group that advocates an end to the trafficking of all forms of forced labour, such as trafficking for the purpose of becoming domestics.

3 Teela Sanders, Male sexual scripts: intimacy, sexuality and pleasure in the purchase of commercial sex. *Sociology*, vol. 42, no. 3, pp. 400–417, copyright © 2008 by Sage Publications. Reprinted by permission of Sage.

Part II
Examining men who procure sexual services

Introduction

The second part of this volume moves into examining why men procure sexual services. Based on empirical research conducted in the state of NSW, Australia between 2009 and 2011, Part II of the volume considers the contexts in which procurement takes place. The main aim of this empirical research is to examine the procurement of female sexual services with a focus on the personal and social aspects of men who procure such services. This aim is underpinned by the following research questions:

1   Are there common demographics amongst a cohort of men who purchase sexual services in NSW and if so what are they?
2   What are the reasons these men give for purchasing sexual services?
3   What services do these men purchase within the sex work industry?
4   In relation to men who purchase sex, what are the views of particular groups in society with an interest in the sex work industry?
5   What contribution does the understanding of the personal and social aspects of men who procure sexual services have on re-theorising this social group in the twenty-first century?

The empirical research underpinning this volume

The following chapters describe and examine the reasons and contexts in which the purchasing of sexual services takes place in order to understand why men purchase sex. This examination is based on a sample of 309 men who procure sexual services within the state of NSW in Australia, while those who sell sexual services were also included in the collection of empirical data. In conjunction with this, the empirical data collected information from groups in society who have a particular interest in the sex work industry and whose position in society can influence policy and legislative debates concerning the selling and purchasing of sex. The examination of these groups' views allows for an assessment of their understandings of why men purchase sex. This is important as it reflects the influence some groups have in political, social and wider public debates on this topic, as already demonstrated in the literature discussed in the first part of this volume.

The empirical research utilised both quantitative and qualitative research methodologies. The methods included a survey of 309 men who procure sexual services and 36 follow up in-depth interviews, including some with men who had participated in the survey, women who sell sex, women's collective groups in NSW, medics and members of the clergy. The production of the qualitative data resulted in those interviewed being assigned a code name to assure anonymity. The codes assigned to interviewees are illustrated by the following format and feature in the forthcoming chapters:

- Male procurer interviewee number 1 was coded MI:1 in the write up of the data,
- Female sex worker interviewee number 1 was coded FI:1,
- Clergy interviewee number 1 was coded CI:1,
- Medic interviewee number 1 was coded MeI:1,
- Women's Collective Group interviewee number 1 was coded WC:1.

The organisation of Part II

The following three chapters, Chapters 4 through to 6, present the findings of the analyses of the quantitative and qualitative data collected for this volume.

Chapter 4 presents the initial demographic data of the cohort of men who procure sexual services from the first phase of data collection. This data is of a quantitative nature and depicts characteristics of the cohort of men sampled. However, some interview data provided by the men who procure sexual services is included in this chapter. This aspect of the data allowed for depth and richness to be added to some of the personal and social data gathered about the cohort of men.

Chapter 5 reports findings based on a more advanced statistical nature. This chapter investigates the logistics of procuring sex and by doing so introduces a mnemonic to guide the research findings presented. This chapter also investigates the reasons offered by the men who procure sexual services for engaging in this behaviour. This is achieved by analysing the responses of those men who returned a survey. A cluster analysis offered in this chapter provides insight into different reasons men give for purchasing sex. The result of this analysis is the emergence of five clusters of men that reflect various reasons in relation to procurement. Considering the cluster analysis in conjunction with key demographic data presented in Chapter 4, further enhancements can be made to this analysis.

The final chapter of empirical research, Chapter 6, brings together all the interview data concerning the reasons why men procure sexual services. This chapter allows for a comparison between the groups interviewed in terms of the similarities and differences amongst men regarding why they pay for sexual services. It also examines why others think men engage in such behaviour. This final chapter of empirical findings provides an important distinction between onset factors for procuring sexual services (why men purchase sexual services for the first time) and continuing factors (why men return to procure sexual services). It is with the presentation of all the data that this volume can move into a discussion of what has been yielded from the study and reflect on the SAPSS model presented in Chapter 3. From the data presented a reconsideration of the applicability of the deviant/immoral frameworks and the normative function frameworks used to understand men who procure sexual services is sought.

Part II of this volume is then brought to a close in the final two chapters, Chapters 7 and 8, in which the procurement of sexual services is reflected upon along with an examination of engaging in the social practice of buying sexual services.

4 Contextualising the cohort

The personal and social characteristics of men who procure sexual services

Analysing the demographic profiles of the men in the survey cohort allows an exploration of whether they 'fit' the beliefs about clients of sex workers that emerge from current theoretical frameworks. For example, do these men fit the profiles presented by Winick (1962), who suggested that all men who procure sexual services are deviant by nature. Or are the profiles of men who procure sexual services more representative of the 'everyman' perspective as presented by Monto and McRee (2005) and discussed in previous chapters of this book. An analysis of the demographic data can also lead to a comparison with the profiles presented in previous research publications. This allows men in the survey to be compared, using these basic and broad characteristics, with men in previous research.

The findings in this chapter are based on the survey questionnaire, described in the introduction of Part II of this volume, answered by 309 men[1] who procure sexual services within NSW, Australia and represent the results of the first phase of the data collection. This chapter presents a range of personal and social characteristics of the cohort of men who procure sexual services. Whilst existing research provides information on the demographics of men who procure sexual services, much of this work is based outside Australia, and on samples of men who live in jurisdictions where sex work is a criminal activity, unlike in NSW. There is also a presentation of some findings from data collected in the second phase of the data collection process, that is, from the in-depth interview data from the 13 men who agreed to an interview. Aspects of the qualitative data offer a deeper understanding and contextualisation of some issues covered in the questionnaire and so it is pertinent to include these data in this chapter. The data presented below provide analyses of variables such as age, marital status and educational background, as well as offering an insight into whether these men disclose their procurement of sexual services to others. The findings report the various reasons given by some men as to why they fail to inform family members and friends of their behaviour. The examination of the public perception of the clients of sex workers was sought from the men surveyed. This along with consideration of whether changing the law in NSW, criminalising sex work and the procurement of such, would in fact prevent them from purchasing sex. It is these latter variables in particular that centre on why men, in some instances, keep their procurement of sexual services a secret. The issue of criminalisation of sex work and the view the men had on this were the final questions of the interview. Therefore, the inclusion of that data in this chapter is important.

At the end of the chapter it is also pertinent to begin considering the data presented in conjunction with the applicability of Monto and McRee's (2005) typologies of men who procure sexual services: the 'everyman' perspective and the 'peculiar man' perspective.

The demographics of men who procure sexual services

The age range of the sample of men who completed the questionnaire was 29–76 ($M=47.5$, $sd=10.9$). This age range and the mean reflect existing data on the age profile of men who procure sexual services in 'Western' countries. Findings from international studies present a broad age range of men who procure sexual services, with most studies finding a large proportion of men are in their early thirties to early fifties (Kinnell, 1989; Brooks Gordon, 2006; Coy *et al.*, 2007). This suggests that regardless of whether sex work is criminalised or not, the age range of those who procure sexual services is consistent amongst Western cultures. The cultural background of the sample is presented in Table 4.1.

The largest proportion of the sample was of Anglo-Saxon/British/Irish background, with the smallest proportion being of Aboriginal/Torres Strait Islander background. This is not a surprising finding considering the cultural make-up of the Australian population. Although, as a key interest to the Australian community, the current study does reflect an under-representation of Aboriginal and Torres Strait Islanders, based on data from the Australian Bureau of Statistics (ABS). According to the ABS 2011 census data, 55.4 per cent of the Australian population is made up of the Anglo-Saxon, British and Irish community, while the Aboriginal and Torres Strait Islander community makes up 2.5 per cent of Australia's population.[2] The particularly small sample of Aboriginal/Torres Strait Islanders in the cohort ($n=0.3$) could be a reflection of a number of cultural differences, in terms of defining and/or

Table 4.1 Ethnicity of men who procure sexual services ($n=309$)

	n	%
Aboriginal/Torres Strait Islander	1	0.3
Anglo Saxon/British/Irish	179	57.9
Western and Northern European	29	9.4
Southern European	15	4.9
Eastern European	16	5.2
North African and Middle Eastern	8	2.6
Sub Saharan African	2	0.6
North Asian	18	5.8
South East Asian	41	13.3

accessing sex work, but also in how the sample was obtained. As outlined in the methodology in Chapter 5, the sample was obtained through the Internet and mainstream Anglo-Saxon newspaper advertisements and may reflect socio-economic status.

As illustrated by Faugier and Cranfield (1995) along with Monto (2000) and Groom and Nandwandi (2006), the ethnic profile of men in studies examining male procurement of sexual services tends to reflect the local population of men who receive a salary that allows them to purchase sex. Much of the existing research shows that the men who procure sexual services are those in professional occupations such as bankers, dentists and university lecturers, as listed by the registrar general's classification of professional occupations (Scott and Marshall, 2009). Table 4.2 outlines the finding in regard to the cohort in this study, and again supports existing literature on the occupational status of those who procure sexual services. There is a reasonable amount of information on the occupational status of men who are involved in the transaction of sexual services, for example, Elliot and McGaw (2002), Ewasiw *et al.* (2006). While these studies reflect a diverse range of occupational statuses of men who purchase sex, Wilcox *et al.* (2009) recognise that 'most studies report a skew towards the higher socio economic classes' (p. 23).

These findings support other work reporting on the occupation of men who procure sexual services, in that the majority of such men are in well paid jobs. For example, Faugier and Cranfield (1995) report 68.9 per cent of their sample are in at least a white collar profession such as hotel manager, or higher such as a marketing manager, lawyer or diplomat. Less than 2 per cent of the sample was unemployed, with some form of manual work making up only 19.4 per cent of the sample's employment. In summary these findings demonstrate that men who procure sexual services earn a salary with enough disposable income to allow them to procure sexual services from within the NSW sex work industry.

The sample members were then asked in the questionnaire to identify their sexual orientation, which is shown in Table 4.3. In the current study the largest proportion of the male sample identified themselves as heterosexual. This finding is reflective of other international studies, for example, Macleod *et al.* (2008),

Table 4.2 Occupational status of men who procure sexual services (*n*=309)

	n	%
Diplomat	3	1.0
Professional A (e.g. doctor, lawyer)	85	27.5
Professional B (e.g. media and marketing)	77	24.9
White collar clerical (e.g. office employee, hotel manager)	48	15.5
Skilled manual (e.g. taxi driver, plumber)	43	13.9
Unskilled manual (e.g. service industries)	17	5.5
Unemployed	6	1.9
Retired	12	3.9
Student	18	5.8

Table 4.3 Sexual orientation of men who procure sexual services (*n*=309)

	n	%
Heterosexual/straight	291	94.2
Bi-sexual	16	5.2
Homosexual/gay	2	0.6

who found that 80 per cent of a sample of men who procured sexual services in Scotland, reported their sexuality as heterosexual.

Although a large proportion of the current study identified as being heterosexual, the current study explored the homosexual experiences of those surveyed in the cohort. Previous studies have indicated that significant proportions of men who are involved in the procurement of sexual services have had sex with men (Prieur and Taksdal, 1993; Day *et al.*, 1993; Faugier and Cranfield, 1995). Prieur and Taksdal (1993) suggest that men who procure sexual services have an increased likelihood of having had a homosexual experience compared to those men who do not procure sexual services. Just over 20 per cent of the current sample declared that they had had a homosexual experience (see Table 4.4). This is 10 per cent and 13 per cent lower than the findings of Faugier and Cranfield (1995) and Day *et al.* (1993), respectively. Nevertheless, the current sample does contain men who, whilst they identify themselves as heterosexual, have had a homosexual experience. Such a finding in previous research has led some theorists to suggest men who procure sexual services are sexually insatiable and risk takers (Prieur and Taksdal, 1993).

Based on the sample members who declared they have had a homosexual experience, the survey explored the type of homosexual experience encountered. This is shown in Table 4.5.

As Table 4.5 shows, those who have had a homosexual experience are likely to have encountered more than one type of sexual experience, as the total number/percentage of acts engaged in, is more than *n*=60/100 per cent. Nevertheless, receiving oral sex is the most common form of homosexual experience the sample had encountered. Receptive anal sex and hand relief were also common experiences of this group. What was not explored in this study was the context in which these sexual encounters occurred. For example, whether or not the homosexual encounter was experienced in a coercive way. A reason for this lack of exploration was due to the fact that none of the men interviewed in the second phase of the study, the qualitative interviews, disclosed ever having a homosexual encounter.

Table 4.4 Homosexual experiences of men who procure sexual services (*n*=260)

	n	%
Yes	60	23.1
No	200	76.9

Table 4.5 Type of homosexual experiences of men who procure sexual services (*n*=60)

	n	%
Receptive anal sex	19	31.6
Insertive anal sex	16	26.6
Oral sex given	23	38.3
Oral sex received	38	63.3
Hand relief received	21	35
Hand relief given	18	30
Group male sex	6	10
Voyeurism	8	13.3

The marital status of the sample was explored through the questionnaire, and as Table 4.6 illustrates, the category with the highest number was that of 'single' men (45.6 per cent). However, if those in the sample who were married and in a 'de facto' relationship are combined, the sample is evenly split between those who are single and those who are currently in a 'relationship' (46.4 per cent). This is an interesting finding, as most research suggests that it is men who are in some form of conventional relationship, such as a marriage, who typically procure sex. Research such as that by Day *et al.* (1993), Sawyer *et al.* (2001), Kennedy *et al.* (2004) and Lowman and Atchinson. (2006) shows that the majority of men (between 50 per cent and 90 per cent) who procure sexual services are married or in a cohabiting/stable relationship. The sample surveyed in this current study is outside that statistical range, with a significant proportion of single men admitting to procuring sexual services. Perhaps the fact that the procurement of sex in NSW is decriminalised results in a more diverse group of men engaging in this behaviour, compared to other parts of the world. Reasons for the procurement of sexual services are explored in detail in the forthcoming chapters.

Monto (2000) argues that men who procure sexual services, who are not married or in a cohabiting relationship may do so as a short term solution to finding themselves outside of a conventional relationship. It is suggested that those who are in a relationship may also procure sex as a short term solution for unsatisfactory sex with their partner. To explore this aspect, the current study examines the sexual satisfaction of those in a conventional relationship within

Table 4.6 Marital status of men who procure sexual services (*n*=261)

	n	%
Single	119	45.6
Married	91	34.9
De facto/living together	30	11.5
Divorced	20	7.7
Widowed	1	0.4

Table 4.7 Sexual satisfaction within conventional relationships of men who procure sexual services (*n* = 141)

	n	%
Very satisfied	17	12.1
Fairly satisfied	20	14.2
Satisfied	32	22.7
Fairly dissatisfied	36	25.5
Very dissatisfied	36	25.5

the cohort, with the findings outlined in Table 4.7. Men within the survey who identified themselves as married or cohabiting with a partner were asked to indicate their sexual satisfaction within that relationship. Existing literature states that men who procure sexual services do so as they are seeking the sexual gratification they fail to achieve within their conventional relationships, as well as other marital difficulties as suggested by Monto (2000). This implies that, for these men, the procurement of sexual services is a deviant act as it involves the breaching of a moral code in society. Men who are in a conventional relationship breach the moral code of monogamy. However, in contrast it could be argued that the procurement of sexual services for sexual gratification is a normative function that sex work plays in society. Reflecting the fact that pleasure and intimacy is a commodity bought by men when engaging in the purchasing of sex.

Based on their experiences of sexual satisfaction within conventional relationships, 51 per cent of the sample stated they were either 'fairly' or 'very' dissatisfied with sexual relations. With only 26.3 per cent of the sample being 'fairly' or 'very' satisfied. This suggests that the sample of men surveyed is likely to experience sexual dissatisfaction within their conventional relationships. As suggested by Monto (2000) this seems to contribute to their motivation to procure sexual services. It is notable though that around half said they were satisfied with their current sexual relations. These aspects will be explored further through the qualitative analysis.

The questionnaire went on to explore the criminal history of men who procure sexual services. As discussed in earlier chapters, men's procurement of sexual services is viewed by some theorists and writers on the sex work industry as 'deviant' and therefore often associated with criminality. It was pertinent, as a result, to enquire about the cohort's criminal history. As documented in Table 4.8, 92.9 per cent of the sample reported having no criminal convictions.

A further question was asked of those men in the cohort with a criminal conviction regarding the offence(s) of which they had been convicted. Each man had only one conviction, and 20 out of the 22 men had a criminal conviction for an offence of 'low seriousness' as defined by the Australian and New Zealand Standard Offence Classification (ANZSOC) (see ABS website, online, available at: www.abs.gov.au/ausstats/abs@.nsf/mf/1234.0). These offences were not related to the sex work industry and included crimes such as driving whilst

Table 4.8 Criminal convictions of men who procure sexual services (*n*=308)

	n	%
No	286	92.9
Yes	22	7.1

disqualified. Two of the offences reported were of a serious nature, murder and attempted murder, and they were both in relation to a sex worker. It should be noted that by far the majority of serious assaults and murders of women are by their husbands or de facto partners (Phillips and Parks, 2006). Both men had served time in prison for these offences. However, by far, the majority of men in this study (92.9 per cent) did not have previous criminal convictions. This finding offers a challenge to the negative narrative of criminality and deviance that surrounds men who procure sexual services.

The questionnaire investigated with the cohort whether they were open about their procurement of sexual services to other people or whether they kept their behaviour a secret. Table 4.9 outlines these findings.

Almost 45 per cent of the sample had not disclosed to anyone that they purchased sex, with most of this group claiming they never would. However, the majority of the sample had disclosed this activity to others (53.8 per cent of the sample). Table 4.10 outlines to whom the sample members have disclosed their procurement of sexual services.

Nearly 80 per cent of those men who had informed someone did not state whom they had told about their procurement of sexual services. However, of

Table 4.9 Have you ever told anyone about procuring sexual services? (*n*=260)

	n	%
Yes	140	53.8
No, but I would like to	4	1.5
No, I never would	116	44.6

Table 4.10 Who have you told about procuring sexual services? (*n*=140)

	n	%
Didn't state	111	79.3
Friends	17	12.1
Family member(s) (other than partner)	3	2.1
Internet forum users (non sex work)	1	0.7
Mistress	1	0.7
Other punters	1	0.7
Partner (other than wife)	2	1.4
Wife	4	2.9

Table 4.11 Reasons for not wanting to disclose the procuring of sexual services ($n=260$)

	n	%
Feel ashamed	36	13.8
Feel embarrassed	59	22.7
Says something about your attractiveness	14	5.4
Stigma attached	78	30
Would be labelled a pervert/sad	45	17.3
Family would stop speaking to me	33	12.7
Friends would stop speaking to me	28	10.8
Unimportant	38	14.6

those who did indicate whom they had told, informing friends was the most common category chosen (12.1 per cent). Whilst this represented a small percentage (6.4 per cent), a proportion of men did tell their wife/partner/family member(s). As with many taboo subjects, the stigma that surrounds the sex work industry could be the cause of the low levels of disclosure.

All the men in the cohort were asked what prevented them from disclosing their procurement of sexual services. This included those men who whilst they had disclosed to someone, typically a friend, had kept it a secret from others, usually their family members. Table 4.11 outlines the reasons men gave for keeping the procurement of sexual services a secret.

The main reasons men gave for not disclosing their procurement of sexual services to others were primarily associated with the stigma that is attached to the purchasing of sex, resulting in shame, embarrassment, being labelled a pervert and being ostracised. They believed the people they disclosed to would see them in an unfavourable way.

Within the second phase of the data collection process for this study, men were asked to discuss their experiences, views and opinions on a number of issues. As a result of this the qualitative data offered further insight into why men may keep their procurement a secret. The following section considers the information of the 13 men interviewed specifically relating to disclosing their procurement of sexual services.

Disclosing the procurement of sexual services: a qualitative understanding

It was common for the 13 men who were interviewed to keep their procurement of sexual services a secret. Family members were identified as the most important group they would not tell. Nevertheless, some men had informed friends about procuring sex, reflecting the quantitative findings on this. MI:5 for example kept the procurement of sexual services a secret from his family. He claimed that generally he was very secretive and selective regarding who he told about his purchasing and therefore he did not tell his previous wife or other family members, including his children and parents. However, MI:5 did tell some friends, and admitted that he would sometimes lie about the amount of sexual services he purchases, increasing the amount he discloses to his friends:

> [My wife] ah well she probably suspected it, but she never actually knew about it, [not like] my mates, in fact I sometimes lie about purchasing sex because I know that it impresses them and especially to my former best man. I often lie about buying sex, because he would think I was less of a man for not buying as much sex as I do.
>
> (MI:5)

The secrecy surrounding the procurement of sexual services was similar for MI:2, who stated his procurement of sexual services was largely kept a secret from his family, however he assumed his father knows:

> Yeh dad probably guessed, I mean after like four trips to Thailand what do you think, y'know? What's he going there for? It's like … I mean the funny thing is, if it's not that, then it'd be something worse, so you'd probably think that, y'know what I mean?
>
> (MI:2)

Generally keeping it a secret from his family, MI:6 did explain that he disclosed to some of his friends, both male and female, about his procurement:

> No [I don't tell the children] because I dunno what their view would be of their father purchasing sex from a sex worker. Although I have got a very close mate of mine that we will occasionally discuss it just in general conversation ummm that's about, that's about it, umm, I've also got a couple of female friends that we also talk about it in general conversation (chuckles) as well yeah.
>
> (MI:6)

Gender was an important issue for some men interviewed when they considered disclosing their procurement of sexual services. This is illustrated by the fact that MI:11 believes he will be judged by some, stating that:

> I don't talk to women about it because they would think that I was some sort of umm … they would judge me on that, like wondering why do I do that. Well I can't say to them because women don't want to have sex with me.… I tell my male mates. I have no inhibitions; I have no problems with it, because they understand. I think most men understand about … men having to buy it. I've got a couple of people, couple of people at work I, I talk to about it umm … couple of my mates, yeah I talk to my mates about it freely I mean I'd say you know, I went down to this really nice place there's this really hot looking girl down there.
>
> (MI:11)

For MI:11, a key inhibition to disclosing his procurement of sexual services to people is a feeling that he is admitting to being unable to engage in conventional sexual relationships. This presents some insight into why some men procure sexual services. This is discussed in depth in Chapter 6.

Although most men kept their procurement a secret from people, some were quite open, even with their partners. MI:7 disclosed his purchasing of sexual services to his wife in 'the early stages of their relationship', with this disclosure occurring after a 'period of courtship, just before they married'.

Overall, based on the interview data with the men, the disclosure of the procurement of sexual services appears to be limited, with men being guarded with whom they tell. There seemed to be no inhibition to telling other 'punters'. However, most of the men interviewed never discussed associating with other procurers of sexual services.

In relation to the cohort of men surveyed through the questionnaire and associated with these beliefs about what would happen if they disclosed their purchasing of sex, the sample members were asked what they thought the general public perception of them was. Table 4.12 lists the six main perceptions that men who purchase sex believe the general public hold about them.

The main perception the men thought the general public had of them was that of being perverse (71 per cent), with another 37.1 per cent of the sample members claiming the general public thought that men who bought sexual services could not be trusted; this was closely followed by being pathological and sick (26.6 per cent). These findings reflect the reasons men offered for not disclosing their procurement. This suggests that men might be more honest about their purchasing of sexual services if such negative views about the act did not exist. Interestingly, a percentage of the sample (27 per cent) claimed that the general public had the perception that men who procured sexual services were wealthy people. A view that in this situation that carries opprobrium, and suggests that these men thought the public believed purchasing sex was the sort of wasteful thing only the rich can afford to do; it may also signify jealousy on the part of those who can't afford it.

Overall, men's non/limited disclosure concerning their procurement of sexual services reflects the fact men believe the public has an image of them as 'dirty' and 'perverse'. This non, or limited, disclosure seems to be a protective behaviour used by these men who procure sexual services to shield them from

Table 4.12 General public perception of men who procure sexual services (*n*=260)

	n	%
Perverse/dirty	184	71
Pathological/sick	69	26.6
Dangerous/menace	36	13.9
Can't be trusted	96	37.1
Wealthy/luxury expense	70	27
Other	23	7.4

opprobrium or even worse outcomes, such as public labelling and stigma. The men believe in the main that society in general holds negative perceptions and maintains a negative narrative about men who purchase sex

Public perception of men who procure sexual services: a qualitative understanding

From the experiences and views shared by the men who were interviewed in the second phase of the data collection, it was evident that they thought that the public perception of men who procure sexual services was largely unfair. This finding provided some depth of meaning to the quantitative data, which revealed that the majority of the men believed that the public perceived them negatively.

MI:3, for example, believed that the public perception of men who purchase sexual services is that they are perverse. MI:3 thought that society had a problem with men procuring sex from women:

> The typical view is we are dirty, sleazy and you've got to be desperate to go [and purchase sex, because], you can't find a partner without going off to pay for it. I think that society has a major issue with it.
>
> (MI:3)

MI:4 thought that society's poor perception of clients is to be blamed on the media and its portrayal of the sex work industry. He also acknowledges the diverse range of reasons why men procure sexual services, including the counselling role that sex workers provide men, and comments on the ignorance of the public regarding the sex work industry. He speaks directly to the theoretical perspective of sex work acting as a normative function within society:

> Surely we are not going to be put on a pedestal like doctors, but I mean, you wouldn't put down somebody that cleans the toilets in a hospital would ya? They [society] only see what is portrayed on the TV. They [society] don't realize that prostitution can take many forms, rather than just the exchange of money. They don't understand that prostitution is not just sex, it's a lot of counselling, a lot of companionship.
>
> (MI:4)

MI:9 carries the comments by MI:4 about the media's culpability in misrepresenting the sex work industry further. The media industry was seen as responsible for constructing an incorrect view of those involved in sex work, with MI:9 also recognising the involvement of religious and feminist groups in the negative portrayal of procuring sexual services:

> I think that society's perception is driven by the conservative religious groups and the feminist groups. I don't think that men, in general, see it as

being a problem although it is unlikely that they would voice this opinion in public for fear of being derided.

(MI:9)

This is substantiated by MI:10, who believes there are negative perceptions in society that are created by religious and political movements:

> ummmmm, probably the vocal part of society doesn't like it. It just goes against their religious principles. I'll tell you the people that are most vocal against us are in the form of religious or political groups. From the general public yes probably umm....! It's all about 'why, what's wrong with you, why can't you get a girlfriend or a wife?'. Things like that.

(MI:10)

A common feeling amongst the men interviewed, was that the perception by some in society, that men who purchase sex are deviant and immoral, was unfair. They felt the media and politics were the key proponents of this view. It is clear from the experiences of the men interviewed that the positive part played by sex work in society is ignored. As MI:6 states, while there is a negative stigma associated with sex work, this stigma and perception, which includes both clients and workers, is both incorrect and unfair, and problematises the sex work industry:

> that umm if you had to go have sex with a prostitute that means that you were unable to pick up a girl ... but the sex industry is fine. There is no problem with it. Ummm I think what happens what clouds people's minds is they think prostitutes, they think Kings Cross, they think prostitutes I dunno why, they think Asians,... the whole sex thing about prostitutes and guys paying ... should be viewed pretty well down the list as far as things that are immoral ... [the social stigma] doesn't phase me cause I don't view myself that way, I'm ok I'm a healthy man, I don't do drugs, I don't drink, I don't do betting, I don't smoke, ummmm. They [society] still think that prostitution is low life ... umm prostitution is for guys that have a warped mind.

(MI:6)

Nevertheless it is important to note that whilst the common feeling amongst the men interviewed is negative regarding the public perception of clients of sex workers, this perception may not be reflective of all members of the general public, over time and in different contexts. For example, Hubbard and Prior (2013) found that communities who resided nearest to sex work markets, such as home based sex work, had a more positive attitude towards the industry than those who did not. This position is reflected in some of the commentary offered by a few of the male interviewees. Whilst acknowledging a negative perception held by the public was most common, it was believed that some members of society held more positive perceptions of sex work. For example, MI:7 believed that the perception by the general public, of those who were involved in sex work, including the clients had improved over time, although he thought there was still hypocrisy involved in the debate:

> There's nowhere near the level [of shame] that there used to be. And if we go back 30 years there was a lot more moralistic finger pointing than there is these days. I think that things in that direction have improved a lot. I think that people do believe that those who go to look for sex are men who are not getting what they're looking for at home ... but ... I wouldn't see that they believe these men are sexual failures or sexually insatiable. I actual think there are a lot of people who on the surface condemn the use of sex workers while in fact, they're doing it or would like to do it themselves. I think there's a lot of uh, two faced hypocrisy around the subject.
>
> (MI:7)

The final aspect to be explored in this chapter is whether men would stop purchasing sexual services if it was re-criminalised in NSW, noting that decriminalisation occurred within this Australian state in 1995 as part of the Disorderly House Amendment Act. Table 4.13 indicates that 69.3 per cent of the sample would not stop buying sexual services if it was made illegal; however, 63.5 per cent of this group claimed they would be more prudent in how they procured such services. Based on the sample survey, less than 20 per cent of men would stop buying sexual services altogether if it became illegal. Overall, the men surveyed claimed that they would not stop buying sexual services if the act was made illegal, which would mean men would be prepared to break the law in order to acquire sexual services. What this finding suggests is the act of procuring sexual services provides men with a fulfilment in their lives that is worth breaking the law over.

Criminalising sex work in NSW, Australia: a qualitative understanding

Through the interviews conducted, men's views were sought on the criminalisation of procurement. The data obtained from the male participants overwhelmingly demonstrated they would not stop purchasing sex if it was made illegal. Although a common pattern was found in the views of the men in that many of

Table 4.13 Would you stop procuring sexual services if criminalised? (*n*=260)

	n	%
Yes	50	19.2
Yes, but it depends on the punishment	30	11.5
No, it would increase my arousal	15	5.8
No, but I would be more secretive/less open	165	63.5

them would be more vigilant whilst procuring sexual services if this became illegal in NSW. The men interviewed also discussed the damaging effects that criminalising the sex work industry would have on those who sold sex. This suggests the men not only considered the impact of criminalisation from their personal viewpoint, but from the viewpoint of others involved in the sex work industry. For example, Male interview 1 indicated that the criminalisation of sex work would not stop him purchasing sexual services but he was concerned that the industry would most probably be driven underground as a result:

> It wouldn't stop me but it'd annoy me.... I'd just have to check out the place more than I do, you know, like what are the chances of getting caught you know, so. I would, I would attempt to carry on. [And] ... it depends how illegal. If there's a policeman standing outside brothels ready to arrest you and throw you in prison, well I'd probably give it up here yeah, I'd just go somewhere else. But ... if it becomes illegal then they're all going to go underground and you're not going to be able to control it then. So I don't know if that's going to be any advantage. And as a result there'd be a lot of girls out of work.
>
> (MI:1)

The issue of the sex work industry being driven underground if the sex industry was re-criminalised in NSW was also a concern for Male interviewees 6, 8 and 10. For example MI:8 suggests that the criminalisation of sex work would simply drive it underground and not deter clients, although he did suggest it would make clients more cautious when procuring: 'Well everything would go underground so you'd have to be in the know to find places anyway. It is a lot easier because it's legal (pause) I guess you're not looking over your shoulder for the law' (MI:8).

An interesting point to note is how some men consider the position of the female sex worker explicitly. For example, MI:6 stated that the criminalisation of sex workers would only serve to make it unsafe, not only for the clients, but also for the female sex workers. This suggests that some clients think highly of the women who work in the industry. Furthermore MI:6 states that his biggest fear in terms of criminalisation is perhaps purchasing sexual services at an unlicensed brothel and the implications of this:

> [I] think it would create more disrespect for females and you would probably get more cases of assaults and rapes.... It would just make it harder to find out who had done it and then it gets driven underground and then all the criminality comes out and then you pay extra high prices. The police thing is always a problem only because there are some places that you will go to that are not licensed to have sex there, only there as um massage and ummmm there might be a sting and so ok you're caught out you're having sex with him and we're now taking your licence away ... so you're implicated. That's probably the only fear, well at least with the places I'm going

to anyway, like I don't go to any high roller places or anything like that umm haven't visited any of the brothels down around the [Kings] 'Cross' so I think where I go is low risk.

(MI:6)

The possibility of the sex work industry becoming unsafe for women, if the laws within NSW were changed and sex work was criminalised again, was discussed by MI:10, who believes that the legislation within the state needs to be set up better, in terms of protecting sex workers, as at the moment the laws do not sufficiently protect sex workers. For MI:10, the current legislation on sex work can make it unsafe for the workers, however, criminalising the industry is not viewed as the way to achieve this:

It is basically open-minded in NSW, yeah it's legal, although I know you cannot just solicit on the street because that creates crime … drug use and that's no good. If the laws change here it will all just go underground um and that would be a bad thing for the workers themselves. Although it is fair to say the way the legislation is set up at the moment, by giving all the power to councils, and with councils being very, very hard about where they let brothels set up, it's creating the illegal side of the industry and is therefore really not helping the workers there, it's unsafe for them.

(MI:10)

Criminalising the sex work industry was also objected to by MI:11, who viewed the decriminalisation of the sex work industry as a positive move for NSW. Similarly to MI:10, MI:11 thought the current sex work industry needed better protection. MI:11 suggested that laws to increase the safety of purchasing sex were needed. However, he stated that the criminalisation of sex work in NSW would not stop him from buying:

I'd love to see them take away the smaller places; you know the ones with all those private houses and make it a more safe environment for everyone involved. But if prostitution became illegal … oh my God, I don't think I'd live much longer though, yes we need to be better protected but that is not done by arresting us. The decriminalisation of the sex work industry was a good move for the state [NSW] because there are obviously times when I need sex because I'm not getting sex. I mean, I went eight years without it and I don't want to go one more second without it. You know, eight years, that just ruined my life, without getting any sort of interest, in my life.

(MI:11)

Unlike other men interviewed MI:5 said that he is unsure of the laws regarding sex work. However, this did not concern him as MI:5 said he is not worried about the possible illegalities, and thinks that if 'prostitution' was made illegal people would still participate in it, much like speeding on the roads:

Well I'm a little bit unsure about the law, sometimes you hear that men are being arrested for soliciting, I think they used a policewoman one time as entrapment and I was like oh … I thought sex work was legal, so I can't exactly understand what the law is. I think it had to do with those men and sex workers crawling and working near a school or something? It's probably part of the excitement. The perceived danger may add to the excitement. I don't worry about that though, I will still buy.

(MI:5)

Overall, the men who were interviewed in the study support the current laws surrounding the decriminalisation of the sex work industry in NSW, Australia. This challenges the debate around how criminalising sex work can support a reduction in the levels of sex work/procurement, as supported by the Swedish model (Wilcox *et al.*, 2009). Most men who were interviewed said that they would continue to buy sexual services even if they laws were changed to criminalise this practice again. A notable discussion was the one in which many of the men considered the impact on the sex workers with reference to criminalisation.

Conclusion

Based on the data presented in this chapter, a picture of men in this study who procure sexual services is created. These men do not form a homogenous group: they differ widely in their personal and social demographics. Analysis of the data from the cohort of men procuring sexual services in NSW, together with analysis of some of the information from the men who were interviewed in the second phase of the data collection reveals a range of factors relating these men. First, men in this cohort who procure sexual services are aged from 29 to 76 and are primarily from Anglo-Saxon-Irish backgrounds. They are men who are mainly employed in high or medium status occupations, such a lawyers and managers. In terms of their marital status there is an even split between men who are single and men who are in some form of cohabiting relationship. There is a tendency however, for the men in relationships to report sexual dissatisfaction with the relationships they have had or are currently in.

Further exploration of the data reveals that men who procure sexual services tend not to have a criminal record and approximately half of those men in the survey have told someone about their procurement of sexual services. Whilst many in the survey sample did not stipulate whom they had told, most of those who did, reported that they told a friend. Analysis of the qualitative data found that whilst disclosure of procurement was most likely to occur with a friend, there is evidence to say there is a gender bias towards male friends. This finding seems to be because the men believe their male friends will understand and not judge them as perverse. The survey data indicated that the reasons preventing men from disclosing their purchase of sex were primarily due to their beliefs that the negative narratives about, and public perceptions of, the sex work industry attached stigma to the sex work industry. Here, the men commonly associated a negative view of procurement with the general public, with the media and politics being blamed for, in their view, this inaccurate representation. Overall, men reported that they believed that the general public thought negatively about men who procure sex. This offers insight into why most men do not disclose their procurement to family members and beyond.

Most of the sample was in agreement regarding the procurement of sexual services and its decriminalised status in NSW. Nearly 70 per cent of the sample indicated that they would continue to purchase sexual services even if the laws in NSW were changed. Although this suggests there would be some reduction in the purchasing of sex should it be re-criminalised, this finding offers support for the claim that the criminalisation of sex work and those involved is an ineffective tool for preventing, regulating and managing the sex work industry. Most men who were interviewed claimed that criminalising sex work in NSW would not prevent the procurement of sexual services, although they indicated that they would be more cautious about buying sexual services if the laws were changed.

This cohort of men does not vary greatly from findings reported in international research on men who procure sexual services. This suggests that the demographics of men who procure sexual services within a state of Australia where sex work is decriminalised does not differ significantly from the demographics of men in other parts of the world who procure sex in a criminalised environment. This is of particular note in countries where the transaction of sexual services is illegal, for example in the United States of America, where only one state out of 50 does not criminalise the act of sex work and the procurement of such. This highlights the incongruities of the civil liberties and human rights afforded to not only those who procure sexual services, but also of those who provide such services across different jurisdictions. What is deemed criminal has long differed between cultures and societies based on the interplay of a range of factors including religion, morality, ideology and history; sex work is no exception.

The findings concerning the personal and social characteristics of this sample of men allow the binary discourse concerning the procurement of sexual services to be reconsidered. From the data presented in this chapter, some of the evidence lends support to the deviance and immoral theorising applied to men's procurement of sexual services. For example, the fact that married men engage in this behaviour can be interpreted as immoral due to the infidelity that takes place as a result. In stark contrast, however, the findings in this chapter also support the normative function that some theorists suggest pertains to the sex work industry and the procurement of sexual services. While seeking sexual pleasure and gratification may be viewed as deviant and immoral by some writers (see Chapter 1), some theorists and writers view sexual gratification as an important and normal aspect of an individual's life (Garza-Mercer *et al.*, 2006). The deviant, immoral and the normative features concerning the procurement of sexual services have been evidenced in the findings reported in this chapter. This therefore, suggests a re-consideration of Monto and McRee's (2005) binary typology of men who are involved in the transaction of sexual services. Monto and McRee claim that those who are involved in this social practice can be understood through either an 'everyman' perspective, suggesting that men who procure sexual services are no different from men in the general population; or by a 'peculiar man' perspective, suggesting that men who procure sexual services are unique in some way that centres around a deficiency, a deviancy or a pathology. Based on the, albeit limited, data presented so far in this volume, the evidence offers support to both positions. But rather than supporting the binary discourse, the findings are beginning to suggest different possibilities that do not categorise men who procure sex into a single category, for example deviant, or do not polarise into two exclusive categories such as 'peculiar man' or 'everyman'.

The following chapter, Chapter 5, extends this inquiry into men who procure sexual services by considering the logistics of their procurement. Based on data obtained from the questionnaire, Chapter 5 considers when and where men procure sexual services. The following chapter builds on the findings presented in this chapter, in order to consider whether the binary position used to understand men who procure sexual services is applicable to their behaviour.

Note

1 Not all sample members answered every question on the survey, as a result $n=<309$ on some responses. While some questions, depending on their nature did not require all sample members to answer and as a result $n=<309$ on these responses.
2 See ABS website, online, available at: www.abs.gov.au/ausstats/abs@.nsf/Lookup/207 1.0main+features902012–2013.

5 The '5WH' of men's procurement of sexual services[1]

The previous chapter presented the demographics and characteristics of men in the survey sample who procure sexual services. While there are similarities amongst these men, it would be incorrect to characterise these men in the cohort as a homogenous group. This second findings chapter considers the five *whats* associated with the procurement of sexual services in order to further explore this notion that men who procure sexual services are not a homogenous group. The five *whats* associated with purchasing sex, which can be better understood by the mnemonic of *the '5WH' of men's procurement of sexual services* has been inspired by the 5WH mnemonic created by Shepherd (1991) in relation to police ethics when interviewing suspects. The five 5WH mnemonic as applied to men who procure sexual services, are: *what* age men begin procuring sexual services; *what* locations are used by men when engaging in the procurement of sexual services, alongside whether this location differs between the first time procurement and future procurement locations; *what* time men engage in their procurement in terms of time of the week, as well their frequency of buying; *what* services are bought during the sexual transaction; and finally, *what* reasons do men offer for why they procure sexual services. In order to explore these five *whats*, the first phase of data collection within the study is used solely. Based on the 309 men[2] sampled, descriptive statistics are used to provide answers to the 5WH. However, a more advanced statistical procedure of cluster analysis is used when considering the reasons men in the cohort offer for why they procure sex. This part of the analysis leads to the identification of five groups of men, based on their reasons for procuring sexual services.

The logistics of men's procurement of sexual services

The first *what* of the 5WH mnemonic is: *what* age do men procure their first sexual service? Men's age when they first purchased sexual services ranged from 12 to 69 (M=25, sd=8.5). This suggests that men in NSW are slightly older on average than their counterparts across the globe when they first purchase sex. Existing data outlined in Wilcox *et al.*'s (2009) REA indicates that men are usually in their late teens to early twenties when this first occurs. However, the finding in the current data may reflect bias in the data created by a few 'extreme' older scores. Taking the 'extreme' scores into account, the median for age at first procurement of sexual services is age 22 (IQR = 19–28), which reflects existing international literature (Graaf *et al.*, 1997; Monto, 2000; Lowman and Atchinson, 2006; and Macleod *et al.*, 2008). See Figure 5.1.

The men surveyed were asked in *what* location they first procured their sexual service (Table 5.1). Most men purchase their first sexual service at an indoor market location (85 per cent), with a brothel being the most common location (51 per cent). The use of the Internet was not a common way to locate a man's first time experience for procurement. This may have something to do with the reasons why men first procure sexual services, and is explored further in the qualitative aspect of the study, presented in the next chapter, Chapter 6. Indoor markets can be understood as referring to licensed premises such as brothels, or a sex worker who sells sexual services from a private residence. It is important to note that internationally some of the terminology can be different when describing the specific markets of the sex work industry. For example, a licensed

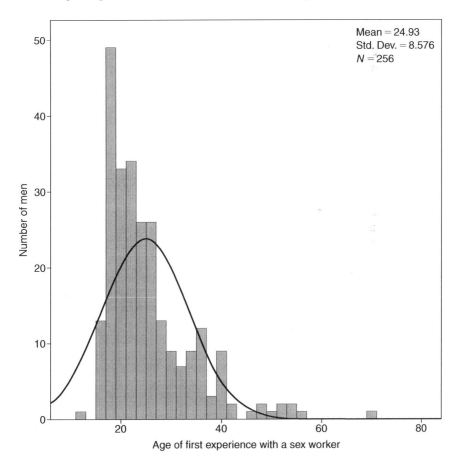

Figure 5.1 Age of first experience with sex worker.

sauna in NSW can be distinctly different to what is meant by a licensed sauna in the United Kingdom, in which the latter is endorsed by the local authority (council) to provide non-sexual services. Outdoor markets specifically relate to sex workers who solicit from the street, and this is typically a universally agreed definition.

Most men procure their first sexual service from indoor sex markets in NSW (Table 5.1). This is not a surprising finding, due to the fact that the sex work industry is decriminalised, with the outdoor market still legislated against in parts, as illustrated in Chapter 2. In Chapter 2 it is documented that within NSW the 1995 Disorderly House Amendment Act legalises brothels, therefore, offering a rationale for the finding in Table 5.1. The street based provision of sexual services in NSW still has legal restrictions on it, with restrictions including the selling of sexual services within view of a school or hospital. This current law in the state of NSW offers a reason why the streets are the least utilised by the cohort of men for procuring sexual services and the indoor markets are the most utilised.

As reported in the first findings chapter, Chapter 4, the mean age of men in the sample was 48. This raises the question as to how long men had been purchasing sexual services, if their first encounter was typically in their early twenties. Based on the data sourced, the third *what* to be examined was *what* length of time the men had been procuring sexual services and the frequency of such procurement. Figure 5.2 outlines the length of time the men surveyed had been procuring sex.

The average length of time men had been procuring sexual services is $M=21$ years, $sd=12$ years. This means that most men with the cohort surveyed had been procuring sexual services prior to the change of legislation decriminalising sex work. It was only in 1995 through the Disorderly House Amendment Act that the procurement of sexual services ceased being a criminal act (within the indoor markets at least). Most of the men surveyed had therefore broken the law at some point in time with regard to their procurement of sexual services. This finding speaks directly to the finding in the previous results chapter, where a large proportion of the cohort of men sampled indicated that criminalising the sex work industry would not prevent them from purchasing sex, because some of them had done so in the past when it was illegal.

Table 5.1 Location of first time procurement ($n=263$)

	n	%
Street	39	14.8
Brothel	134	51.0
Massage parlour	32	12.2
Advertisement (non Internet)	36	13.7
Internet	16	6.1
Recommended sex worker	5	1.9
Other	10	0.4

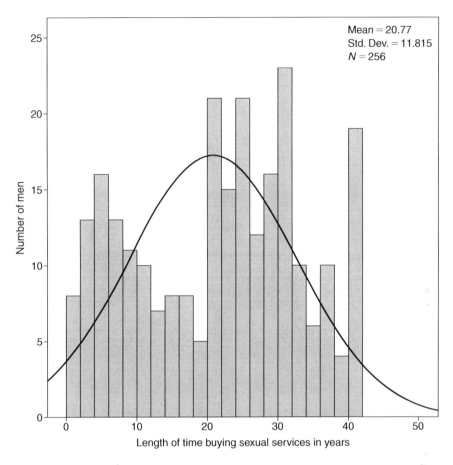

Figure 5.2 Length of time buying sexual services in years.

In relation to men's current procurement of sexual services, the sample could be termed 'regular' clients of the sex work industry. Almost 59 per cent of the men who answered this question claimed they purchased sex weekly, fortnightly or monthly (see Table 5.2). The term 'regular' client has been used consistently in the literature in reference to men who procure sexual services, in work such as Freund *et al.* (1991); Plumridge *et al.* (1997) and Kennedy *et al.* (2004). These scholars describe clients who buy sexual services at least once a month as a 'regular' client. For example, Plumridge *et al.* (1997) apply the term 'regular' procurement to men who have been purchasing sexual services once a month for at least a year. Some men in Plumridge *et al.*'s study acknowledged they had been procuring sexual services for as long as 20 years. As supported by Figure 5.1 and Table 5.2, this international definition of 'regular' client is reflected and supported in this current cohort of men. Whilst the current sample is not necessarily a representative sample, the

Table 5.2 Frequency of procurement (*n*=262)

	n	%
Daily	2	0.8
Weekly	44	16.8
Fortnightly	47	17.9
Monthly	63	24.0
Every 2 months	39	14.9
Every 3–6 months	48	18.3
Every 7–11 months	6	2.3
Yearly	13	5.0

current study's data can be used to support the claim that a man who procures sexual services on a monthly basis over a year or more appears to become a regular client. More importantly the act of procurement becomes a regular part of his life, over his lifespan.

The time of the day and week that men procured sexual services is outlined in Table 5.3. This data maps onto the third *what* of men's procurement of sexual services – *what* time of day and week.

From the data presented in general, men do not have a set time when they procure sexual services, with 56.7 per cent of the sample buying sexual services when it is convenient. This finding challenges the work of Blanchard (1994) who claimed that men bought sex like a regularly purchased commodity. She claimed men were highly disciplined and focused in their procurement by frequenting the sex work industry at specific times. Brooks Gordon (2006) documents in her study of men who procure sexual services in the United Kingdom that week days tend to be the most common days for men to be involved in the transaction of sexual services. The rationale offered for this trend by Brooks Gordon (2006) was that most of the men in her sample were married and/or had family commitments and this would prevent them from purchasing at the weekend.[3] However, when the demographics presented earlier are taken into account, what Table 5.3 suggests is twofold. First the large proportion of single men in the cohort may account for the greater spontaneity in the procurement of sexual services reported in the survey; and second, that men viewing the procurement of sexual

Table 5.3 Time of week/day of procurement (*n*=263)

	n	%
Monday–Thursday during the day	44	16.7
Monday–Thursday in the evenings	33	12.5
Friday and/or Saturday during the day	9	3.4
Friday and/or Saturday in the evening	23	8.7
Sunday during the day	4	1.5
Sunday during the evening	1	0.4
I have no set time, just whenever is convenient	149	56.7

services as nothing more than a commodity, may be opportunistic in their purchase of sex. The viewing of sex in this latter way – as a commodity – reflects the idea men may procure sex if he has the time, or when it is more convenient, or when they have the extra money to do so. However, it cannot be overlooked that the effects of decriminalisation may have an impact on this finding. For example the more relaxed approach to sex work, along with ease of availability make 'walking in off the street' less problematic. The spontaneity of procurement of sexual services within a decriminalised system may reflect an aspect of the contemporary market society, that is, an unplanned purchase or a shopping spree is possible. The spontaneity of the act in this way may be a product of how an individual with disposable income buys something they had not intended to buy yet have the money and time to acquire it.

The locations men used in their continued procurement were also investigated in order to establish if locations differ between the sites men use for their first procurement and sites used for repeat visits to the sex work industry. The analysis shows that within NSW the location men made their first procurement of sexual services, mostly in the indoor sex markets, is the preferred procurement site when they return to the sex work industry (Table 5.4). The indoor arena where procurement commonly takes place is typically a brothel, with 67.2 per cent of the sample often buying sexual services within this location. As indicated earlier, this finding maybe a reflection of the legislation in NSW. The sex worker's home is the second most popular indoor site, suggesting trust, confidence and longevity in the relationship. Sex workers who work from home tend to be older workers who have a few clients they see on a regular basis and have known these clients over a number of years. These men tend to be the regular clients of such sex workers.

In order to examine the fourth *what* in the mnemonic '5WH' of men's procurement of sexual services, the sample was asked about the type of services they purchased. The sample reported that the main procurement was vaginal sex with a range of other types of sex, more specialist services such as fetishes like BDSM[4] being uncommon reasons for procuring sexual services. As Table 5.5 outlines, over 90 per cent of the sample reported vaginal intercourse as the main service bought, with oral sex (received by the men) being the second most popular (77.1 per cent).

Table 5.4 Typical location for continued procurement (*n*=262)

	n	%
In a car	1	0.4
In a safe house	17	6.5
In a brothel/sauna	176	67.2
Hotel	23	8.8
Your home	10	3.8
Sex worker's home	35	13.4

Table 5.5 'Sexual' services procured (*n*=262)

	n	%
Hand relief	136	51.9
Oral – sex worker on you	202	77.1
Oral – you on sex worker	122	46.6
Vaginal intercourse	238	90.8
Anal intercourse you on sex worker	64	24.4
Anal intercourse – sex worker using toys	20	7.6
Anal stimulation	35	13.4
Fetish	30	11.5
More than one sex worker	70	26.7
Massage	134	51.1

The image often created of men who procure sex is one of perverseness or sleaziness. Men who purchase sex have been constructed as outlandish and being more inclined to engage in violent forms of sex. These views are commonly associated with theorists such as Winick (1962) and Stroller (1975), and are consistent with some radical feminist views on sex work. The belief that men are entering the sex work industry to engage in more perverse sexual acts is found not to be the case for this cohort of men. The types of sexual acts men purchase reflect acts that are commonly associated with conventional romantic relationships and map onto conventional behaviours. These behaviours are typical within conventional relationships as documented by all writers on conventional sexual behaviour in marriage and long term heterosexual relationships, and also recognised in research by Sanders (2008a).

Whilst the data already presented in this chapter offers further context for the procurement of sexual services started in the previous chapter, what is of particular interest is the reasons why men procure sexual services. Why do men purchase sex from the sex work industry? The next section of findings considers this position in terms of the reasons men offer for procuring sexual services. The data presented in the following section uses the statistical technique of cluster analysis to provide five groups of men based on their reasons for procurement, in order to reconsider how men's procurement of sexual services is theorised and understood.

Men's reasons for procuring sexual services – the fifth *what*

The following analysis reports on the key factors for why men purchase sexual services, this finding reflects the fifth *what* of the reasons men offer for understanding their behaviour. The initial analysis is descriptive (Table 5.6), followed by a cluster analysis of such reasons (Table 5.7). The cluster analysis provides the groupings or clustering of reasons that are the most typical amongst the sample for their procurement of sexual services.

Table 5.6 indicates the key reasons for men procuring sexual services, with some of these reasons being understood as an outcome achieved by procuring.

Table 5.6 Reasons for procuring sexual services (n=262)

	n	%
Single	103	39.3
Lonely	88	33.6
Cheaper than a date	56	21.4
Devoid of all responsibility	108	41.2
Non emotional sex	97	37
Live out a fantasy/fetish	72	27.5
No regular sex with a partner	89	34
Don't have good sex with partner	49	18.7
Thrill/excitement	142	54.2
Attractiveness of sex worker	138	52.7
Use of sex toys	17	6.5

This level of analysis has not separated initial or onset reasons (why men visit a sex worker for the first time) from continuing reasons (why men continue to visit sex workers). The analysis at this stage simply presents the reasons men offer in order to make sense of their procurement of sexual services. Exploration of initial or onset reasons and continuing reasons; as well as potential differences between the two will be presented in the next chapter, Chapter 6. The list of reasons presented in Table 5.6 are from a prescribed list on the questionnaire that was generated through consultation with services working alongside the sex work industry as well as sex workers themselves. Men were required to tick as many reasons as applied to them, and there was an option for men to add additional reasons that specifically applied to them.

As presented in Table 5.6, the most common reason for men to procure sexual services are: thrill/excitement (54.2 per cent) and the attractiveness of the sex worker (52.7 per cent). Being single (39.3 per cent), lonely (33.6 per cent) and the lack of responsibility involved in purchasing sex (41.2 per cent) are also important reasons why men engage in this behaviour. Interestingly, previous research into why men purchase sex, has not reported 'attractiveness of the sex worker' as a common reason for this behaviour. Most previous research tended to report more negative or less savoury reasons for the procurement of sexual services. For example, some studies report difficulties in romantic relationships as the key factor (Jordan, 2005; Monto, 2000), separation from a partner (Jordan, 2005; Monto, 2000, Xantidis and McCabe, 2001) and violence and control of women (Grubman Black, 2003; Busch et al., 2002) as primary reasons for men's procurement of sexual services.[5] The finding that the attractiveness of a sex worker is a key reason for the procurement of sexual services reveals a more positive aspect to this social practice. Research that reports reasons such as clients finding a sex worker attractive is emerging more frequently. For example there is a small but growing body of literature reporting that men consider the 'girlfriend experience' to be a key reason for their procurement of sex (Sanders, 2008a; Coy et al., 2007). This current study's findings support this more recent work. It finds that men procure sexual services based on factors that can have a more positive impact on their lives, such as experiencing the closeness and familiarity with a sex worker that is more commonly associated with conventional relationships.

Aside from attractiveness being a key factor, the findings of this study also reflect the work of Lau *et al.* (2004) and Monto (2000) for example, who have claimed that men purchase sexual services because of the thrill and excitement associated with the act. A large proportion of this sample (54.2 per cent) stated that this is a key factor. This will be examined in more depth using cluster analysis. The following section presents the cluster analysis, which contributes to establishing a new approach in understanding men's reasons for purchasing sex.

A hierarchical cluster analysis was conducted because this statistical technique allows for groups of cases with common characteristics to be clustered together (Francis, 2001). Table 5.7 illustrates the outcome of the cluster analysis that has generated five clusters, or groups, of men. The main reasons specific to each cluster of men with similar characteristics are also shown in the table. The main reasons men offer in explaining why they procure sexual services differs across the five groups, and some reasons can be understood as an 'outcome' that men achieve by procuring sexual services, this distinction is outlined below with a detailed analysis of Table 5.7.

Table 5.7 Reasons for procuring sexual services – cluster analysis

Main reasons	*% of overall sample*
Cluster group 1	
Attractiveness	
Thrill/excitement	27
Cluster group 2	
Devoid of all responsibility	
No regular sex with partner	20
Cluster group 3	
Devoid of all responsibility	
Non emotional sex	
Living out a fantasy	
Thrill/excitement	
Attractiveness	26
Cluster group 4	
Single	
Loneliness	
Attractiveness	16
Cluster group 5	
Thrill/excitement	
Living out a fantasy	
Non emotional sex	10

Defining and examining the reasons for procuring sexual services

Figure 5.3 lists those reasons offered by the men surveyed indicating why they purchase sexual services, with some reasons being classified as an 'outcome' achieved as a result of procurement.

The findings from the cluster analysis are worthy of detailed attention and closer analysis. Cluster 1 represents the largest proportion of the sample. The attractiveness of the sex worker and the thrill and excitement associated with the procurement of sexual services are the key reasons given for engaging in this social practice by this group of men. The latter of which represents an outcome achieved as a result of their procurement of sexual services – experiencing the thrill/excitement. The attractiveness of the sex worker, which is not explicitly reported in the existing research, yet features in three of the five clusters, including Cluster 1, represents an emotional or intimacy link to the procurement of sexual services. In other words there is a link between men procuring sex, displaying emotions and being intimate.

The association between emotions and intimacy and the procurement of sexual services is particularly evident with the men in Cluster 4. These men are addressing their loneliness and singleness through their procurement. These life circumstances and feelings are the main reasons given as to why this group of men purchase sex. Cluster 4 exemplifies the normative function that sex work can play in the life of the procurers. The procurement of sexual services allows this group of men to meet the human desire of achieving intimacy.

Cluster 5 represents a group of men who procure sexual services for three reasons, which include both identified outcomes of purchasing sex in Figure 5.3 – experiencing a fantasy and experiencing excitement. It would appear that this group of men is not procuring sex for reasons associated with seeking intimacy,

Reasons for procuring	Outcome achieved by procuring (but given as reason by men)
Attractiveness of sex worker	Experiencing the thrill/ excitement of procuring
Being single	Experiencing the living out a fantasy
No regular sex with partner and wanting/needing sex	Feeling no responsibility
To overcome loneliness	
Having non-emotional sex	
Having sex that is devoid of all responsibility	

Figure 5.3 Reasons for procurement, outcomes achieved by procurement.

as are their peers in Clusters 1 and 4, as having non-emotional sex drives the men in Cluster 5 to procure sexual services. Such a finding signifies that not all men purchase sex for emotion and intimacy reasons. The men represented in Cluster 5 may reflect those men who simply view sex as a commodity, the purchase of which provides goods such as thrill seeking.

Cluster 3 features a range of reasons men give for procuring sexual services. While men in this cluster share a reason for purchasing sexual services with their peers in Clusters 1 and 4, the 'attractiveness of the sex worker', it could be inferred from this analysis that this cluster reflects a group of men who are not driven by reasons associated with seeking intimacy. The men represented in this third cluster reflect a group of men who procure sexual services for non-emotional reasons, such as living out at fantasy. Cluster 3 men are therefore more alike with men represented in Cluster 5 in terms of the reasons for their procurement.

Finally, the men in Cluster 2, have two reasons associated with their procurement of sexual services. 'Not having regular sex with a partner' could be associated with seeking intimacy; however, Cluster 2 men procure sexual services as it allows them to have sex that is devoid of responsibility. This latter reason for procuring sexual services does not reflect the more expressive reasons that men in other clusters offer as reasons for engaging in this social practice.

In summary, based on this volume's quantitative findings regarding the reasons men procure sexual services, it can be understood that men are driven by particular wishes and needs that can involve the physical need to have sex because, for example, some men are not having regular sex with a conventional partner. However, there is a strong presence of expressive reasons that men give for purchasing sexual services, which can include the attractiveness of the sex worker. While all five clusters of men vary in terms of the reasons for their procurement, what can be concluded is that none of the reasons represent a deviant act. Men procure sexual services in order to seek a level of intimacy, or address a particular need or feeling. Some men simply view the transaction of sexual services in the same way as acquiring any other commodity.

Table 5.8 reveals a more detailed analysis of the reasons surrounding the procurement of sexual services. It cross-references the clusters outlined above with key demographic data of the men surveyed in this study, with a more complex picture of men's procurement of sexual services emerging. The personal and social characteristics data presented in Table 5.8, in conjunction with the cluster analysis data, bring together the variables considered in both this chapter, and the previous chapter, Chapter 4. These data contribute to an extension of the analysis, adding knowledge to our understanding of the type of men who procure sexual services and their reasons for doing so.

From Table 5.8, a number of interesting findings emerge. First, and as noted in Table 5.7, Cluster 1 represents the largest percentage of the sample; these men have an average age of 49. The two reasons offered for purchasing sexual services include one outcome achieved through the act – experiencing the thrill/ excitement, while the other reason can be considered expressive – the attractiveness

Table 5.8 Reasons for procuring sexual services linked with men's demographics

% of overall sample	Age (M)	Occupational status	Age 1st time (M)	No. of years procuring (M)	Marital status (mode) (%)	Frequency of procuring (mode) (%)	Told others? (%)[1]	Stop if illegal?[2] (%)
Cluster 1: attractiveness, thrill/excitement								
27	49	Professional A	23	26	Married/ de facto 49.3	2 weeks or monthly 21.4	No 53.5	No 73.3
Cluster 2: devoid of all responsibility, no regular sex with partner								
20	50	Professional B	24	26	Married/ de facto 52.9	3–6 months 26.4	No 57.7	No 69.2
Cluster 3: devoid of all responsibility, non-emotional sex, living out a fantasy, thrill/excitement, attractiveness								
26	48	Professional B	21	27	Married/ de facto 50	Monthly 26.5	Yes 61.8	No 75
Cluster 4: single, loneliness, attractiveness								
16	40	Professional A	24	16	Single 79.4	Monthly 27.7	Yes 67.4	No 55.8
Cluster 5: thrill/excitement, living out a fantasy, non-emotional sex								
10	51	Professional B	22	29	Married/ de facto 84.6	Every 2 months 33.3	Yes 53.8	No 65.3

Notes
1 Variable discussed in Chapter 4.
2 Variable discussed in Chapter 4.

of the sex worker. There is, however, a level of deviancy associated with some of the men's behaviour in this cluster. This is based on the fact that approximately half of the men in the cluster are engaged in a conventional relationship (married or cohabiting), and having sex outside this relationship can be viewed as deviant as it is a form of infidelity. Men in Cluster 1 would also be unlikely to stop purchasing sexual services if procuring such a service was made illegal in NSW. This finding adds another element of potential deviancy to their engagement in procuring sexual services, as these men would break the law in order to procure sexual services. Cluster 1 men are also regular users of the sex work industry based on the length of time they have been procuring (Coy *et al.*, 2007[6]). This cluster of men has engaged in procuring sexual services for 26 years, on average, with 21.4 per cent of these men purchasing services at least every two weeks. This represents the highest frequency in terms of purchasing, compared with the remaining four clusters of men.

Second, Cluster 3 whilst representing a slightly smaller percentage of the sample compared to Cluster 1, contains the largest number of reasons relating to men's purchasing of sexual services. These reasons include an outcome achieved through their procurement, the experience of living out a fantasy. However, most of the reasons these men engage in this social practice tend to reflect less expressive reasons such as non-emotional sex. Similar to the men in Cluster 1, half of the men in Cluster 3 were married or cohabiting and therefore the issue of deviancy caused through their infidelity is apparent in this group of men. Cluster 3 men, however, acknowledge that their procurement of sexual services is associated with the act of being 'devoid of responsibility'; this may be a reflection of this cluster's marital status. A key difference between Cluster 3 and Cluster 1 men is their professional status. While both clusters represent a 'professional' occupation, as classified by the registrar general's classification of professional occupations (Scott and Marshall, 2009) Cluster 1 men were of a higher status than their Cluster 3 counterparts. This may have some impact on the difference in procurement habits between the two clusters of men. However, Cluster 3, like Cluster 1 men, would be unlikely to stop purchasing sex if it was made illegal in NSW. Men grouped in Cluster 3 were the youngest when they first procured sexual services, with the average age of first procurement in this cluster being 21. On average, this group of men have been procuring sexual services regularly over a 27-year period, on a monthly basis.

Cluster 5, whilst the smallest proportion of the sample, is the oldest group in comparison to their counterparts, with an average age of 51. Men in Cluster 5 are similar to Cluster 3 in terms of the reasons given for their procurement of sexual services, reflecting less expressive reasons for their procurement. However, this cluster of men is the group most likely to procure sexual services less frequently than a 'regular' user as defined by Coy *et al.* (2007). Nevertheless men in Cluster 5 have been the longest procurers of sexual services, with an average number of years procuring equalling 29 years. One notable feature of this cluster of men is that 85 per cent of them are married or cohabiting; this is the largest percentage of a cluster reflecting this variable. Due to their marital status, as for Cluster 1 and 3 men, men in this cluster who are married can be classified as deviant due to the breaking of the moral code of monogamy. Yet their marital status, in conjunction with their age could be viewed as a reason for their infrequent procurement compared to others in the cohort. Finally, the majority of this group of men would not be inclined to stop procuring sexual services if such as practice was made illegal in NSW (again another common finding amongst the sample). This may be a reflection of the number of years these men have been purchasing sexual services.

Cluster 4 represents the youngest cluster of men, by approximately ten years, compared to the other four clusters (M = 40). This group of men procure sexual services for reasons associated with their single status and their feelings of loneliness. Men in Cluster 4 were more likely to have told someone about their procurement of sexual services, compared to the men in other clusters. This finding may be a reflection of a more liberal view of purchasing sex in this generation and their single status. Such differences between the generations may also reflect a difference in terms of the stigma perceived to be associated with the sex work industry. For example, younger single men may not feel the same stigma as older married men. Cluster 4 included the men who would be most likely to stop procuring sexual services if sex work was made illegal in NSW. This finding, again, may reflect a generational difference between those in Cluster 4 and those in other clusters, as Cluster 4 men are unlikely to have purchased sex illegally in the era of a criminalised sex industry in the way some of the older men may have.

Finally, Cluster 2 men procure sexual services because they are not having regular sex with their conventional partner and because they considered the act of procurement devoid of all responsibility. Furthermore, this cluster of men could not be described as regular clients of the sex work industry as their procurement is typically every 3–6 months, which is outside of the common definition for a regular client (Coy et al., 2007). However, men in this cluster represent one of the highest percentages reported regarding continuing to procure sexual services even if it became illegal in NSW again (69.2 per cent). The profile of this group of men infers a strong commodity aspect to their purchasing of sexual services.

This cluster analysis can be brought to a conclusion by the following summary; the five clusters represent a range of reasons for procuring sexual services. Some men procure sexual services for reasons associated with addressing feelings of loneliness or seeking intimacy, reflecting expressive reasons for engaging in this social practice. For other men, procuring sexual services relieves them of the responsibilities they may associate with more conventional relationships and reflects a more commodity-based rationale for engaging in this social practice. Some of the reasons men purchase sex are outcome driven, nevertheless, none of the clusters are motivated by criminal intentions or by means that represent the domination or controlling of women, as some scholars and writers on the sex work industry would claim. It could be argued that the reasons the men in the cohort have offered as to why they procure sexual services are driven by a goal to feel good about themselves. The procurement of sexual services therefore could be seen as contributing to their positive sense of self and a healthy well being.

Table 5.8 reveals the benefit of conducing a cluster analysis on this cohort of men. It shows that men who procure sexual services have a variety of personal and social characteristics. They are not homogenous. What emerges from this analysis is a complex picture of why men procure sexual services. Different men purchase sex for different reasons, but usually men do not have just one reason – there is a combination of reasons.

This research suggests that to use a binary typology such as that developed by Monto and McRee (2005) or a theoretical framework that understands this behaviour in a single factorial manner is misleading. The findings of the cluster analysis may lend support to the 'everyman' perspective (Monto and McRee, 2005) as it could be argued that any man could procure sexual services. But a problem arises in that this view implies that everyman in society is procuring sexual services. As the prevalence data of procuring sexual services does not support this notion (e.g. Atchinson *et al.*, 1998), to use the term 'everyman' as a means of understanding men who procure sexual services is inaccurate. Furthermore, the findings from the cluster analysis offer no evidence to imply that these men are 'peculiar' – there is no evidence to suggest these men are inherently different to other men in society. However, it cannot be ignored that there is an aspect of deviance and immorality to the behaviour of some of the men sampled. As noted in the analysis many men are engaging in the procurement of sexual services whilst married. But as a counter to the view that this is unusual, it must be recognised that many men are 'unfaithful' to their wives or partners but not necessarily through the purchasing of sex, rather through having 'affairs'. So this behaviour, of having sex outside a marriage relationship, is not peculiar or outside the norm. Therefore, a more accurate and useful term to refer to men who procure sexual services maybe '*any man*'. Any man in society may procure sexual services at some stage in their life and may do so for different reasons at different times. And the findings of this research indicate that it is inaccurate to set up a binary opposite of 'peculiar man' as the men in the sample do not appear to be, while not everyman procures sexual services.

These findings imply that a revision to the SAPSS model presented in Chapter 3 is needed. The SAPSS model was devised to reflect the current theorising of procurers of sexual services. If the SAPSS model is to become a tool that supports a more accurate understanding of men who purchase sex then the model needs to reflect the findings presented in this book also. This consideration of reworking the SAPSS model will take place in Chapter 7, upon the presentation of all the results collected for the study.

Conclusion

The key findings in this chapter have emerged from the cluster analysis. Through this, and other simpler, statistical procedures, an overview of the diversity of men in the sample who procure sexual services within NSW, Australia has been presented. From the analysis presented so far, and using the '5WH' mnemonic, a profile of men who procure sexual services is emerging. Men who are involved in the transaction of sexual services in NSW have been involved in such an activity on average, since their early to mid-twenties. Most of these men become 'regular' users, spanning many years of purchasing. The primary market from which this cohort of men procures sexual services is within the indoor markets and the preferred sexual act purchased is vaginal sex, but with men seeking a range of sexual experiences. A common feature of these men's procurement of sexual services is that there is no set time for engaging in the act; this challenges some existing beliefs that men are highly disciplined and have a set time for procuring sexual services (Blanchard, 1994) and may be a reflection of the significant proportion of single men in the study. Single men, may not have the same commitments as those men in conventional relationships and who have children, leading these single men to be more sporadic in their procurement practices.

The cluster analysis revealed five distinct groups of men and their reasons for procuring sexual services. The reasons vary and when such findings are mapped onto to the personal and social characteristics of men in the sample, the diversity of this cohort of men is evident. Men purchase sex for reasons that make them feel good about themselves, whether that be because they are single and want sex or to be with someone (closeness), they find the sex worker attractive or because they are feeling lonely. This finding offers a complexity concerning the procurement of sexual services in that there are many reasons men purchase sex. Yet, there is a simplicity surrounding the understanding of men's procurement, based on the notion that the act simply allows men to feel good about themselves, for whatever reason they choose to purchase sex. The findings of Chapter 5 offer evidence to support the claim that sex work plays an important role in the lives of the men surveyed. This position challenges current thinking, which is based on a binary discourse for understanding why men engage in this activity. The data demonstrates that men do not procure sexual services driven purely by deviant factors, as some current literature on the subject argues. Rather, an interplay of factors, which may be specific to a period in one's life course or particular circumstances at a given time, appear to drive the purchasing of sex. However, it seems to be, for the cohort of men sampled in this study, that once purchasing sexual services has begun, it is likely to become a regular part of a man's normal life activities rather than a sporadic and unusual activity. Men who procure sexual services are not a homogenous group, and therefore, it can be claimed that this social practice cannot be understood using the theorising that currently exists concerning men who procure sexual services. Men's procurement of sexual services cannot be accurately understood using a framework that centres solely on a deviant/immoral framework or on a normative function as such a binary understanding of this behaviour underplays the multifactorial nature of procuring sexual services. If this is the case the typology created by Monto and McRee (2005) maybe an unhelpful tool to support an understanding of men's procurement of sexual services.

The following chapter, Chapter 6, builds on the interplay of reasons that surround the procurement of sexual services by men. Using the interview data collected in the second phase of the data collection process of this study, the experiences and views of men who procure sexual services are analysed, to help explain the quantitative data. The qualitative data that is presented in the forthcoming chapter allows for a distinction to be drawn between reasons men first procure sexual services and the reasons men continue to procure sexual services. Interview data collected from the experiences and viewpoints of female sex workers and groups with an interest in the sex work industry, are also analysed to examine why men purchase sexual services. Chapter 6 adds depth to the claim that the procurement of sexual services is a complex interplay of factors more accurately understood by men attending to their well being. By examining the interview data from the perspectives of those who are involved in the sex work industry, as well as those who are not directly involved in the purchasing of, or the providing of such services, namely the interest groups, an assessment can be made concerning the representations common in society, of the procurement of sexual services.

Notes

1 A summary of this chapter has been accepted for publication and is in press in the *British Journal of Forensic Practice*.
2 Not all sample members answered every question on the survey, as a result $n = <309$ on some responses. While some questions, depending on their nature did not require all sample members to answer and as a result $n = <309$ on these responses.
3 It is worth noting that samples in these studies were not as large as the current study.
4 Bondage and discipline, sadism and masochism.
5 These studies draw upon a variety of different research designs, methodology and methods.
5 The researchers define 'regular sex buyers' as all those paying for sex once a month or more (p. 14).

6 Examining why men procure sexual services

The following chapter presents an analysis of the data collected in the study from the 36 interviews, to provide an in-depth understanding regarding why men procure sexual services. Evidence within the findings chapters thus far, has provided a description of the types of men who purchase sexual services from the NSW sex work industry, as well as the logistics of this procurement. These findings challenge the simplicity of the binary discourse currently used to understand this social practice, as evidenced through the questionnaire and interview data. The findings presented so far have also considered reasons for procurement, based on the survey data in the previous chapter. The cluster analysis, for example presented in Chapter 5, indicated a variety of reasons for men's procurement of sexual services. In this chapter, these reasons are further examined using the qualitative data.

The previous chapter highlighted the finding that a common pattern amongst the cohort of men sampled was that they were 'regular' users of the sex work industry, as defined in the work of scholars such as Coy *et al.* (2007). A variety of reasons for men's procurement of sexual services were presented, which included wanting no commitment, being attracted to a female sex worker and helping to address loneliness. Analyses of the in-depth interviews with the 13 male purchasers of sex provide substantive meaning, from their perspectives regarding the reasons for and their experiences of purchasing sex. There are three major themes the data presented in this chapter fall under: first, early life experiences and impact on procurement; second, reasons for first time procurement; and third, reasons for the continuation of procurement.

Analyses of the sex workers' interviews in this chapter reveal their understandings as to why men procure sexual services as well. As such these accounts act as a means by which to validate or counter the claims of the male clients, in particular with reference to why men first purchase sexual services and reasons why they continue. Sex workers are a valuable data source for any research that aims to unpack the features, processes and issues relating to the sex work industry. By drawing upon the experiences and views of the sex workers a deeper understanding of why men procure sexual services emerges.

This chapter also uses interview data from interest groups. The groups canvassed are women's collective groups (seven interviewees), medical practitioners (five interviewees) and clergy (four interviewees). As outlined in the previous chapters of this volume, these groups have played an important role in shaping and defining the sex work industry over time. This history of these groups' influence on the sex work industry makes this data set an important feature of this volume, as it provides a means to understand the views of these groups. It opens the opportunity to evaluate if their knowledge, which over time has been used to shape policy and debate concerning the sex work industry, is accurate in relation to the features of the industry. It is not of course claimed to be representative, but rather a window into some of the views and thinking of people in these social and cultural groups. The interview data reveals that some of the views held by these interest groups, whilst accurate, are limited in relation to a deeper understanding of men's procurement of sexual services. Analysis reveals a difference between what male clients offer as reasons for purchasing sexual services and what some of the interest groups believe. These findings suggest that the influence and impact such groups have had on shaping policy and debate concerning sex work may be due in part, to poorly informed views of some aspects of the sex work industry. These views may be based on prejudice and personal attitudes and beliefs, rather than evidence. This position resonates with the work of scholars such as Weitzer (2005; 2009) who has claimed that many theoretical debates and writings concerning this area have been based on opinion rather than evidence.

Interview data was categorised and then thematically analysed to provide meaning and allow further interpretation regarding the reasons men purchase sexual services that emerged in the statistical and cluster analysis. In particular, attention is paid to the reasons influencing men's choice in purchasing their first sexual service compared with what influenced their continuation of procuring sexual services. By bringing together this and other data presented in the previous two findings chapters, this final section of this chapter provides a further justification for rejecting the binary discourse surrounding the practice of procuring sexual services, which began in the concluding parts of Chapter 5. In conjunction with this Monto and McRee's (2005) typology of men who procure sexual services, which can be considered as facilitating the use of the current discourses on purchasing sex, will be reviewed and considered in terms of its relevance to a twenty-first-century understanding of men's procurement of sexual services.

Early life experiences and the impact on procurement

Some men in the interview group believed that aspects of their early life had impacted negatively on their relationships with others later in their lives and contributed to why they procure sexual services. Some believed these early life experiences made it difficult to engage in romantic relationships and enjoy sexual activities. They said, however, that access to the sex work industry helped address these issues. Men who experienced such inhibitors in relationships with others found that the sex work industry supported them in overcoming issues such as a lack of self-confidence and in addressing the inability to experience 'closeness' with others. As such it could be argued that the procurement of sexual services for some men allowed them to attend to aspects of their 'well being'. However, the men's accounts relate to some theorists' views, as discussed in Chapter 2, theorists such as Freud, who considered that men's procurement of sexual services was deviant and originated from disruptions in an individual's psycho-sexual development. Analysis of the interview data revealed that some of the men had encountered challenging experiences concerning poor socialisation processes and poor perceptions of themselves. This resulted in experiences of shyness and poor body image. Some recounted sexual abuse. These early experiences and the belief of some men that those experiences had affected their sexual lives as adults, offers support to a psycho-sexual explanation regarding why some men procure sexual services.

For example MI:4 said he was raised in a very sheltered and closed environment, where his mother kept him away from other children. He believes that this contributed to his lack of social skills in adulthood and his inability to engage in conventional relationships:

> I was screwed over by my mother because my mother is a queer little biscuit. She said to me when I was 13.... You stay away from girls, they'll say you took them into the bushes and put your hand down their pants.... The thought never occurred to me until my mother suggested it ... this is the sort of thing my mother did. My mother kept us away, myself, my brother my sister, she kept us away from the other children.... As a consequence of that, you don't develop the social skills. So if you don't develop the social skills, then you can't interact with society.
>
> (MI:4)

MI:4 offers an angry account about the socialisation process in his early life that he believes has impacted negatively on his relationships with females. It is impossible to know whether this is the only reason but it is important that this man believes it to be so and believes it is one of the drivers for him to purchase sex. This case provides some support for the theory that poor socialisation processes explain why some men engage in less common sexual activities, such as purchasing sex. It could be argued that this position applies to MI:5 as well. As a child, he was sexually abused by a family friend. He believes that this is one reason for his procurement of sexual services:

> The [procured] sex has to be impersonal and not intimate ... and it stems from the sexual abuse that I experienced as a child. My first introduction to sex was when I was about nine or ten and I was sexually abused by a friend of the family and I'm not talking about a grab at the swimming pool, it was sustained and patterned abuse spreading over a couple of years.
>
> (MI:5)

While MI:5 recognises he does not procure sexual services as a means of intimacy, it would seem that this social practice does address an adult need that cannot be achieved through more conventional outlets. This, he believes, is a product of the child abuse he suffered. This would suggest that sex work provides this man with a safe means through which to express his normal sexual needs and desires.

Finally, shyness, lack of self-confidence and poor body image were offered by some of the men interviewed as issues in their childhood/youth. These issues were claimed to be reasons why they began to procure sexual services – a clear reflection of how early life experiences impact on the procurement of sexual services. MI:4, already discussed above, made this point. It can be understood that having a poor body image and experiencing shyness inhibits social interaction with others in a number of ways. In terms of 'wooing' a partner, people who suffer such problems may struggle to attract a partner. As a result the procurement of sexual services could be a perfect outlet for some men who experience such difficulties. For example, MI:10 recalled shyness as a feature of his childhood and adolescence. He was reclusive and shy until his late teens, and as a result did not have many friends and failed to develop the social skills men use to engage in attracting a female partner. He said:

> Um sort of hadn't had any girlfriends by that time, a little bit frustrated so um it's ... very um, I was quite shy, I was a very very shy, I was a reclusive person when I was younger so um ... that's how I got into [procuring sex].
>
> (MI:10)

It is evident that the sex work industry has provided some men the means to address their shyness and isolation and engage in sexual relations with women. As a result of these findings, the data presented thus far suggests that the sex work industry plays a role in supporting some men in enhancing their well being.

In summary, some men interviewed had experienced problems in the early stages of their lives. These experiences, they believe, have inhibited them in their social interactions with others in adulthood. Some men have linked their concerns about their self-image with their poor sexual and social skill development and view their poor self image as the reason for significant social problems faced in their lives. Ranging from child sexual abuse to reclusiveness and bullying, these factors have negatively impacted on their lives. This lends some support to the theorists who argue that difficulties in developing successful intimate relationships in adulthood and the consequent use of the sex industry to fulfil that aspect of their lives, can be traced in part, to experiences in childhood (Freud, 1962). However, through the procurement of sexual services, such inhibitors may, according to the men interviewed, be positively addressed. This challenges the attribution of deviance to the sex work industry, when sex work supports some men to overcome personal problems such as reclusiveness. In contrast there is the interpretation that sex work and its purchase can be viewed as having a normative function in the lives of these men. This social practice of procuring sex allows some men with low self-esteem and poor body image or who have had repressive or abusive experiences in life, to express their sexuality and potentially improves their psycho-social well being.

These findings have implications for Monto and McRee's (2005) 'everyman' and peculiar man perspectives. Reflecting on some of the men's stories of negative life experiences, perhaps Monto and McRee's 'peculiar man' may be an appropriate typology to explain and understand men who procure sexual services. However, not everyone who has experienced abuse or poor socialising as a child can be characterised as 'peculiar', and not all the men who were interviewed recalled difficult experiences in their childhood or later lives or having had a poor sense of self. Experiencing poor self-image or bullying, therefore, does not make a man 'peculiar' or deviant. Rather these experiences disclosed by the men suggest that they cannot be pigeon holed into binary categories as a means of understanding their behaviour.

Why men procure sexual services for the first time: the men's perspective

Reasons why men first purchased sexual services were explored explicitly in the interviews. It emerged that the reason or reasons for purchasing a sexual service for the first time were not necessarily the same as those for future purchasing by the men. The majority of men acknowledged that the first time reasons were mainly to do with the end of a romantic relationship or the lack of sex in their relationship, resulting in them not having had 'sex' for a period of time. Therefore, a main reason for the initial purchase of sexual services was found to be responding to a physical need – the act of sex. Here a commonality is evidence between this finding and the evolutionary psychologists' perspective on sex for pleasure (Kauth, 2007) as discussed in Chapter 1. These scholars have argued that sex is not always for procreational reasons and that sex for pleasure is part of the genetic constitution of humans. Sex for pleasure is something important to men in this study and is a key reason for them purchasing sex. The end of a relationship was noted as the main reason for MI:8's initial procuring of sex. Whilst he reported a lack of sex in a previous relationship, after his divorce he went to a massage parlour for sexual services that were for pleasure purposes:

> It got to the stage where maybe if I was lucky, I got it once a year in my previous relationship. Post-divorce though I went into a massage parlour and it was like a sauna; I would get a massage, rub-down, full body stuff, there was no intercourse involved it was just hand relief stuff.
>
> (MI:8)

Evidence for 'sex for pleasure' is outlined in this account by MI:8. He reveals that not only was sex procured for pleasure but, in the first instance, was as a result of the end of a relationship that had not been a positive one sexually for him. MI:8 acknowledges that within his conventional relationship he did not have regular sexual activities with his partner. This finding resonates with the cluster analysis presented in Chapter 5, where cluster group 2 members cite an absence of regular sex with a partner as a reason for procuring sexual services. However, this implies that the sexual act itself, whilst a reason for some men first procuring sexual services, may not be the only reason for men's procurement. In contrast, some men may seek 'closeness' with someone from the opposite sex as an emotional response to the lack of sex within a current relationship, or as a result of a relationship ending.

Fulfilment of fantasies and fetishes

It is noted by some scholars that men procure sexual services because they want to enjoy a sexual experience they may not be able to access through a conventional relationship (McKeganey and Barnard, 1996; Monto, 2000). While some of the findings in Chapter 5 suggested that men in the cohort surveyed primarily engage in sexual acts such as vaginal intercourse and oral sex, experiencing a sexual fantasy was acknowledged by some as a reason for purchasing sex for the first time. MI:7 said this was the main reason he first procured sexual services. He also said that, while the fulfilment of fantasies and fetishes were, for him, reasons for procuring sex initially, purchasing sex was also a mechanism to address his low self-esteem and confidence issues:

> I wanted to fulfil some fantasies, but most of all it certainly helped me out [going to sex workers], helped me over my fears of sex. And working through that to the point where I am now very active. It wasn't until I was 50 that I discovered that I was able to give pleasure to a woman, and uh, that's when I started to enjoy it.
>
> (MI:7)

Through the narratives of the men interviewed, the matter of confidence in regard to sexual relationships with 'another' emerges. Traditionally, men are viewed as confident and self-assured, yet some of the men offered an alternative narrative of men's 'sense of self'. These alternative accounts indicate that poor self-esteem and confidence are not uncommon but can be addressed through the procurement of sexual services. This reflects the positive impact that procuring sex has on the lives of men, and as a result challenges the deviancy discourse that some writers have promoted with regards to the sex work industry.

Male bonding and the expression of masculinity

Extending the point raised above, MI:13 discussed the 'male bonding' experience through his first experience in the sex work industry. MI:13 went with his cousins to a brothel for the first time when he was 19. He talked about his confidence being positively impacted through his procuring of sexual services. His view was that the sex work industry provides a perfect environment to support young men, who experience a low sense of self, in their sexual development:

At the time I was 19, I was with my two cousins ... it was just like a bonding session I guess. Just a way of bonding. But there was ... um ... body and self-confidence issues too ... it was a way of just building up confidence and learning how to interact with people as well. It builds up your confidence in regards to communicating with potential girlfriends. And it's actually much more safer with a sex worker than a girl you meet out.

(MI:13)

There is clear recognition by MI:13 that his first time experience within the sex work industry was in the context of a bonding session with his peers. However, as a result of this experience he began to develop self confidence in relation to sex with the opposite sex. Scholars such as O'Connell Davidson (1998) have recognised that groups of men visit sex workers as a male bonding exercise, as a means of demonstrating their manhood, and to assert their masculine identity. However, O'Connell Davidson's work underplays the more sensitive aspects of men's procurement of sex. As MI:13 indicated, a poor level of self-confidence was also a key factor for his first procurement of sex. MI: 13's account exemplifies the interplay of these factors.

Sex as a commodity?

Some of the men stated the main reason they had purchased sex for the first time was based on their view that sex is a commodity, it is 'something' that can be bought. This position speaks directly to the economic theories some scholars such as McLeod (1982) (discussed earlier) have advocated as reasons for men's procurement of sexual services. Men consume the product on offer in the sex work industry in the same way they would consume another product in any other market setting. This is highlighted by MI:12, who describes the first time he bought a sexual service as a 'non emotional' experience that required no ongoing commitment. He likened it to visiting a hairdresser:

It's like going to see a hairdresser. Y'know, there's no commitment; sometimes there is a bit of a spark there, but it's just part of, it's just part of life, its natural ... just like eating or sleeping or drinking.

(MI:12)

The commodity position is further supported by MI:1 claiming the rationale for the procurement of sexual services for the first time is based on the notion sex is something that can be bought:

I think most men initially buy sex because sex is fun, they are very aware of the type of sex they are purchasing and are pleased to be able to have their sex packaged and contained within a commercial transaction.

(MI:1)

However, MI:1 also makes reference to the fact that some men procure sexual services because they lack sexual contact in a conventional relationships. This again reveals an interplay of reasons why men procure sexual services:

> I would say most men who I know who buy sex for the first time are not getting the amount of sex they desire in their personal lives. It may just be spontaneous after a few beers or without much preconceived planning, but men do it because they are not getting it elsewhere and can buy it like anything else.
>
> (MI:1)

The idea that men procure sexual services, because they view sex as a commodity, was considered in Chapter 3 of this volume. Commercial sex has been recognised in the work of a number of scholars such as O'Connell Davidson (1998), Monto (2000), and Jordan (2005) for a variety of reasons, ranging from objectifying women to experiencing sex with no long term commitment. Based on some of the men's accounts, it would seem that commercial sex gives men the opportunity to experience their first sexual encounter as they would any commodity. Yet, intertwined with 'sex as a commodity', men acknowledge that they also procure sexual services because their relationship has ended and/or they have not had sex for some time, or they have low levels of self-confidence.

In summary, the men interviewed shared a number of experiences that offer a number of reasons why men first procure sexual services. These range from using procurement as a means of addressing a poor sense of self to experiencing a fetish. For most men though there is an interplay of reasons for procuring sexual services and the men's interviews speak to a more complex understanding of men's engagement in this social practice. This complexity is not evident in the current binary discourse on men's purchasing of sex.

In order to gain another perspective on men's initial purchasing of sex, female sex workers were interviewed. The purpose of this was to examine the similarities and differences between the two main social actors in understanding why men purchase sexual services.

First time reasons for the procurement of sexual services: the sex worker perspective

The data from the female interviewees provided some rich insight into their experiences as providers of sexual services to first time clients. In their experience, most first time procurement is driven by the need or desire for sex as a result of the end of a relationship. However, the sex workers acknowledge different reasons that drive men to first procure sex. These reasons included, for example, the desire to lose one's virginity, and peer pressure. Commonalities and differences can therefore be seen between the men's and the female sex workers' accounts, providing the opportunity to triangulate the data obtained in the study.

The loss of virginity and ease of the transaction

Sex workers said that the procurement of sexual services for the first time may be driven by a man's desire to lose his virginity. FI:3 indicated that clients who came for their first experience with a sex worker were aged between 18 and 26 and commonly wanted to lose their virginity. She describes how these men were often pressured by their peers to lose their virginity by dating a 'girl' or going to a sex worker. She believed that the latter option was most favoured by men, as the 'transaction' was more convenient and easy: 'Visiting a sex worker is often a result of a man wanting to lose his virginity and it is seen as "cheaper" and "easier" than conducting the "wining and dining" experience' (FI:3).

Similar to the accounts offered by some men interviewed, FI:3 recognised the peer pressure/male bonding experience this first encounter features. Parallels can be drawn here between the accounts of men who procure sexual services and females who sell sexual services in terms of why men procure for the first time: 'A large proportion of clients visiting a sex worker for the first time were also doing so with groups of friends, they are pressured into it [lose their virginity] a little by their peers' (FI:3).

However, FI:6 suggested that regardless of the reasons for purchasing sex for the first time, the fact it is easy to do so was the main reason men came to the see a sex worker for the first time: 'It's easier to just pay for it and get it over and done with whatever the reason you are buying for' (FI:6). Whilst the ease of the transaction is offered by the men and female sex workers who were interviewed as a first time reasons for purchasing sex, FI:6 offers an additional reason, as she states the onset reasons also include the fact that some men are just lonely: 'Although men are purchasing for a range of reasons, essentially they don't want to be lonely and then at the end of it [sexual act] they actually want to talk to you' (FI:6).

In this part of FI:6's account, she recognises men's feelings as a reason for purchasing sex for the first time. This is not the first time in this analysis that men's procurement of sexual services is linked to men's feelings. For example, men reported (as noted in this chapter and Chapter 5) that they purchased sex to build self-confidence and address feelings of inadequacy. What the data set is evidencing is the emotional aspect of men's lives that procuring sexual services addresses. This is further evidence that procuring sexual services attends to some men's positive sense of self and their well being. In support of this position, FI:2 added to this evidence by recognising that some men enter the sex work industry for the first time as a means of receiving affection.

The need to seek affection, regardless of age, regardless of circumstance

While it was recognised that men were wanting someone to connect with and talk to, as noted by FI:6's account above, an implicit reference to men emotionally connecting to someone through the procurement of sexual services is made by a number of the sex worker interviewees. FI:2 extends this idea and claims men ultimately purchase sex for the first time as they are seeking affection. She discussed the fact that men who procured sexual services seek a level of intimacy from the sex worker that they do not get elsewhere in their lives. FI:2's narrative indicated that this need for affection arose for a range of reasons such as shyness, or because their wives were pregnant or had just had a baby, or they were going through a divorce or were simply 'horny'. Regardless of these various factors, these men felt they were experiencing some form of sexual and/or emotional neglect and were seeking affection:

> The dominant [age for first timers], is probably about ... 20 ... because they didn't have a girlfriend so they are lonely and starved of affection. For others, some of them would say that they weren't happy in their marriage or that they weren't getting any affection from within their marriage. Some of the first timers will tell me that their wife is ill ... again they are looking for affection. The guys in their thirties, this is from my experience, umm, either their wives were pregnant, or had just had a baby. There were a lot of those cases, or umm, they'd just come out of a divorce. The guys in their forties and fifties, well the married guys, umm, were just bored in their relationship, ignored ... yes, and umm, yeah the 50- and 60-year-olds, well (laughs), they are just horny men. They are all looking for affection for whatever the reason – this is why men buy sex.
>
> (FI:2)

While offering a multifactorial account for the reasons men procure sexual services for the first time, FI:2 believes there is one underlying issue why men procure a sexual service. This underlying factor is simply men are seeking affection. Regardless of whether a man is lonely because he is not in a relationship, or feeling neglected as his wife has just had a baby, or if a man is experiencing a sexual urge – feeling horny. What the sex work industry offers is a resolution for men experiencing a lack of affection in their lives. FI:2's narrative suggests that the sex work industry responds to the needs of men in relation to their physiological, psychological and social well being. This account of why men first purchase sexual services is reflected in the accounts of members of the interest groups interviewed.

First time reasons for the procurement of sexual services: the interest groups' perspectives

The views of the interest groups were sought regarding what they thought were the reasons men procured sexual services for the first time. Many had insight into some of the reasons revealed by the men and the sex workers who were interviewed. The clergy viewed the primary driver for men's initial procurement of sexual services as peer pressure; drawing a parallel with the narratives of the sex workers and some men interviewed. Nevertheless, the clergy as a group still felt that purchasing sex was the wrong thing to do. The clergy believed that the procurement of sexual services breached religious teachings. This is exemplified by CI:1 who stated that the individual making his first visit to a sex worker would know what they were doing was wrong, yet recognised they had outside influences that pressured them into it:

> Yes even the first time [for procuring sex], no doubt the Church would teach that the person knew what they were doing was the wrong thing, regardless of their age or social background. I'd say it is always, always negative, it couldn't be positive, whether its friends that are kind of pushing them into it or you know, I've heard examples of even fathers taking their sons there as a, you know, kind of coming of age thing, it is all sinful.
>
> (CI:1)

It is interesting to see that Cl:1 believes men seem unable to resist the peer pressure, that they are unable to control their choices and their behaviours as they are 'pushed' into procuring sex by others and that once men are subjected to such an influence it is a 'fait accompli'. This is reminiscent of how the Church and medical science historically, portrayed men. In regard to their engagement in the sex work industry, men have been portrayed by some social institutions as being unable to control themselves. It would seem that this belief is still held by some.

Multi-factorial reasons for first time procurement

There were some members of the clergy, along with other interest group interviewees who acknowledged multiple reasons for men procuring sexual services. Levels of stress and poor sense of self were commonly cited reasons by some of the interest groups interviewed for men's first purchase of sex from the sex work industry. CI:3, for example acknowledged that men who purchase sexual services for the first time could be influenced by a range of factors, recognising that men could be:

> insecure in terms of their own sexual expression, lonely or some may be ... curious, some may be drunk, um..., some may be unfulfilled in their sexual relationships ... Um ... perhaps they are in the midst of a relationship breakdown and longing to continue that ... regardless of such reasons, the Church still views the act as sinful.
>
> (CI:3)

CI:3's understanding of why men first procure sexual services is insightful, offering a range of reasons such as feeling lonely, being single or experiencing a relationship break-up. Nevertheless, similar to CI:1, CI:3 held the view that the act of procurement is morally wrong in the eyes of the Church. It is this type of perception that lends support to the theorising that those who purchase sex are deviant and that has informed, and continues to inform, knowledge about and understanding of the procurement of sexual services contemporaneously.

The range of reasons that influence men to engage in the transaction of sexual services for the first time is reflected in the accounts of the medics interviewed. Although, the medics acknowledged a range of factors that contribute to the first time purchase of sexual services, this interest group tended to offer more physiological reasons for men procuring sexual services. For example, MeI:2 believed stress was a primary reason; however, this view was extended to recognise that men may also purchase sex for the first time for the experience and feelings of thrill and excitement. For MeI:2 the act provides men a means of experiencing sexual fantasies and fetishes they may not be able to access elsewhere in their lives:

> Men may initially visit a sex worker for many reasons, however, I would think commonly due to events in their personal life such as stress at work and at home. These men need to relieve stress, they want a distraction. However, there is always the excitement of procurement, that will contribute to why men begin to buy sex, they get to live out a fantasy.
>
> (MeI:2)

The recognition of an emotional factor (stress) contributing to men's initial procurement of sexual services was also acknowledged by MeI:3, who outlined stress as a reason for purchasing sex for the first time, as well as a number of other emotional and intimacy reasons:

> Yes, stress leads men to buying sex for the first time, it's a release for them, but other personal reasons such as shyness, sexual inexperience and losing one's virginity could be reasons why men first buy sex. It is also a way of seeking affection, for example for someone who has lost a partner and who is experiencing loneliness.
>
> (MeI:3)

MeI:3 offers a range of factors that they believed influence a man to procure sexual services for the first time. It is important to note how this narrative reflects the many reasons the male interviewees, who procure sexual services, offer. Furthermore, MeI:3's narrative reflects some of the female sex workers' accounts. This multifactorial understanding of why men first purchase sex was also seen in the accounts of the women's collective group members. The overarching view of the women's collective group members was men procure sex for the first time for a variety of reasons. These interviewees suggested similar onset reasons to those noted above by the medics, including loneliness, curiosity and fulfilling a fantasy. For example, WC:1 stated that 'curiosity, peer pressure, fulfilling a fantasy and as a means of meeting their sexual needs regardless of their current relationship' were reasons for men first purchasing sexual services.

It is worth noting thus far that in the narratives of those who purchase and sell sex, and in the narratives of the interest groups, there is broad recognition of the variety of factors for men first purchasing sexual services. Most of those interviewed recognised that the reason(s) men purchase sexual services for the first time from the sex work industry are as a means of addressing a poor sense of self, such a poor body image, and to address levels of stress and feelings of loneliness. It is also recognised by some, that men seek affection through their encounter with a sex worker. Nevertheless, in contrast, one member of the women's collective group failed to share the understanding offered by her peers or of men and women involved in the sex work industry regarding first time purchasing: one women's collective group member who was interviewed believed that men procure sexual services for the first time because they are deviant, saying that men purchase sex as a result of patriarchy and the desire for power.

Procuring sex and desire for power

Some writers on the procurement of sexual services have viewed men's reasons for purchasing sex as misogynistic or as a means of controlling women (O'Connell Davidson, 1998; Grubman Black, 2003). While this position is not evident in the interview data presented thus far, WC:5 provided accounts that support this position. She stated men procure sexual services due to patriarchal social dominance, and that their behaviour is a result of: 'A desire for power, this is the main reason why men procure sexual services for the first time' (WC:5).

WC:5 believed patriarchy was the cause of the 'social problem' of procuring sexual services:

I believe that a strong influence on men to purchase sex for the first time is growing up in a patriarchal culture with certain beliefs about male and female sexuality for example that men 'need' sex, the women are sexual objects. This culture 'conditions' many men to think and interact with women in particular ways, which results in the purchase of sex.

(WC:5)

Summarising why men procure sexual services for the first time

In summary, the data presented thus far in Chapter 6 and drawing on findings in earlier chapters, suggests the reasons men procure sexual services are diverse. As a result of this finding it could be argued that the binary typologies and discourses surrounding the understanding is reductive. The variety of reasons for purchasing sex, according to the men surveyed and interviewed and according to the women sex workers, generally relate to pro-social impacts on men's physiological, psychological and/or social well being. The initial procurement of sexual services, as described in most of the interviewee's accounts, is not necessarily always about the act of sex. However, some women's collective group members believed men procure sexual services for the first time due to deviant and negative reasons that also have negative outcomes. Such a negative understanding of men's initial purchase of sex from the sex work industry reflects some of the existing literature, which theorises that men are driven by the need for power over women and misogynist attitudes. Nevertheless, most of the views held by the women's collective group members in regard to why men purchase sexual services for the first time did not reflect this position.

Table 6.1 summaries the main first time reasons, that emerged from analysis of the data, for men who procure sexual services, by each of the five groups interviewed.

As Table 6.1 indicates, there are many of reasons for men's initial procurement of sexual services, with a significant number of reasons centring on dealing with/addressing emotions such as feeling lonely and having a poor self-image. These reasons reflect expressive reasons for procuring sexual services; however, physical reasons are also acknowledged as drivers behind men's first engagement in this social practice. These are commonly shared views held by all groups interviewed. In summary, and using the table above, it can be concluded that the

Table 6.1 First time reasons for the procurement of sexual services by interview group

Men who procure	No regular sex with partner
	Experience shyness
	Lack of self confidence
	Relationship breakdown
	It's a commodity
	Spontaneous act
Female sex workers	No regular sex with partner
	Feeling lonely
	Experience shyness
	Lack of self-confidence
	Loss of virginity
	Peer pressure
	Wanting affection
	Feeling horny
Clergy	Peer pressure
	Feeling lonely
	Curious/living out a fantasy
	No regular sex with partner
Medics	Stress relief
	Feeling lonely
	Loss of virginity
	Experience shyness
	Sexual inexperience
Women's collective groups	Living out a fantasy
	Peer pressure
	Feeling lonely
	Power and control over women
	Influence of pornography

many reasons why men procure sexual services impact positively on a man's well being, and may be reflective of why men continue to purchase. To extend and explore this line of enquiry further, the following section of this findings chapter considers the reasons that contribute to why men *continue* to purchase. This analysis allows for an assessment of the similarities and differences, if any, between why men purchase sex for the first time and why they to continue to purchase sexual services.

The reasons for the continuation of procurement: the men's perspective

The previous findings chapter, Chapter 5, presented the reasons men claimed they procured sexual services. Nevertheless, no distinction was made between whether these reasons influenced the first time purchase of sexual services or a continuation of purchasing sexual services; and whether there were differences between the two. Through the interview data thus far in Chapter 6, consideration has been given as to why men first procure sexual services, Consideration is now given to why men re-enter the sex work industry to purchase sex and the reasons why they continue in this practice. The data that follows shows that different reasons do contribute to men's continuation of procuring sexual services. Nevertheless, the overarching themes of viewing sex as a commodity and attending to one's emotional needs and levels of intimacy are still prominent reasons why men continue to procure sexual services.

A desire for intimacy, a 'girlfriend experience'

Achieving a level of intimacy through the procurement of sexual services has been recently acknowledged in the literature as a reason why men procure sexual services (Kennedy *et al.*, 2004; Sanders, 2008a; Milrod and Weitzer, 2012). This is commonly offered in the accounts of the male cohort interviewed in this study in relation to why they continue to purchase sexual services. MI:1 for example indicates that the emotional aspects drive him to keep purchasing sexual services:

> I think it's my girlfriend I mean, I think that's what going around in my mind – this woman's my girlfriend. The fact I've never seen her before, doesn't seem to worry me too much but I think I try and make it as … as close to normal sex as possible, it's kind of intimate.

> (MI:1)

MI:1 is viewing the sex worker as his girlfriend; he sees the transaction of sexual services with the sex worker in the same way as he would an intimate relationship interaction between him and a girlfriend. MI:1 views the sex that takes place between him and the sex worker in the same way he imagines he would have with his girlfriend (if he had one). This finding draws parallels with the work of Sanders (2008a), who concludes from her research into men who procure sexual services that these men want a 'girlfriend' experience. The fact that MI:1 in the current study has paid for the sexual service is missing completely from his perception and consideration of the experience. The data presented accords with the accounts of men, and others interviewed above concerning men seeking affection through their first time procurement. In the continuation of procurement men are extending this need for affection and experiencing levels of intimacy and closeness they associate with a 'girlfriend', as would occur within a more conventional setting. This account is reflected in MI:3's narrative.

MI:3 acknowledges he likes the feeling of intimacy he gets from the sex worker he sees regularly. MI:3 reports that the emotional intimacy he receives from the experience is a reason he returns to the sex work industry, he sees the same sex worker each time, suggesting his attempt to make this akin to a conventional setting in which the procurement takes place:

> I take in the funny emails, the joke emails from work, not the dirty ones, but the funny ones. We sit at the end of the bed, have a drink and go through the jokes and then we have a cuddle and a kiss. I will always tell her, like you're really beautiful and love being with you, that sort of thing.
>
> I'm very open with her and I listen to her stories. That's part of the enjoyment for me. We talk about family things and she would ask how my wife is or how is this and that going? I enjoy it, you know, the friendship, the pseudo love I guess.
>
> (MI:3)

As with the findings of Sanders (2008a) and Holt *et al.* (2007), MI: 3's engagement in the transaction of sexual services is more commonly associated with a conventional romantic relationship. MI:3 describes a setting that is intimate and tells of his engagement in behaviours that are non-sexual. Aspects of his experience that contribute to the continuation of procurement, are the exchange of information between him and the sex worker regarding each other's lives. In Chapters 1 and 3, it was recognised that human beings seek closeness and proximity to each other, which in turn fosters a positive sense of self. From the accounts offered by the men, a reason they continue to procure sexual services is to nurture this positive sense of self through the closeness and intimacy experienced between the sex worker and themselves.

For the male clients interviewed, the emotional interaction contributes to their continued procurement of sexual services. MI:6 provides further evidence of this in his claims that his continued procurement of sexual services is an interaction that is not only physical but emotional as well:

> an interaction of both emotional and ummm physical because it fills that void for that moment … she is my wife, my girlfriend, it's a set of emotions and physicality that's thrown into the equation. I need some companionship

for the moment, I need to be emotional for a moment, I need to put my hands on a body, I get all that from her.

(MI:6)

MI:6 indicates, as with the other men interviewed, that the 'girlfriend' experience is an important reason for the continuation of procurement. This is suggesting that for many men, whilst the procurement of sexual services has many positive features, a common continuing reason is that the act provides a level of intimacy for men: the 'girlfriend experience'. The girlfriend experience in part is what MI:5 seeks through his continued use of the sex work industry. He believes that because he is old and single; he will not find anyone else to settle down with. However, he still has a desire for intimacy and to feel close to someone: 'because I'm single, and whilst I've had short term relationships I'll never get into a long term relationship now at my age, so it basically comes down to being close to someone, having sex with them' (MI:5).

MI:5 acknowledges being 'close' to someone is achieved through his procurement of sexual services. The purchasing of a sexual service is important to him as it allows him to engage in a relationship with a sex worker, which encompasses and meets his emotional and sexual needs at his time of life.

The achievement of intimacy is also a reason for MI:11 continuing to purchase sexual services. The intimacy for MI:11 ultimately reflects his inability to have sexual relationships outside of paid transactions.

Every time I talk to a girl and I befriend her … they just want to be friends. And when you're friends with a girl they don't want to have sex with you … it was very hard for me to get, to get sex; I've been rejected probably 150 times this year already, this doesn't happen to me when I buy sex.

He also likes to experience intimacy in ways other than having sex:

I like to have a bit of a chat with her [sex worker], I couldn't just walk in have sex with her and jump off … that's not me umm…. I like to talk to her a little bit about things and what she has done recently I think it's good, I mean they're human beings they're not robots … umm but I think people can class them as that [robots] … I mean they have got souls, they have got a heart, and they're doing it for a job.

(MI:11)

The commodification of intimacy

As with other men interviewed, the closeness and level of intimacy MI:4 experiences through the procurement of sexual services, which he doesn't experience in his life outside the sex work industry, are the reasons he continues to purchase sexual services. However, there is a recognition by MI:4 that through procurement, intimacy is bought. He recognises the fact that purchasing sex, means intimacy is also purchased and he views sex as a commodity:

> Well you can buy sex, and the main reason for me purchasing sex, for me anyway; is for closeness and intimacy. I went to a parlour and I met a lady at a parlour, and uh, sort of fell in love with her, that's why I go back.
>
> (MI:4)

While MI:4 describes a 'closeness' he has found with the same sex worker that contributes to the reason he returns for sexual services; his account also evidences implicitly the commodity aspect attached to his involvement with the sex work industry. Nevertheless MI:4 declares he 'loves' the woman he sees, which is also a reflection of the normative function that the procurement of sexual services plays in these men's lives. This account by MI:4 reflects a relationship typical of a more conventional relationship.

In summary, the main reason some men offer for their continued procurement of sexual services, is a desire for intimacy. Having the 'girlfriend experience', which is closely aligned with experiencing intimacy, is also a common reason given. Earlier in the chapter it was recognised that a reason for men first procuring sex was the need for affection, which can be associated with a 'girlfriend experience'. One conclusion emerging from these analyses is that men's *feelings* are central to the initial and continued purchasing of sexual services. Men first enter the sex work industry, as they feel they lack affection in their lives, whilst the continuation of procurement centres on the 'girlfriend' experience, which involves preventing loneliness and sustaining levels of intimacy.

Minimal commitment, maximum benefits

Not all of the men interviewed considered their transaction of sexual services to be driven by intimacy factors. Some men recognised that their procurement of sexual services meant they did not need to engage in the same level of commitment that was required in more conventional relationships. However, men who claimed this to be a reason for their purchasing of sexual services also recognised the positive impact their involvement in the sex work industry had on their lives. Men provided accounts that claimed that procuring sexual services provided sustained healthy levels of well being in their lives. This they said was because purchasing sex contributed to de-stressing after work, and/or limited the stresses caused by the demands of a conventional relationship. Such factors reflect the reason some men enter the sex work industry for the first time. MI:1 stated that he had been a client for over 20 years and had seen the same sex worker each time. MI:1 recognised that the convenience of purchasing sexual services was now part of a normal routine and the procurement of sexual services was a substitute for a conventional relationship. MI:1 viewed the relationship as one that did not make demands on his settled way of life and therefore provided no conflicts in his life:

I am getting older and probably finding it harder to meet women … if I go and pay for sex it actually fits in good with me, if you wanna watch the football or something like that there is no conflict, it's a lot less stressful than marriage.

(MI:1)

MI:1's account suggests that sex work plays a normative function in his life; it fits in with his everyday life. This is a similar situation for MI:6 who acknowledged that the reason he continues to purchase sexual services is that it is a reward for working hard:

It serves a need and a purpose. If I just feel like going I go … I might go over to see a sex worker after I've had a really good training run … like umm it's a reward for me.

(MI:6)

Some of the male interviewees consider the continuation of their procurement as the purchasing of a commodity, but this is by no means the only or main way they think of purchased sex. They say it provides stress relief and that it maximises a sense of thrill and excitement in their lives. MI:3 for example, believes that it is the excitement, enjoyment and stress relief from work that sustains his involvement within the sex work industry:

It often coincides with a pressured time at work. It is a form of relief, an enjoyment … these are the reasons I keep going back, that's the beauty of it, and it's legal. To me it is a business transaction. I don't want a long term relationship.

(MI:3)

MI:3 offered reasons for the procurement of sexual services that are the same as some of the primary reasons for the onset to procurement, such as stress relief and the excitement of the transaction. However, MI:3 acknowledges that procuring sexual services means he is devoid of all the responsibilities typically linked to a long term relationship. MI:3 finds this appealing. The fact that MI:3 addresses high levels of stress and excitement in his life through the procurement of sexual services, lends support to the notion that the act of procuring sexual services is associated with attending to one's psycho-social well being. Attending to one's well being through purchasing sexual services, is also evident in the account of MI:9. However, this is due to his lack of sexual activity in his current relationship, his inability to have various sexual experiences in that relationship and his need for sexual intimacy.

Lack of sex in marriage and the continuation of procurement

MI:9 recognises that through the transaction of sexual services he is able to have the various sexual experiences he wants to encounter in life. These experiences he believes are not available to him through his marriage. His narratives provide links between the reasons for first time procurement and the continuation of procurement with regard to not having regular sex with his partner:

> It's an opportunity for me to explore the many things that were either discussed or just dismissed within my relationship. Some things she [his wife] would just not discuss, and some things I just didn't discuss with her as I expected to get a very negative response anyway. I don't have this problem when I go and buy sex, that's why I keep going back.
>
> (MI:9)

Summarising why men continue to procure

In summary, from the accounts of those men interviewed, the reasons men give for continuing to purchase sex range from the 'ease of a transaction' to having the 'girlfriend experience'. However, what can be surmised from these reasons is how men attend to maintaining a sense of 'well being' through their transaction of sexual services. Men continue to procure sex as it assists in creating a healthy sense of self. Their first experience of purchasing sex produced positive feelings, including the experience of intimacy and excitement that they may have been finding very hard to experience in conventional relationships. In comparing why men first purchase sexual services to why they continue to do so, a shift is evident, between men seeking affection to men wanting to develop that affection over time. The continuation of procurement involves most of the aspects and experiences of a conventional girlfriend or marriage relationship, and this leads to the prevention of loneliness and relieves stress. There is a strong expressive rationale why men continue to procure sexual services. While expressive reasons reflect why men first purchase services from within the sex work industry, there is more emphasis on such reasons when men return to the sex work industry. The procurement of sexual services for men contributes to a healthy sense of self by seeking out closeness, proximity and familiarity on a regular basis with someone they like. The continuation of the procurement of sexual services does not necessarily centre on a sexual act per se, but often also includes talking about everyday things, enjoying each other's company, sharing jokes over a drink, seeking solace for problems and difficulties, and caring about the other; these are all things that contribute to one's sense of well being. From the accounts offered by these men, they find this can be done more easily with a sex worker than within a conventional relationship.

In conclusion it is worth restating the positive impact that surrounds men's procurement of sexual services. It is not just one type of man with one particular reason involved in procurement, yet a range of different men with a variety of reasons. However, in amongst this diversity a common goal for these men through the purchasing of sexual services is addressing social and health issues, which in term contributes to a positive sense of self – well being. This conclusion lends support to the findings presented in Chapter 5, along with the rejection of some current theories and binary typologies concerning men who procure sexual services which were also discussed in Chapter 5. The procurement of sexual services, through the accounts of the male clients reflects a complexity in so far as men's engagement with the sex work industry is an interplay of factors and is not influenced by a single factor. Nevertheless, the behaviour of procuring sexual services can be simply summarised as a men attending to his psycho-social well being.

The next part of this chapter will focus on the sex workers' and interest groups' views. The data from these groups on why men continue to procure sexual services can be used to assess if there is a shared understanding regarding why men continue to procure sex. This is of interest, as these groups in society have over time contributed to shaping policy and legislation regulating the sex work industry.

The reasons concerning the continuation of procurement: the sex worker perspective

The female sex workers interviewed offered similar responses to the male participants in terms of an understanding of why men continue to procure sexual services. They acknowledged the complexity of and interplay between reasons for the continuation of men's procurement of sexual services. Female sex workers, overall as a group based on their experience of selling sex, claim the continuation of purchasing sex was due to a mixture of factors, which centre on men attending to their emotions and need for intimacy. For example, FI:2 indicated that clients continued purchasing sex in the pursuit of affection and over time they formed an attachment to sex workers:

> umm, well with my regulars, the guys that I used to see more than once, I sort of formed a bit of an ahh, I don't know, not emotional, not on my side anyway, but I sort of formed some sort of a friendship with them.... And umm, I guess I used to give them a lot of affection, which is what they were lacking. So a lot of my regular clients came back not always for the sex, it was more for just to sit and chat, have a cigarette and have a bit of affection, you know. In the second booking usually, or a lot of the time you just have this rapport with someone, you would have sex and then you would spend the rest of the time sort of just chatting and if he felt good in your company then he would come back and see you – it is intimate on some level, umm, sometimes the guy would get a little bit attached. The clients that I've had, umm, I'd say about 95 per cent of the clients have been, umm, respectful, umm, nice, in the sense of, just you know, wanting affection.
>
> (FI:2)

The account of FI:2 not only supports the earlier findings of the generally positive interaction between client and sex worker. FI:2's account also confirms that men's emotional needs and their need for intimacy, that they have fulfilled the first few times they visit a sex worker, are key reasons men continue to purchase services from sex workers. Similar factors were referred to by FI:6 who said that clients keep returning to the sex work industry in order to prevent feelings of loneliness: 'men keep coming back because they don't want to be lonely. Buying sex gives them an outlet to this and to the lives they want to lead' (FI:6).

What the accounts of the female sex workers and male clients provide is agreement that men's emotional and intimacy needs are reasons for continuing to procure sexual services. Seeking affection, seeking the girlfriend experience, and preventing loneliness are all common reasons given for men's continued use of sex workers. This reflects the positive role sex work plays in lives of men and wider society. Without the sex work industry some men may not be able to meet some of their basic human emotional and sexual needs.

The ease of the transaction recognised by female sex workers

Another notable theme in the continuation of the purchasing of sexual services, recognised by some sex workers interviewed was the convenience of the transaction; this convenience has been noted by Monto (2000) and Jordan (2005). Such scholars highlight that the transaction is easy and convenient, as it fits more easily with the particular shape of the working and personal lives of men who procure sexual services, than a conventional relationship. Furthermore, some of the men interviewed noted this as a reason for continuing to procure sexual services. FI:3 expands on this theme by acknowledging that men considered the purchasing of sexual services as a long term solution to the costs, frustrations and disappointments of dates. She also recognised that it served a purpose for satisfying specific needs such as fetishes:

> Cheaper and easier than maintaining or participating in a relationship with a partner, that's why clients keep coming back to us. Clients will often tell you 'I just want sex, I don't want the bullshit'. But also, I find many male clients want to be a little bit more adventurous in the bedroom, that's why they keep coming back. Businessmen often come in because they were looking for a party time, lawyers because they are motivated to buy dominatrix services, they want to be dominated and want to be submissive. I think this is because they were dominating [elsewhere] within their life so much.
>
> (FI:3)

In summary, whilst sex workers offer a range of reasons, based on their experience, for men continuing to procure sexual services, there is an agreement amongst the sex workers. A key factor the sex workers share in their understanding of why men continue to procure sexual services is the men's need for intimacy. Men want to have a 'girlfriend' experience. Furthermore, the female sex workers also recognise the differences between different types of clients and their reasons for continuing to purchase. Such findings reflect a shared understanding between those who purchase sexual services and those who sell sexual services. Overall, men who procure and females who provide sexual services recognised that the act of sex is not always the primary reason for procurement and that non-sexual needs influence the continuation of purchasing sex worker services; this understanding is not shared by most members of the interest groups.

The reasons concerning the continuation of procurement: the interest groups' perspective

Evidence has emerged in this study, that there is a shared understanding between male purchasers of sexual services and those who provide such services, regarding reasons for purchasing and what men want and need from purchasing sex worker services. These two groups also offer an insight into the different reasons men first procure sexual services compared with the reasons influencing continued procurement. This is not necessarily the case with the interest groups' views and understandings, in particular with reference to why men continue to procure sexual services. Interest group members tended to think that the reasons for the continuation of purchasing sex are deviant and immoral compared to the stated views and understandings of those who purchase and sell sexual services.

Desensitisation and the procurement of sexual services

The clergy as a group commonly identified a main factor in the continuation of the procurement of sexual services was desensitisation. CI:1 for example stated:

> as sexual pleasure becomes more of a numbing experience or some kind of coping experience for men, whatever that underlying stress is in their life, then no doubt it would [the purchasing of sexual services] become a way of life.
>
> (CI:1)

The understanding shown by CI:1 of why men continue to purchase sex is in stark contrast the accounts of men who purchase sex and those who sell such services. CI:1 offers an understanding that suggests that men are shut off from their emotions and feelings of intimacy when procuring sexual services. This position is in stark opposition to the reasons given by those involved in this social practice of purchasing sex from sex workers, although CI:1 does recognise how the stress of life can contribute to a man's procurement of sexual services. CI:1's view is extended by CI:2 who agrees that men are desensitised after a time in relation to their procurement of sexual services. CI:2 describes the male purchaser as a passive agent, who cannot help himself:

> their tendencies, their passion for sex, their desire has grown, it is like a cancer, in such a way that umm ... the person looks for a disproportionate level of satisfaction ... ultimately the sexual urge and procurement of sex is

not felt by them after a period of time, it grows out of hand. He cannot stop himself and so he will continue to go out and look for more.

(CI:2)

CI:4 thinks it is the advancements in technology that is the problem, that is, technology has aided men in the procurement of sexual services. Such technological advances make the sex work industry more accessible. CI:4 construes men who procure such services as men who have fallen victim to their 'temptation':

We live in a world today with the Internet and all of this is in your face ... everything is at your fingertips and you see all this at your fingertips and it becomes very tempting to men to then follow this up. It is easy for them to access, so why would they stop with all this temptation.

(CI:4)

The clergy view of men who procure sexual services is arguably, inaccurate. The clergy hold a view that these men are passive agents in the procurement of sexual services. The data collected from the clergy suggests an understanding that is at odds with the views, experiences and understandings of those involved in the procurement of sexual services. Overall, while the clergy have acknowledged there were some understandable issues that explain why men first procure sexual services, they portray men as passive agents who are victims to uncontrollable urges and forces such as the Internet and temptations. But, this was not the case for all the interest groups interviewed such as the medics. The medics, by comparison to the clergy, offered a more positive view about the continued use of sexual services.

It is just about having fun

The medics understanding of why men continue to procure sexual services focuses on reasons such as thrill seeking and excitement. For example, MeI:1 believed the continuation of procurement by men was due to the thrill and excitement of the chase, but MeI:1 implies that this is triggered by the lack of sex within a current marriage: 'Most men quite like sex as a fun activity, and hope to have some fun/exciting sex with a sex worker, in particular within sexless marriages' (MeI:1).

Extending this idea were the views of MeI:3 who believed some men who cannot find a regular partner in life are engaged in the purchasing of sexual services over a sustained period of time. The fact men can keep having fun with a range of different partners ensures that men return to the sex work industry according to MeI:3. MeI:3 believed men continue to procure sexual services because they were:

Having fun with different sexual partners, each time they have sex – it keeps them hooked. It is convenient for them too, they know where to go, how it works, they know how to get it, what they want, no fuss. These guys have some kind of handicap in life, they can't find regular partner, they are addicted to brothels, the women. These men have no time or desire to date, they want it [sex] quick and now.

(MeI:3)

Here MeI:3 recognises that some men who procure sexual services have a form of disability or some form of social inability. There is something 'wrong with them' and they cannot get or keep a conventional relationship. But they can get sex and have fun with a sex worker and this leads men to continue to use the sex work industry. MeI:3 understands that the sex work industry supports men who may struggle to engage in more conventional relationships by providing a place to engage with members of the opposite sex. This view supports the normative function the sex work industry plays in society and suggests that the procurement of sexual services has a positive impact on the lives of men.

MeI:2 extends the acknowledgement of the normative function sex work can play. For MeI:2 men continue to procure sexual services as it allows some to:

obtain a basic activity in life. They may be in a loving relationship with regular partner but their sexual needs are not met, men get stressed due to family and work commitments and other lifestyle stressors. Their purchasing of sex is less risky than having an affair, yet it addresses a number of functions for men.

(MeI:3)

Overall, while some of the medics recognise 'fun' as a key reason for men's procurement of sexual services, they also suggest that men are attending to their psycho-social well being by continuing to purchase sexual services. Particular needs and desires are met within the sex work industry that are not achieved elsewhere in their lives. The medics interviewed reported that men continue to procure sexual services to address stress levels and/or to achieve closeness to members of the opposite sex. In conclusion, there is general agreement amongst the medics interviewed, and those who purchase and sell sex, that such a social practice can support a man's well being. This position is not found in the accounts of the women's collective group members interviewed. This group, in contrast have a simple yet negative understanding of why men continue to procure sexual services.

To dominate and control: no difference from why men first purchase sex

Finally, in relation to the women's collective group members interviewed, many did not distinguish between men's reasons for first purchasing sex and why they continue. This is an important finding in itself because it is at complete odds with the lived experience and views of those who purchase and sell sex. It is also in conflict with the views of medics and to some extent the clergy, who all think there is an interplay of reasons. Members of the women's collective groups on the other hand offer a simplistic understanding of this behaviour. WC:7 for example claims men continue to procure sexual services in order to extend their power and control over women:

> Men keep going back to sex workers because of the difficulties they have relating to women, these men have desires to dominate women, which is supported due to the ease of access and the belief that it is their right to this 'service'. These men have a compulsion, they have a sex addiction. Also because the sex industry exists, there is not enough social and legal condemnation to discourage men from purchasing sex, the sexualisation of women is normalised within mainstream culture, as is the unrelenting and biological male sex drive. They are taking advantage of their male privilege and their position in a culture in which women continue to be in an economically and socially subordinate position, these women have few choices but to sell their bodies for sex.
>
> (WC:7)

WC:7 portrays the women who sell sex as victims, and men who purchase such services as taking advantage of them. The interviewee, whilst reflecting on a number of factors surrounding this practice, has no view of the sex work industry other than as an environment that is exploitative of women and supportive of men's power and dominance. WC:7 considers that the procurement of sexual services centres on the act of sex itself. She does not think that factors, such as intimacy and emotional attachment (earlier discussed as 'the girlfriend experience'), as outlined above by men who procure, and women who sell these services, play a part. By comparison, none of the female sex workers' accounts suggested they were being victimised by their clients or thought of themselves as victims. Sex workers, in fact, portrayed a setting in which sexual services are exchanged within a mutually respected setting. Again it must be noted that this study has surveyed and interviewed only men who purchase and women who sell sex in a non-coercive, legalised environment.

Who, what and why: summarising the data in order to make sense of men's procurement of sexual services

In drawing this final section of Chapter 6 to a close, Table 6.2 summarises the key reasons that each group associates with the continuation of the procurement of sexual services. Those factors in italics represent the crossover between those factors associated with first time purchase of sex, indicated in Table 6.1.

Overall, Table 6.2 indicates that men continue to procure sexual services based on their social and psychological well being; these are mainly emotional and intimacy based reasons, while for some men this form of well being is based on the fact the procurement of sexual services comes with no obligation. Those

Table 6.2 Continuing reasons for the procurement of sexual services by interview group.

Men who procure	*No regular sex with partner*
	Attractiveness of the sex worker
	Prevent loneliness/the 'girlfriend' experience
	Thrill/excitement of procurement
	It's a commodity
	It is devoid of responsibility
Female sex workers	Emotional attachment
	Convenient/ease of procurement
	Prevent loneliness
Clergy	Temptation
	Desensitised to emotions and feelings
Medics	*Stress relief*
	No regular sex with partner
	Thrill/excitement of procurement
Women's collective groups	To dominate women
	Cannot relate to women
	The men are sex addicts
	Take advantage of subordinate women

who provide sexual services and the medics interviewed also make reference to these reasons. The clergy and women's collective group members present an understanding of men's continued procurement of sexual services as deriving from 'bad' and socially negative needs with negative outcomes.

This chapter has illustrated the complexities surrounding the procurement of sexual services and the range of reasons men purchase sexual services. These reasons can differ between why men first procure sexual services and why they continue to engage in this act and within the process of procurement, over time, there is an interplay of reasons contributing to the purchasing of sexual services. Furthermore, this chapter has revealed how the understanding and perception of such reasons and needs differ between those who procure and sell sexual services and the interest groups. What is notable though is the significant difference between those who are involved in the sex work industry and those who are not. Table 6.3 brings together data from Tables 6.1 and 6.2 presented in this chapter and represents the common reasons identified by the groups interviewed. The data represents both first time reasons and continuing reasons for purchasing sex.

Table 6.3 shows the similarities in understanding between men who procure sexual services and the female sex workers in terms of why men purchase sex, and shows these similarities for first time as well as continued purchasing. From the data presented in Table 6.3 it is evident that only three common reasons influence men's purchase of sex for the first time as well as continuing to do so.[1] These reasons are: not having regular sex with a partner, stress relief, and viewing sex like any other commodity. The issue of loneliness also appears as a

Table 6.3 Reasons for the procurement of sexual services by interview group – first time and continuing

	First time reasons for the procurement of sexual services	Continuing reasons for the procurement of sexual services
Men who procure	No regular sex with partner Experience shyness Lack of self confidence Relationship breakdown It's a commodity Attractiveness of the sex worker Sex for pleasure Spontaneous act	No regular sex with partner Prevent loneliness/the 'girlfriend' experience Thrill/excitement of procurement It's a commodity Stress relief Devoid of all responsibilities
Female sex workers	No regular sex with partner Experience shyness Lack of self confidence Loss of virginity Peer pressure Feeling lonely Wanting affection Feeling horny	Emotional attachment Convenient/ease of procurement Prevent loneliness
Clergy	Peer pressure Feeling lonely Curious/living out a fantasy No regular sex with partner	Temptation Desensitised to emotions and feelings
Medics	Stress relief Feeling lonely Loss of virginity Experience shyness Sexual inexperience	Stress relief No regular sex with partner Thrill/excitement of procurement
Women's collective groups	Living out a fantasy Peer pressure Feeling lonely Power and control over women Influence of pornography	To dominate women Cannot relate to women The men are sex addicts Take advantage of subordinate women

reason why men first purchase sex, as well as why they continue; however, loneliness is a complex concept in the context of men who procure sexual services. As described above through the interview data, the need to address loneliness can have multiple meanings in that it can be a reason a man first purchases sex because he wishes to address his *feelings of* loneliness, whereas loneliness as a continuing reason to procure of sexual services reflects a need to *prevent* loneliness from recurring (men find their loneliness overcome at least in part by first procurement and want to prevent loneliness returning so continue purchasing).

In relation to why men procure sexual services for first time, issues such as shyness, self-confidence and to lose one's virginity are common drivers, and it is important to recognise that these reasons are shared by most groups interviewed. However, a shared understanding is not evident between all the groups concerning the reasons men continue to procure. What seems to be the significant finding for understanding the continuation of procurement is how the men who procure sex and the female sex workers both recognise the emotional connections and attachments many (but not all) men establish with sex workers. Some men, nevertheless, continue to procure sexual services as they view sex simply as a commodity. Considering the data emerging from this chapter it is evident that a distinction can be made between reasons for first time procurement and reasons for continuing to do so. However, in some instances some reasons influence both first time procurement and future procurement. In conclusion, the data presented in Table 6.3, and the narratives of men who procure sex and the female sex workers, suggest that the procurement of sexual services can positively impact on the lives of men and enable them to achieve positive outcomes. Men procure sexual services in order to maintain a healthy sense of self, and they therefore attend to their well being through the procurement of sexual services. The men in the sample who are involved in the procurement of sexual services represent a variety of different groups and social actors. They are our fathers, brothers, uncles, work colleagues and friends. They are our neighbours, people who represent us in the law courts and invest our money on the stock markets. They are the men who help us buy our next house and edit the newspapers we read. And whilst differences amongst the cohort are also found due to age, first time reasons for the procurement of sexual services and reasons for continuing the procurement, a common theme of attending to one's well being consistently emerges from within the dataset.

The following chapter, Chapter 7, will reflect on the findings of this study and argue for a re-theorisation of men's procurement of sexual services. This will support the presentation of a new way of understanding why men engage in this social practice. Chapter 7 will reflect on the data, in conjunction with the current discourses that surround this social practice and present a contemporaneously informed theoretical framework to apply to the procurement of sexual services. A theory of 'well being' based on the psychological perspective of positive psychology will be used and justified as a more suitable discourse to use in order to make sense of men's procurement of sexual services in the twenty-first century.

Note

1 These three reasons are also reflected in Table 6.2 in italics.

7 Making sense of men's procurement of sexual services

A new understanding and conceptualisation of this social phenomenon

The following chapter brings together the findings of the current study in order to make sense of men's procurement of sexual services and re-theorise men's engagement in this social practice. This chapter addresses the key aim of the empirical research underpinning this book, 'to make sense of men's procurement of sexual services' by challenging current views regarding this behaviour. Through this challenge a rejection, in part, of previous theorising on this social issue can be formulated. Based on the data set presented in this volume, a new understanding of the procurement of sexual services emerges, which centres on 'well being', based within the theoretical framework of positive psychology with a more fitting understanding and conceptualisation of the purchasing of sexual services emerging. This new understanding suggests that policy and law makers could reflect on their position in relation to this social practice. This applies in particular to those countries that criminalise the procurement of sexual services. It is also important to note again, that within this volume the procurement of sexual services has been referred to as a 'social practice'. As recognised in the introduction of Part I of this book, this is a fitting term to apply to the procuring of sex in adult and consensual contexts, as it is one of the most consistent practices in and across societies and time. Sex work has been woven into societies' fabric. It is also a repeated practice in the lives of some men (and women, see the work of O'Connell Davidson, 1998) through which they acquire a range of personal and social benefits.

Reviewing the findings in light of the theoretical considerations outlined in Chapters 1, 2 and 3, which explored sexuality, the deviancy of men's procurement of sexual services and the normative function that sex work plays in society, it can be argued that the current way of making sense of men's procurement is inadequate. The monolithic, homogenising, dichotomous and binary approaches to understanding the procurement of sexual services fail to reflect the complexities and realities of this social practice. Drawing upon the data presented in Chapters 4 to 6, a new way of making sense of men's procurement of sexual services emerges. First though, this chapter will reconsider the procurement of sexual services using the literature presented in Chapters 1, 2 and 3. This reappraisal will allow the problematising of the conventional understanding of this social practice to occur in the light of this volume's findings.

Revisiting 'deviancy' as a label for men who procure sexual services

Beliefs, concerning the reasons men purchase sex, held by those who are not involved in the sex work industry help reinforce and sustain the discourse of deviancy and pathology that has been applied to this practice. This has been evidenced in this volume, from the interview data obtained from the clergy and feminist participants in particular, but also from how men understand what society thinks of them. The analysis of data presented in this volume strongly suggests that deviancy, as a single explanation for understanding the procurement of sexual services, is both inadequate and misleading. In part this is a result of the procurement of sexual services being shown to be a multi-faceted phenomenon. As Roach Anleu (2006) recognises, deviancy can encompass a range of behaviours, from deviating from social norms to the breaking of a law that criminalises certain behaviour. In the case of purchasing sex, in the majority of jurisdictions in the world the practice is formally constructed as deviant through legislation. The term 'deviancy' though, as noted in this book, is itself problematic. The term deviance does not necessarily reflect the seriousness, impact or consequence of an act. Furthermore the term fails to reflect the seriousness, impact or consequence on the individual being labelled as someone whose actions are classified as deviant. Nevertheless it has become a term synonymous, globally, with men who procure sexual services. The findings reveal that some men who procure sexual services may be deviant, in as much as many are married and therefore are breaking the social norm of monogamy. The label, however, is not an accurate reflection of the procurement of sexual services, because neither the range of sexual acts nor the reasons of pleasure seeking are out of the range of other conventional relationships observed in the general community.

The use of the term 'deviant' reflects the social construction of the sex work industry and sexual services as 'bad', immoral and criminal by various groups in society. A clear link can be made here with labelling theory (Becker, 1963), in which deviant behaviours are not necessarily about the actions or behaviours themselves, but the context in which they occur. Men who purchase sex are seen as deviant for purchasing sex and intimacy, as these 'things' are generally considered to not be appropriate for purchase. In contrast other pleasurable things such as buying tickets to the movies or a concert, holidays, online games and so on, are viewed as appropriate. This construction is not though, an accurate way of understanding the actions and behaviours of men who purchase sexual services. Such a construction fails to reflect the personal, social and health benefits many men obtain through their procurement of sexual services. This position exemplifies the point made by Heidensohn (1968), considered in Chapter 2, who coined the phrase 'process of definition'. The term reflects how the social commentary of others can construct something or someone as deviant. The motivations, actions and behaviours, as described by the men who purchase sex from sex workers and women who supply sex in this research, do not appear deviant.

Therefore, 'deviancy', by itself, is a poor theoretical lens through which to make sense of men's procurement of sexual services.

The rationale for and purpose of defining the act of procuring sexual services as deviant can be understood, although not justified, when Lemert's (1951) work is considered. His definition of deviancy can be understood as behaviours that exhibit unusual and excessive desires. If the prevalence data of men's procurement of sexual services are taken as accurate (see the work of Wilcox *et al.*, 2009 for an overview), then it would seem that a small number of men are responsible for a large volume of sex work. This makes the practice an unusual one as only a minority of men are engaged in the practice, reinforcing an aspect of Lemert's definition of deviancy. Whilst Lemert's claim that deviancy is a reflection of excessive desire can also be applied to men's procurement of sexual services, as many men procure sexual services on a regular basis over a long period of time, this would mean that men who have sex with their wives or partners regularly have an excessive desire for sex, and are therefore deviant – a clearly ridiculous conclusion. These seem dubious reasons for automatically labelling all purchasing of sex as deviant.

Criminalising the 'John', is it evidence based?

Labelling sex work and those who purchase it as deviant can result in the criminalisation of men. There are many examples across jurisdictions nationally and internationally. For example, the 'John' schools established in the United States of America for men caught engaging in the procurement of sexual services has been documented in Chapter 2 of this volume. Such an approach, which is fundamentally the application of a moral judgement to the criminal code, that purchasing sex is immoral and therefore criminal, has negative consequences on men in terms of termination of employment and family break-ups. This also demonises men in many Western countries who purchase sex. One intention of this criminalisation is the reduction and prevention of sex work. Based on the subjective view or belief that such action is always immoral and criminal whether or not it is freely chosen and consensually entered into (as a chosen line of work) or is associated with trafficking and is coerced (a criminal act). This construction is ideological in nature. Policy and legislation criminalising all sex work and the purchasing of sex, as outlined by Weitzer (2005), is often politically motivated and not based on robust, social science research methodology, design and analysis. This calls into question the appropriateness of this social construction of those involved in the sex work industry, in particular those who procure sexual services.

If, as this volume has suggested, purchasing sex is deeply associated with some men's sense of self and well being, the criminalisation of men for purchasing sexual services is to be challenged. Analysis of men's reasons for procurement, suggest that there is no basis for criminalising sex work that is voluntarily undertaken and respected by purchaser and provider alike as a legitimate form of work. Of course, as noted a number of times in this volume, there are some behaviours and acts associated with sex work such as trafficking women, slavery and coercive sex work that are criminal and should remain so. But voluntary sex work, as discussed in this research, is like any other legitimate work. Criminalising it is associated with the political, social and moral context of a country's/ state's jurisdiction. As Wilcox *et al.* (2009) highlighted, the method of criminalisation as a tool for reducing and/or preventing the sex work industry is mixed in terms of scientific evidence. For those who are engaged in the sex work industry, criminalisation is considered to be the least effective. Based on the data presented in Part II of this volume, the men who procure sexual services agree that if criminalisation measures were re-applied to the NSW sex work industry this would not prevent a large proportion of them from future procurement. It has also been recognised within the dataset of this volume that criminalising sex work again in NSW would make the selling of sexual services more dangerous for the sex worker. Understanding sex work and the procurement of sexual services using a deviance theoretical framework, therefore, is not only unhelpful, but also misleading.

Understanding this social practice in this way has resulted in many people involved in the sex work industry across the globe being classified as criminal, leading to members of the sex work community having criminal records, in contrast to the current situation in NSW. The ripple effect of having a criminal record is wide ranging, impacting on the lives of 'offenders' on matters such as employment, travelling overseas and future relationships. This appears an unnecessary dissonance in light of the data presented in this volume.

Radical feminists and the criminalisation of purchasing sexual services

Labelling men who procure sexual services as deviant has also been supported and perpetuated by some feminists, notably radical feminists. This supports the notion that sex work is harmful, a school of thought within (radical) feminism better known as 'prostitution as harm' (see Chapter 2). Within this school of thought, it is claimed that men's procurement of sexual services is a means by which men dominate women. Feminist scholars such as Catherine MacKinnon draw comparisons between men who procure sexual services and perpetrators of rape, child sexual abuse and intimate partner violence. This is a universal approach to constructing men who purchase sex and treats all men who procure sex as a homogenous group. But, as the findings in this volume indicate, men who purchase sex do not form a homogenous group. There is a range of needs men seek to meet by engaging in this social practice. The motivations and context in which procurement takes place rarely involve the domination or ill-treatment of a female sex worker. There are of course instances of rape and ill treatment of sex workers, but there is also significant evidence of rape, violence and ill treatment of women in marriage. Such behaviour is criminal wherever it happens and is not, according to the evidence gathered in this study, a common experience or behaviour in sex work in NSW. Female sex worker accounts support the male clients' accounts of what takes place during the procurement of sexual services. They say that conventional needs and behaviours, such as the prevention of loneliness and the 'counselling' roles sex workers play for the majority of men purchasing sex, are common. They also indicate that legalised and regulated sex work ensures far greater safety of sex workers than criminalising sex work, which makes it more dangerous.

Radical feminists assume that purchasing sex is always committing violence against women. This ignores the free choice many women make to enter (and exit) the sex work industry. It can be further argued that the radical feminist position dehumanises women and ignores individual agency. Adding to this criticism of the radical feminist position on sex work is that its social construction is based on limited empirical evidence (Weitzer, 2005, 2009).

Radical feminism's position on sex work can also be criticised for being built on a limited definition of sex and what is involved in the context of procurement. For radical feminists, sex especially in the context of sex work, is merely sexual intercourse where a man uses a woman and where men disregard the emotional and intimacy aspects that are involved for both parties engaged in the act. As discussed throughout this volume, and as presented in Chapters 4 through to 6, sex has a much broader scope than the act of intercourse. It encompasses love, affection, pleasure, stimulation and a range of other pleasurable emotions, and, as Kimmel and Plante (2004) recognise, the act of sex has just as much to do with how to people interact together as with the actual act of physical sex. Radical feminists' narrow definition of sex makes their position on the sex work industry inaccurate, and also overlooks sex work between male providers and purchasers as well women who procure sexual services from male providers. Of course, radical feminists make important and vital arguments in regard to the involuntary, coercive and criminal nature of some activities associated with aspects of the sex work industry, such as sex trafficking. However, they fuse voluntary sex work and coerced prostitution into the same argument, so that all sex work is labelled as abusive and coercive. This is a universalising argument that, if the evidence in this book is accepted, inaccurately and unjustly constructs all men who procure sexual services as deviant and all women who provide sex for purchase as victims of abuse and rape.

Some feminists, for example Marxist feminists, argue that the domination of men over women within the sex work industry is evidence of women's economic dependency, that is sex workers are financially dependent on the men who purchase sex. If sex work provision, however, is understood as a small business, this same argument can be made in regard to all small businesses in that the providers of the service are dependent on purchasers, whether the business be a hairdresser, a shoe shop, a corner store or a brothel. It also ignores emotional and other related dependencies that men who procure sexual services have on the women who sell such services. This way of constructing the purchasing, and provision, of a sexual service as mutual dependency resonates with the social exchange theory outlined in Chapter 3 and supported by the findings. It supports the argument that sex work has a normative function within society, a position advocated by particular factions in feminism but rejected by many radical feminists.

Legitimate work, mutuality and relationship building through the procurement of sexual services

The factions within feminism that are supportive of the sex work industry, identified as sex work feminists in Chapter 3, recognise sex work as legitimate when it is voluntary sex work. Such feminists, as one would expect, oppose the coercive and criminal form of prostitution exemplified by sex trafficking. The data from the empirical research in this volume goes some way to offering further insight into why this differentiation is important. Evidence in the findings for men procuring sexual services in order to have a 'girlfriend experience', to address loneliness or to overcome shyness offer support for voluntary and coercive forms of sexual services provision to be differentiated. Such findings also provide support for the work of Sanders (2008a, 2008b), who found these same reasons expressed by the men in her study in the United Kingdom for engaging in the procurement of sexual services. In her work, Sanders recognises that men who purchase sex are involved in an emotionally driven practice that is no different from other conventional relationships. Sanders (2008a) recognises that the 'normalisation techniques' such as courtship rituals and sexual familiarity, traditionally found in other non-commercial relationships, are a feature between male clients and female sex workers, and where the commercial aspects of the procurement of sexual services are 'temporary moments' (p. 410). These findings are in stark contrast to the radical feminist's perspective that promotes men who procure sexual services as sexually insatiable and objectifying of women.

The notion that voluntary sex work involves mutual dependency between men who procure sexual services and women who sell sexual services, suggests that the aspect of social exchange theory, considered earlier in this volume, is a realistic understanding of the procurement of consensual sexual services. Levinger and Huesmann (1980) provide a definition of social exchange that can be applied to the procurement of sexual service. As applied to procuring sex it involves a number of transactions, including costs and benefits for both the purchaser and provider. Women provide a range of services to men, both of a sexual and non-sexual nature, which men 'consume', with men's consumption spanning a number of years, in some cases decades. For Levinger and Huesmann, the length of an exchange is reflective of reciprocity and is established in the first encounter. It is worth noting that whilst the current study did not focus on the 'consumption' by women who sell sex, information on this aspect was gathered, with one clear 'consumption' being money. Women obtain money from their clients, just as in any other business, and in some instances are given gifts by men. By understanding sex work and the transaction of sexual services in this way, both parties can be understood as being mutually dependent on each other. This undermines the argument that sex work entails, by definition, domination by men of women sex workers and inequality between the male purchaser and female provider. Social exchange theory (Levinger and Huesmann, 1980) applied to sex work is supported in as much that both parties involved in the procurement of sexual services indicate its benefits. Levinger and Huesmann's work opens up an understanding of such 'pay offs' as short term, instant payoffs. These payoffs are termed behavioural rewards, e.g. the feeling of proximity, the receiving of money for goods, while longer term payoffs are termed relational rewards, reflecting the level of involvement indicated in sustained interaction and men's continued use of the sex work industry. Nevertheless, while social exchange theory can in part explain why people engage in sex work, as a theoretical framework it does not encompass the breadth and depth of why men procure sexual services that emerged in the analysis of the data and as presented in the findings.

Being a 'man': the emotional and intimacy needs of procurers

As the data analysis indicates, the frequency of men's procurement of sexual services and its longevity results in a large amount of money being spent on this social practice over a man's life. One understanding of this is that this amount of expenditure signals power and wealth and fits a definition of masculinity that emphasises these status symbols, including how much disposable income one has for luxuries (as considered in Chapter 1).

However, 'masculinity' can also be problematised in making sense of the procurement of sexual services. The main theme for men's procurement of sexual services emerging from the analysis of the data in this volume centres on psycho-social needs, where men acquire levels of intimacy and attend to their emotional needs, such as dealing with stress. Men attending to their emotional needs, traditionally is not associated with 'maleness' and being masculine (as outlined in Chapter 1). Therefore, traditional ways of understanding what it is to be a man and what masculinity is are not reflected in the key reasons men procure sexual services, such as the need for affection. As noted by Hearn and Pringle 'masculinity operates within the context of patriarchy or patriarchal relations' (2006: 7). This widely held view could explain why men's emotions and well being have been overlooked in the analysis of men's procurement of sexual services. The recognition of men's psycho-social well being, and how they attend to emotional needs when procuring sexual services, or in other aspects of their lives, is an under-researched area and requires further attention. The neglect of this area of research is perhaps because, as Shields *et al.* (2006) acknowledged, the gendered nature of emotions determines who is allowed to have and display particular emotions. As noted above, particular literature on masculinity suggests that society expects men to be brave and have bravado, and not to be emotionally needy. Leafgren (1990) argues that the cultural expectations of men and men's achievements throughout life may have a negative impact on their mental health. There is an implication here that the social construction of masculinity may be harmful to men's well being. Drawing this conclusion from the theorising of masculinity is evidenced in studies showing that men who restrict their emotions tend to experience more conflict in relationships and encounter higher levels of stress at work (Thompson *et al.*, 1985; Campbell and Snow, 1992). From the evidence presented in this volume, the procurement of sexual services is used by some men to improve their well being by addressing feelings of loneliness, reducing stress and seeking affection.

The empirical research presented in this volume provides a critique on some of the definitions of masculinity and socially constructed ways of understanding what it is to be a 'man', which position maleness and men's perception of their maleness, as always being brave and in control. Loneliness and other emotions such as stress are experiences many men in the cohort cite as reasons for their procurement of sexual services. This is despite some men in this study claiming they purchased sex to demonstrate they were real men, especially first time purchasers, providing some support for some radical feminists', such as Carole Pateman's argument. The narrow understanding of what is to be a man does not encompass the need for emotional engagement and intimacy, that men in the study claimed to be among the main reasons for their procurement. These men freely admitted to procuring sexual services in order to address emotional needs.

The findings also challenge the position many radical feminists take, namely that men's procurement of sexual services is a reflection of hyper-masculine heterosexuality. Research into the expression of emotions provides evidence that the displaying of emotions by men threatens male identity (Seidler, 2007), and has led men to be conditioned to feel wrong about displaying emotions and their need for intimacy. The evidence presented here describes how services from a sex worker allow men to address emotions and feelings of loneliness. For example men can be initially motivated to procure sexual services in order to address feelings of loneliness, with the continuation of procurement acting as a means of *preventing* loneliness. While the concepts developed in masculinity studies can be useful in understanding aspects of why men procure sexual services, they are limited. The definitions of masculinity fail to recognise the importance of men expressing their emotions and displaying intimacy, and these play an important part in men's choice to procure sexual services.

Scholars such as Gaia (2002) for example, have identified that establishing a sense of intimacy within a conventional or procured relationship is important for avoiding loneliness. This is evident within the sample of men researched, as well as in the accounts of the female sex workers, and some interest groups in the study. It is useful to remember that intimacy is defined by scholars such as Sternberg (1997) and as presented in Chapter 3, as a bond between two people that reflects mutual trust and acceptance. The findings provide a link between emotional intimacy and the already considered social exchange theory. Men are purchasing sexual services to address an emotional need, and for a significant amount of men in this study this takes place on a regular basis over a long period of time. Chapter 5 provided evidence in the cluster analysis, that some groups of men have been procuring sexual services for, on average, 29 years. During this time mutual trust, respect and dependence develop between the men and women involved, just as in a conventional relationship. Sanders (2008b) identifies five behaviours that men who procure sexual services display that relate to conventional courtship behaviour: communication, courtship rituals, sexual familiarly, the want for mutual satisfaction, and emotional connections. All these behaviours were evident in the self-reported behaviour of the men in this study and in the reports of the sex workers. Most men in this study engaged in behaviours that do not reflect traditional maleness or hyper-masculine heterosexuality. They displayed intimate behaviours like buying personal gifts for the sex workers and enjoying relating to the sex worker without the physical act of sex. A finding emerging from this study is that men, through the transaction of sexual services, are not only attending to their emotional needs, but also to something broader. They are attending to their sexual health and their psycho-social well being. In order to consider this proposition fully it is important to revisit the literature on human sexuality.

Human sexuality and the context of procurement

As Millett (1970) claimed, sex does not take place in a vacuum; it is more than just a biological and/or physical act and is enmeshed in a larger context. This applies to sex purchased from sex workers and is evident in the findings. Purchased sex, for most of the men in this study, does not involve just a physical act, but is embedded in a 'context' in which emotional needs are met and non-sexual behaviours are conducted. These findings lend support to the recently established and growing scholarship on emotions within the sex work industry, led by scholars such as Sanders (2008a) and Milrod and Weitzer (2012). As already documented, Sanders argues that men who procure sexual services engage in behaviours and acts that are closely associated with conventional romantic relationship behaviours, rather than those associated with deviant behaviour. Milrod and Weitzer (2012) report that men procure sexual services for the first time for reasons that are associated more with the physical act of sex, but their future procurement is related to more expressive reasons. The empirical research presented in this volume can offer further evidence to support these claims, with particular reference to the data presented in Chapter 6. In Chapter 6, why men procure sexual services for the first time, and why they continue to procure were examined. Through this examination, a distinction similar to that found by Milrod and Weitzer (2012) emerged.

More contemporaneously than Millett's (1970) position that sex is far more than a physical act, Kimmel and Plante (2004) established that sex is one of the means by which people interact with each other. This reaffirms the importance of understanding the context and what takes places in the environment in which a sexual act of any kind is taking place. Men in this current study display a wide range of behaviours and give a number of reasons for engaging in this social practice that resonate with positive factors and outcomes experienced when purchasing sexual services. But inaccurate and universalising representations of sex work have been created by interest groups and have been instilled in the social consciousness. This has contributed to the distorted view of human sexuality promoted by some religious and morally conservative groups. Weitzer (2005) argues that these inaccuracies are maintained by interest groups, often for political gain, and are typically created by people who have never worked within or used the sex work industry. This is reflected in some writings and theories used to understand men's procurement of sexual services, as they mainly overlook the context and environment in which procurement takes place. Scholars such as Kimmel and Plante (2004) claim the context and environment to be important aspects to consider when examining any sexual behaviour, including that exchanged in the sex work industry.

The positive function that sex work plays within society has been recognised in the work of evolutionary psychologists. As discussed earlier in this volume, evolutionary psychologists argue that there are many reasons for engaging in sex, other than for procreational purposes. Added to this, Kauth (2007) and Sefcek *et al.* (2007) recognised that the needs of human sexuality are satisfied by a range of pleasure sensations other than just sexual acts. Men in the study cohort indicate a range of pleasures they obtain from purchasing sex. For example, men overcome loneliness and indicate that they gain emotional pleasure through the affection they experience in engaging with a sex worker, whilst another common reason, stress relief, was also associated with the act of procurement. Evolutionary psychologists such as Kauth (2007) recognised that proximate factors such as stress impact on how an individual will play out their sexuality. This current study offers support to the evolutionary psychology position that proximate factors are important in a person's execution of sexuality as well as that humans seek sex for a range of reasons. As presented in Chapter 5 through the cluster analysis, and the consideration of reasons men give for their procurement of sexual services for the first time and subsequent visits, the empirical findings presented in this volume support the evolutionary psychology perspective that the act of sex is triggered by multiple reasons, suggesting that there is a need to re-theorise the procurement of sexual services to reflect this.

However, even this broader view of human sexuality and pleasure has been argued to be too narrow by Vance (1991). Scholars such as Vance have suggested that sexual behaviour and attitudes are shaped by our culture, in other words they are socially constructed. What we perceive as acceptable and non-acceptable behaviour is influenced by the social, political and religious fabric of one's culture. This position is reflective of the symbolic interactionist perspective of sexuality, as discussed in Chapter 1. Symbolic interactionists claim that there are social aspects to sexual behaviour and that sexuality has to be understood within its enacted context (Waskul and Plante, 2010). This perspective assists in making sense of men's procurement of sexual services. The men who participated in the study are engaged in the purchasing of sex not only for sexual gratification at a biological level, but to address things that are distressing in their lives, such as loneliness and stress.

So the procurement of sex involves emotional, psychological and social aspects, and these multidimensional understandings of sex are important in theorising the purchasing of sexual services. The reasons men give for engaging in this social practice resonate with all aspects that evolutionary psychologists and symbolic interactionists associate with the act of sex. The criminalising of sex work and its purchase has resulted in the dismissal of these many dimensions to the purchasing of sex and of men's reasons for procuring, in particular to the positive impact this social practice has on some men's lives. This has added to the sex work industry being constructed in a negative way with a negative narrative surrounding those involved in this social practice.

Why do people have sex?

Stakeholders in the sex work industry have identified numerous reasons for men's procurement of sexual services. These reasons have been cited as physical attraction, the ease of having sex (commodification of sex), stress relief, seeking affection and preventing loneliness. In keeping with the recent work by Sanders (2008a, 2008b) and Milrod and Weitzer (2012), this book situates the purchasing of sex in the normal range of sexual behaviour, with the findings being partially explained by the evolutionary psychology perspective, as discussed above.

It is therefore apparent that this study's findings may be best explained using mainstream sex research examining and theorising why humans have sex. As already discussed, the men in this study give, as reasons for their procurement of sexual services the same reasons people in general give for seeking and having sex in conventional relationships. They discuss their experiences of purchasing sex in the same way as men in conventional relationships discuss their relationships. Reflecting on the reasons mainstream society offer for engaging in sex therefore, could offer further support for rejecting current theorising on the procurement of sexual services, in particular theories that are framed by the deviancy and immorality of sex work. Leigh (1998) lists several reasons why humans have sex, which include for pure pleasure, to achieve a conquest and as a means to relieve sexual tension. The reasons offered in that 1998 study resonate clearly with but are more limited than those offered by the men in this current study for example, stress relief has been recognised as a need that can influence some men to procure sexual services for the first time, as well as contributing to why men continue to purchase.

In a more recent and larger scale study, Meston and Buss (2007) also investigated why humans have sex. These researchers were focused on the motivations for human engagement in this practice. Their two-phased study, involving 1,983 men and women found that nine themes represented the breadth of reasons humans have sex. The themes they noted were: 1. Pure attraction to the other person; 2. Experiencing physical pleasure; 3. Expression of love; 4. Having sex because of feeling desired by the other; 5. Having sex to escalate the depth of the relationship; 6. Curiosity or seeking new experiences; 7. Marking a special occasion; 8. Mere opportunity; and 9. Sex just happening due to seemingly uncontrollable circumstances[1] (Meston and Buss, 2007: 480). These themes reflect the theorising offered by symbolic interactionists such as Kimmel and Plante (2004) and evolutionary psychologists such as Kauth (2007), who claim that sex occurs for a variety of reasons, not just the desire for the physical act and for purposes other than procreational ones.

Of importance to this volume however, is whether these themes reflect the reasons offered by the men who procure, and female sex workers who provide sexual services, sampled in the current study. The themes derived from the analysis of this study's data are very similar to Meston and Buss's themes. Based on the empirical findings of this volume it can be argued that men procure sexual services because they find the sex worker attractive; they want an emotional connection and deeper experience of intimacy achieved with the same person over time; being with someone in an intimate setting enhances self-image and confidence; just wanting to have physical sex; and sex as an opportunity for pleasure. As already noted in the findings chapters of this volume, attractiveness is a key reason emerging from the current study for men procuring sexual services. However, such a finding is not well documented in existing sex work research. Nevertheless, notably, attractiveness is a common motivational factor within the findings of Meston and Buss's study (2007). Meston and Buss's research signifies this motivation as being the *most common* amongst the wider population for having sex. This similarity of findings between the two studies adds weight to the assertion that sex work has a normative function within society. Men are engaged with the sex work industry for similar reasons that men and women engage in sexual activity in the wider community. If men who procure sexual services are motivated by the same reasons that people engage in conventional sexual relations, why are people in wider society not considered deviant or pathological?

Meston and Buss also reported the least given reasons in their study for having sex. These included reasons such as 'I wanted to give someone an STI', 'I wanted to hurt an enemy' and 'I wanted to hurt/humiliate the person' (2007: 482). In the current study, some interest groups, namely the radical feminists said they believed that men procure sexual services to control women and thought men had similar reasons to those perverse ones named by Meston and Buss. There is no evidence to support this claim in the current study.

Meston and Buss (2007) acknowledge that there is a range of reasons people have sex. Sex is motivated by a complex interplay of factors, including the context in which the sex takes place. The concurrence between Meston and Buss's findings and those of the current project suggest that general sex research is a valid source for supporting the claim that the procurement of sexual services falls within the range of normal sexual behaviours. A complex interplay of factors are at work in the purchasing of sex by men, and therefore a theoretical framework applied to the procurement of sexual services needs to reflect this. Current binary and single factorial theories for understanding the procurement of sexual services are inadequate as they fail to recognise this complex interplay of factors, while some of these theories overplay the extent to which the procurement of sexual services falls outside the normal range of sexual behaviours. Current theorising on the procurement of sexual services fails to recognise a broader definition of sexuality and the act of sex as offered by symbolic interactionists such as Kimmel and Plante (2004) and evolutionary psychologists such as Kauth (2007). Such broader understandings of sexuality and the act of sex encompass not only biological aspects, but also the context and environment in which the behaviour is conducted. This allows for the recognition of more expressive behaviours, for example, feeling connected to another human being and acquiring affection.

As a result of the failings of current theorising on men's procurement of sexual services, a multifactorial theory is required to more accurately make sense of this social practice.

Sexual health, sexual rights and 'well being'

By considering the current data and extending Vanwesenbeeck's (2001) claim discussed earlier in this volume that there are rational and positive reasons for selling sex to the procurers of sexual services, it can be argued that the procurement of sexual services can contribute to an individual's positive 'sexual health'. As Braun-Harvey (2011) indicates, sexual health is concerned with a state of well being in relation to one's sexuality across a lifespan. It can be argued and supported from within the current study that some men procure sexual services as a means of attending to their sexual health and their psycho-social well being. In 2006 the WHO defined sexual health as:

> A state of physical, emotional, mental and social well being in relation to sexuality; it is not merely the absence of disease, dysfunction or infirmity. Sexual health requires a positive and respectful approach to sexuality and sexual relationships, as well as the possibility of having pleasurable and safe sexual experiences, free of coercion, discrimination and violence. For sexual health to be attained and maintained, the sexual rights of all persons must be respected, protected and fulfilled.[2]
>
> (WHO, 2006)

This definition demonstrates the breadth encompassed by sexual health, and that to ensure well being is achieved, all human beings have sexual rights that must be acknowledged. These sexual rights:

> Embrace human rights that are already recognized in national laws, international human rights documents and other consensus statements. They include the right of all persons, free of coercion, discrimination and violence, to:
>
> • the highest attainable standard of sexual health, including access to sexual and reproductive health care services;
> • seek, receive and impart information related to sexuality;
> • sexuality education;

- respect for bodily integrity;
- choose their partner;
- decide to be sexually active or not;
- consensual sexual relations;
- consensual marriage;
- decide whether or not, and when, to have children;
- pursue a satisfying, safe and pleasurable sexual life.[3]

(WHO, 2006)

The definition of sexual rights by the WHO outlines several components that both men who procure sexual services and the females who provide sexual services in the current study acknowledge are part of the procurement context. These components include being respectful of bodily integrity; choice in their partner; a decision to be sexually active or not; consensual sexual relations and pursuit of a satisfying, safe and pleasurable sexual life. Furthermore, the findings indicate the positive impact and influence this social practice can have on a man's life (noting that this study is only of men who procure sex, but the same could apply to women who procure sex). To deny men the 'right' to procure sexual services is in fact the denial of a human being's sexual rights. This claim can be extended to those who sell sex. Considering the procurement of sexual services in this way is not new. Sexuality has been documented in previous chapters of this book, as an expression of love, affection and pleasure (Kimmel and Plante, 2004). Within the current data set, there is evidence that those involved in the selling and procuring of sexual services experience these emotions and behaviours. The procurement of sexual services is complex; it is multifaceted in nature and is engaged in for a range of reasons. These reasons include the expression of love and affection as well as achieving pleasure. These components and elements are not only reflected in the work of Sanders (2008a, 2008b) and Milrod and Weitzer (2012) but also within this current study. In light of the definition of sexual health and sexual rights offered above, the procurement of sexual services can be understood in the broader context of sexuality and through the recognition that sexual acts do not take place within a vacuum.

With the consideration of sexual health and sexual rights, and the recognition that humans execute their sexuality for reasons other than just the physical sexual act, a new means for making sense of men's procurement for sexual services begins to emerge. This framework takes account of the psycho-social well being of procurers of sexual services, and recognises the positive influence the purchasing of sexual services from within the sex work industry can have on the lives of men. Furthermore, the proposed framework is multifactorial in nature, recognises the importance of context and environment and is informed by a theory of 'well being'.

Well being and the procurement of sexual services

Well being is 'a complex, multifaceted construct that has continued to elude researchers' attempts to define and measure' it (Pollard and Lee, 2003: 60). However, there has been a growth in research on well being in recent times and it has become a feature of many government policies globally. For example, in Australia a national institute of well being has been established, and according to the National Wellness Institute of Australia (NWIA), 'well being' can be defined as the existence of positive factors present in a person's life. This is characterised by a person who actively seeks such positive factors, whilst maintaining a balance of these attributes (NWIA website, no date). The NWIA also states that well being is achieved through the pro-social behaviours one engages in that allow positive attributes to be achieved. Having the opportunity to experience a fulfilling and pleasurable sexual life, should one want that, is an aspect of this well being. What is clear in this definition of well being is that it is multifaceted in nature. Acknowledging well being as a multi dimensional construct (Diener, 2009), a theory of well being is an appropriate lens in which to understand the procurement of sexual services, due to the variety of reasons men give for engaging in this social practice. This resonates with NWIA's position on understanding and defining well being. In order to apply a theory of well being to the procurement of sexual services though, first it is important to consider the two main approaches used to encapsulate a consensus in what is meant by well being.

There are two approaches commonly associated with a theory of well being. The first is the hedonic tradition, which considers this construct in terms of happiness, positive affect, low negative affect and satisfaction of life, as recognised in the work of Lyubomirsky and Lepper (1999). The second approach, the eudaemonic tradition, is associated with positive psychological functioning and human development (Waterman, 1993). There is recognition, in these two approaches, of a relationship between psycho-social factors and well being. The correlation between psycho-social factors and well being has been well documented, for example, Fredrickson (2001) has drawn connections between the experience of positive emotions and well being. Research in this area has also provided support for positive emotions fostering and evolving through social and physical behaviours experienced by an individual (Ellsworth and Smith, 1988). The diversity of experiences that foster such a positive sense of well being are present in the diversity of behaviours and actions displayed by those involved in the purchasing and provision of sexual services. The men who procure and the females who sell sexual services have provided evidence of this in the current study. Based on the findings presented, both approaches for understanding the construct of well being are reflected in the views and experiences of those who procure sexual services. Men surveyed in the study, for example, spoke about the positive effects they experience through their procurement of sexual services, e.g. a form of stress relief, being with an attractive women, with such experiences having a positive influence on their psychological functioning.

In summary well being is associated with a person's quality of life, a goal of increased life satisfaction (Selgiman and Csikszentmihalyi, 2000) and with positive psycho-social factors and relationships with others. Well being has been theoretically associated with the discipline of psychology (La Placa *et al.*, 2013), which has been argued to be the most dominant discourse in this area of study. Within psychology, the term has more recently become synonymous with the psychological perspective of positive psychology (Dodge *et al.*, 2012; Norman, 2013). Seligman stated: 'the topic of positive psychology is well being ... the goal of positive psychology is to increase flourishing' (2011: 13). As outlined by the work of Seligman and Csikszentmihalyi (2000), positive psychology recognises that individuals who experience closeness in relationships experience a sense of intimacy in such relationships, and being engaged in relationships where similarity and familiarity is a feature generally produces high levels of well being. From the experiences outlined by the men in the current study, as well as the female sex workers interviewed and some interested group members, it is apparent that the purchasing of sexual services leads to many aspects associated with high levels of well being. For example, men have reported that they seek intimacy through their procurement of sexual services and acquire a feeling of closeness and proximity with a sex worker. This is evidence of the relationship between procurement of sexual services and a person's well being. As 'well being' has been associated with positive psychology, a growing disciplinary area within the study of psychology (Selgiman and Csikszentmihalyi, 2000), the results of this study imply that understanding the procurement of sexual services through a theory of well being may well be best achieved using the framework of positive psychology.

Positive psychology as applied to men who procure sexual services

Positive psychology has gained momentum in the study of human behaviour and society. It is presented as a response to the limited research within psychology and the wider social sciences that focuses on reasons that make life worth living. Through the framework of positive psychology (Selgiman and Csikszentmihalyi, 2000), questions concerning well being such as, what conditions make people flourish, and what contributes to individuals being autonomous, self-regulated and fulfilled, are asked. The focus of this theoretical lens aims to address the past criticisms of psychology, a discipline that over time has pathologised human behaviour. Therefore, applying the psychological perspective of positive psychology to the procurement of sexual services is twofold. First, it addresses the criticism of current theorising that pathologises the procurement of sexual services and demonises men who purchase sex. It does this by providing a framework for investigating and considering factors that increase a person's quality of life. Second, this theoretical framework is built on a notion of well being and as a result relates explicitly to the data presented in this volume. Positive psychology aims to change the focus of research on human behaviour and society: 'from

[the] preoccupation only with repairing the worst things in life to building also positive qualities' (Selgiman and Csikszentmihalyi, 2000: 5).

The theoretical framework of positive psychology aims to understand and explain the subjective experiences of an individual in terms of happiness, optimism, hope, self-determination – in short well being. In recent times this theoretical approach has contributed to understanding, in a new way, a range of behavioural and mental health issues. An example of this is how positive psychology has been used to theoretically underpin the 'Good Lives Model' (GLM) (Ward and Brown, 2004), traditionally applied to behaviours deemed as deviant such as substance abuse. The GLM is a positive strength based approach that supports humans to acquire 'primary goods' such as intimate experiences in a social acceptable way (Ward and Brown, 2004: 246). According to Ward and Brown, people:

> are by nature active, goal-seeking beings who consistently engage in the process of constructing a sense of purpose and meaning in their lives. This is hypothesized to emerge from the pursuit and achievement of ... valued aspects of human functioning and living. [This allows] individuals to flourish ... achieve high levels of well-being.

> (ibid.)

Based on the premise of positive psychology, the GLM recognises ways in which humans can flourish and attend to their psycho-social well being.

As with the GLM, positive psychology can underpin an understanding of the behaviour of purchasing sex. A range of reasons for men's procurement of sexual services that have emerged from the findings can be related to the premise of positive psychology and the listed elements of well being. For example, men flourish and feel fulfilled through the procurement of sexual services as an array of emotional, psychological and social needs are met, from seeking affection, to gaining confidence, to experiencing a personal thrill and engaging in courtship rituals. By re-theorising the procurement of sexual services through a theoretical lens of positive psychology, which is based on a framework of 'well being', the interplay of needs, drivers and outcomes can be explored in relation to the well being of men who purchase sex. Making sense of men's procurement utilising this theoretical framework, takes into account the context, behaviours and actions involved in the selling and purchasing of sexual services as well as the relationships formed between the men and women. Therefore, the broader understanding of sexuality and the act of sex in human society, as offered by scholars such as Kimmel and Plante (2004) and Kauth (2007), can be applied to men's procurement of sexual services by using a positive psychology perspective.

Recently, positive psychology has been extended to focus on human flourishing (Seligman, 2011), defined by Gable and Haidt as 'the conditions and processes that contribute to ... optimal functioning of people, groups and institutions' (2005: 104). The focus of positive psychology reflects the various components that are associated with well being, making this psychological framework an important lens to use when making sense of the procurement of sexual services. For example, Seligman's more recent work defined five elements associated with a person's well being, reflected in the mnemonic PERMA (Seligman, 2011): positive emotion, engagement, relationships, meaning and accomplishment are reflected in a person's well being, and the data in this study reflects all aspects of PERMA. Men procure sexual services to seek affection and prevent loneliness, the first aspect of PERMA – positive emotion. Men who procure sexual services immerse themselves in the sex work industry and in most cases over a substantial period of time, with men in the cohort having been procuring sexual services for, on average, 29 years. This finding reflects the second aspect of PERMA – engagement. Men who procure sexual services describe a girlfriend experience and the conventional behaviours they engage in when purchasing sexual services. This experience of men's procurement is supported in the accounts of the female sex workers in this study. This evidence reflects the relationship established between those who purchase and those who sell sexual services, the third aspect of PERMA.

Meaning is the fourth aspect of PERMA, and is evidenced in the reasons men give as to why they procure sexual services. The procurement of sex offers a purpose to men, whether it is a physical purpose, acquired through the act of sex or living out a fantasy, or a more expressive purpose and meaning such as intimacy and preventing loneliness. The final aspect of PERMA that is reflected in the reasons men offer for purchasing sexual services, is accomplishment. Through the procurement of sexual services men accomplish of a number of physical, psychological and social things, including feelings of excitement, losing one's virginity, relieving stress and experiencing closeness with a member of the opposite sex. Positive psychology examines human development at a subjective level by considering the subjective state of a person in conjunction with objective elements such as the context and environment in which people live (La Placa *et al.*, 2013: 117). Diener *et al.* (1999) conducted some of the first research into the subjective aspects of well being and concluded that: 'well being is a broad category of phenomena that includes people's emotional responses, domain satisfactions and global judgements of life satisfactions' (p. 277).

In sum, positive psychology understands well being through the experiences of emotions and life satisfaction. The findings presented in this volume, provide evidence of the link between men's procurement of sexual services and positive effects. There are many aspects of the data set that one would expect to be associated with high levels of satisfaction, such as relieving stress and experiencing pleasure. When humans pursue an experience that results in feelings of pleasure, a sense of achievement and/or the satisfaction of needs, they are attending to their well being as understood by positive psychology. Men who procure sexual services pursue and experience these feelings. So a theory of well being within a framework of positive psychology appears to be an appropriate theoretical framework for making sense of men's procurement of sexual services.

In light of the theory building above and the data presented in this volume, this chapter now reconsiders the SAPSS model, first presented in Chapter 3.

Recognising that through the findings presented within this volume, the procurement of sexual services is multifactorial in nature, the development of the multifactor analysis choice model for the procurement of sexual services (MAPSS) model, which supports a more accurate understanding of the choices men make when engaged in this social practice, is presented.

Rethinking the SAPSS model: introducing the MAPSS model

From the analysis of the data in this volume, there is a clear need to reconsider the SAPSS model presented in Chapter 3. The primary aim of this model when it was initially presented was to summarise and make sense of the existing literature. In light of the current research though, the SAPSS model fails to account for and accurately reflect the findings presented in this volume. Upon revision, this model can be used as a tool to understand the procurement of sexual services. The MAPSS model has been developed and is presented in Figure 7.1. The 'deviant/ immoral' and 'normative function' choice routes derived from existing theories do not accurately reflect men's procurement of sexual services that has emerged in this volume. Therefore, these terms can be assigned to the 'historical context' box within the revised version of the model. This is a symbolic and important shift of these labels. Placing the terms 'deviant/immoral' and 'normative function' into the 'historical' box, indicates their place in developing understandings of men's procurement of sex but also that they have shortcomings. Both perspectives fail to acknowledge the interplay between the diverse factors and aspects of men's lives contributing to their procurement of sexual services. These perspectives also fail to account for the different legalisations and regulations of the sex work industry in a jurisdiction like NSW, as well as impacting negatively, in some part, on the way purchasers and providers of sexual services think of themselves. These observations further suggest that Monto and McRee's (2005) typology of men who procure sexual services – the 'everyman' perspective and the 'peculiar man' perspective – are not contemporaneously valid. This is primarily due to the typologies association with the binary argument that has surrounded the debate on men's procurement of sexual services. The everyman perspective (discussed in Chapter 3) represents the position that men who procure sexual services are no different from men in the general population, while the peculiar man perspective represents the view that men who procure sexual services are inherently different from men in the general population. While it could be argued that the current data set offers support for the use of Monto and McRee's 'everyman' perspective, I am rejecting using this characterisation because it is based on the use of a binary approach – these men must be either one or the other. In order to develop a fresh, contemporary lens for examining and understanding the procurement of sexual services the MAPSS model needs to offer new terminology to enable a new, more accurate discourse to emerge concerning the procuring sexual services.

The revised model reflects the interplay of reasons that surround men's procurement of sexual services. The MAPSS model indicates that the many reasons why men procure sexual services are not mutually exclusive, but interlinked. This

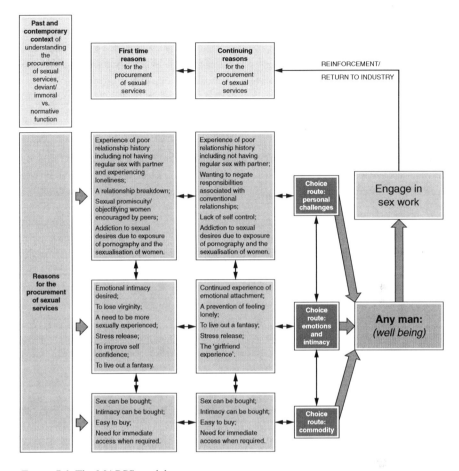

Figure 7.1 The MAPSS model.

finding is based on the data that has emerged from the current study. The new model, the MAPSS, also makes clear the differences between reasons men first procure sexual services and continuing reasons, yet recognises there can be overlap, and illustrates the type of men within contemporary society who procure sexual services. The model also acknowledges the pro-social influence procuring sexual services has on the lives of men. Represented through the three choice routes, these influences include losing one's virginity; preventing loneliness and achieving emotional attachment to another, in order to achieve well being. The MAPSS also recognises some less savoury influences behind men's procurement of sexual services, represented through the 'personal challenges' choice route. Men can be influenced to purchase sexual services due to a relationship break-down, wanting to negate responsibilities associated with sexual relationships, as well as experiencing poor relationships in the past; however, addressing these issues still leads to men achieving well being. As evidenced through the empirical research presented in Chapters 4 through to 6, some men have encountered difficult childhood experiences that have impacted on their adult lives, while a significant proportion of the data in this book has reflected more pro-social views and experiences of those who procure sexual services. Nevertheless, the MAPSS model captures the fact there has been some recording in the data of some negative views and experiences, such as cheating on a marital partner, by those who procure sexual services. The MAPSS captures not only the different reasons why men purchase sex, and draws a distinction between the first time and continuing reasons whilst at the same time recognising that some first time and continuing reasons are the same; but the model also captures how these influences ultimately lead to acquiring an end goal of 'well being'. Overall, based on the findings of this volume, I will argue that these men can be understood as 'any man', as already has been suggested in Chapter 5 of this book. This acknowledges that there are differences between men, they are not a homogenous group, yet amongst men 'any man' could be a procurer of sexual services. The term 'everyman', used by Monto and McRee (2005), does not denote that men who procure sexual services are different from each other on many personal and social levels. The term 'everyman' suggests homogeneity amongst the group of men. On the other hand the term 'any man' provides a sense that not every man is buying sexual services, but it acknowledges the fact that any one (man) could be procuring. Equally, evidence in this research indicates that men who purchase sex should not be labelled as 'peculiar men' either, as there is no evidence to suggest that men who procure sexual services are deviant or 'abnormal'. Furthermore, the 'peculiar' label implies that the act of sex is odd, whilst scientific evidence within the disciplinary areas of biology and psychology suggest the act of sex is a natural human behaviour and desiring it is a normal instinct. The man who procures sexual services is 'any man'.

The MAPSS model becomes a tool that accurately reflects the procurement of sexual services in the twenty-first century. It is a tool that can be used as a platform for future sex worker–client research.

Conclusion

In conclusion, the findings of this volume lead to an understanding of the procuring of sexual services, in the context of a voluntary and regulated industry, as a positive social practice for the purchaser and the provider of such services. This supports the adoption of a theory of well being, understood within a framework of positive psychology, for making sense of men's procurement of sexual services. Dodge *et al.* (2012) recognise that while research into well being has been growing over recent years, an agreed universal definition of the construct fails to go beyond a 'description of well being itself' (p. 222). However, there are some commonalties shared amongst researchers in their definition of well being. For example, positive affect with specific reference to moods and emotions is recognised in the constitution of well being (Diener and Suh, 1997; Lee and Ogozoglu,

2007; Singh and Duggal Jha, 2008), along with positive psychological functioning (Duckwork *et al.*, 2005; Liney and Joseph, 2004). Those aspects of well being are evident in the previous findings chapters of this volume, where stress relief and seeking affection, for example, are reasons men give for purchasing sexual services. These findings suggest the appropriateness of using the theory of well being as a means of making sense of the procurement of sexual services. But due to a lack of agreement in defining well being, a definition applicable to the procurement of sexual services and that reflects the constitution of well being as applied to this social practice, was sought. Based on evidence of the empirical research presented in this volume, the following definition of well being in the context of the procurement of sexual services is offered:

> A process that respects the sexual rights of both men and women who engage in consensual sexual and other intimate behaviours with another willing adult within a commercial setting to attend to aspects of their physical, psychological, social and emotional wellness over a period of time.

The definition of well being in the context of the procurement of sexual services reflects the reasons men procure sexual services and is a significant development in this book. This definition of well being becomes a resource to be used in the future to support an understanding of and promote the sexual rights of those who procure sexual services. As a result of this development a further rejection of current binary typologies, in particular those promoting a deviant narrative of sex work and its purchasing, is mounted.

This chapter has also considered the existing literature in light of the findings of this current research in order to make sense of men's procurement of sexual services. In doing so, it has been recognised that sex, with particular reference to 'sex' within the sex work industry, is rarely considered in the context of well being. Sex in the sex work industry, is typically considered as a negative and bad activity, for example, as immoral, as transmitting STIs, as producing unwanted pregnancies and as being synonymous with sex trafficking. This universalising negative focus leads to the misrepresentation of this social practice, suggesting that negative outcomes (as would be suggested by the characterisation of the purchasing of sex as a deviant behaviour) are the dominant experiences of men and women involved in purchasing and providing sex. In contrast, when the findings of this research are considered in relation to sexual health, sexual rights and well being, positive aspects of this social practice are revealed. The empirical research suggests that the importance that the procurement of sexual services has in men's lives has been underestimated, supporting the small body of research on the emotional impact of procuring sexual services (see Sanders, 2008a, 2008b; Milrod and Weitzer, 2012).

As highlighted by Meston and Buss (2007) 'historically, the reasons people have sex have been assumed to be few in number and simple in nature' (p. 477), while Hill and Preston (1996) state that caution must be applied to reducing the reasons humans have sex to a small number as this can lead to poor understanding of this social practice. While research into the reasons humans have sex has resulted in a generally positive understanding of this act, a negative understanding has traditionally been constructed in relation to procured sex. This study challenges the binary, single factorial theories along with the binary typologies of those who procure sex. The procurement of sexual services is a complex social practice. While it is clear that a main reason for the onset to procurement centres on the physical act of sex itself, other reasons given, such as the need for affection, should not be ignored. It also emerged that reasons for procuring sex can alter over time, with new reasons influencing long term procurement. The reasons for continuing to purchase are more in line with a man's need for intimacy along with related emotional and health based reasons. In general, across the cohort, men are procuring sexual services in order to attend to well being aspects of their personal and social lives.

The narrow definitions offered for the phenomenon of 'sex', in particular within the context of the sex work industry, as purely physical and/or biological, have been called into question by the findings of this book. They reveal that a broader understanding of sexuality and sex, an understanding that recognises social and emotional aspects, as well as physical reasons for 'doing sex' should be applied to the procurement of sexual services. An acknowledgment of the importance of the context in which the purchasing and doing of sex takes place has been introduced into the theorising of sex work. By examining the context of the procurement of sexual services within the sex work industry, it becomes evident that the physical act of sex is only one of many reasons for the purchasing of sex and that for many men the physical act of sex is not the dominant reason. This lends support to a broader definition of sex and sexuality being proposed in regard to men's procurement of sexual services. Understanding the procurement of sexual services in this broader way challenges, in particular, deviant understandings of this social practice. It puts aside the legacy of stigmatisation and stereotyping by the Church and medical science. While the work of Freud for example, would suggest that a conflict in the early stages of one's life explains why men procure sexual services, from the data supplied in the empirical research, doubt can also be cast on such a theory. Although some men in the study who procure sexual services have experienced, what could be viewed as disruptions in the early stages of their childhood, this is not the case for the majority of those sampled.

Adopting a broader and more realistic definition of sexuality, one that encompasses sexual health and sexual rights, allows for the negative construction of the sex work industry to be challenged and changed. Existing theories and typologies of men's procurement of sexual services do not explain or encompass the reasons for and nature of this social practice emerging from this present study. The use of deviance theory to understand the actions of men who purchase sexual services by social groups and commentators, such as radical feminists, has been based on very limited evidence but has led to the stigmatisation and stereotyping of people who are involved in the procurement of sexual services. To redress this, civil liberties and human rights, including sexual rights, should be brought to bear in the rethinking of the place and nature of sex work.

Sex work as a normative function in society is a theme that emerges consistently in the findings of this study. Social exchange theory suggests that the behaviours and actions engaged in during the procurement of sexual services, demonstrate a mutual dependency between the men and women involved in purchasing sex. This mutual dependency involves intimacy. When definitions of intimacy, such as a person experiencing a warm and close connection with another, along with trust in that context (Sullivan, 1953), are considered it is evident that connectedness to others and trust between those involved in the procurement of sexual services occur during the procurement process. The procurement of sexual services involves meeting psycho-social needs including intimacy and therefore reflects the normative function this social practice plays in a person's life over a period of time.

While social exchange theory offers insight into the nature of purchasing sex, it underplays the place and role of sexual services in the lives of men who purchase sex. The current study has provided strong evidence for adopting a theory of 'well being' with a framework of positive psychology, for making sense of men's procurement in a more accurate way. The theory of well being acts as a means of offering a new way of understanding this social practice. It is through a theory of well being situated within the framework of positive psychology that the breadth and depth of why men procure sexual services can be recognised. To provide a focus for well being in the context of purchasing sex, a definition of well being specifically applied to the procurement of sexual services has been offered in this chapter.

Finally, in light of the theory building, within this chapter a reconsideration of the SAPSS model, presented in Chapter 3, for understanding men's procurement of sexual services was sought. This reconsideration and development also extends from the findings presented in Chapters 4 to 6. With a reconsideration and redevelopment of the SAPSS model, a new model is presented, which acts as a means of reconceptualising the discourse that surrounds the procurement of sexual services. In this chapter the MAPSS model, the enhanced version of the initial SAPSS model, is introduced. By adopting these 'tools' for understanding men's purchasing of sex, this book presents a re-theorising of men's procurement of sexual services to make sense of men's procurement of sexual services in the twenty-first century. This new platform can be used in future research on this social practice.

The following chapter, the final in this volume, provides a conclusion, summarising the main findings of the empirical research. Also in the concluding chapter is a consideration of new directions in research of the procurement of sexual services. These new directions involve not only men who procure sexual services, but other groups in society who also purchase sex. These new directions in research allow the use of the theory building presented in this volume, definition of well being for the procurement of sexual services and MAPSS model to be adopted.

Notes

1 Meston, C.M. and Buss, D.M. (2007) Why humans have sex. *Archives of Sexual Behavior*, vol. 36, no. 4, © Springer Science+Business Media, LLC 2007. Reproduced with kind permission of Springer Science+Business Media.
2 Reproduced, with the permission of the publisher, from the World Health Organization website. Geneva, World Health Organization, 2006.
3 Ibid.

8 Conclusion, recommendations and implications for further study

This final chapter comprises two sections in order to draw this volume to a close. First, the main points the volume has brought to the debate on the procurement of sexual services in the twenty-first century are summarised, this includes the mnemonic '5WH' that reflects the five core questions used to reveal the key aspects of the procurement of sexual services. The development of the definition of well being, specific to purchasers of sexual services and the MAPSS model are also reflected upon in this chapter. Finally, at the end of the chapter there is reflection on the limitations of the empirical research presented within this volume; these limitations are not only reflected on, but also used to build up a series of new directions for future research into the procurement of sexual services.

The contribution of this work: a new understanding of men who procure sexual services

This volume has explored the way in which sex that is purchased from a sex worker in a non-coercive environment is experienced and understood. The work presented in this book has found that sexual services are experienced not just as physical acts for procreational purposes or simply for pleasure; it has found that a sexual service in this commercial context is made up of many components. The complexities of the procurement of sexual services are revealed in the empirical findings presented in this work. The empirical research presented within this book has examined the personal and social characteristics, reasons and experiences of men who procure sexual services in NSW, Australia. By doing so, the work presented in this volume has sought to critically reflect on the current theorising of the clients of sex workers and assess the usefulness and applicability of such theories. In order to critically reflect on existing knowledge literature the SAPSS model presented in Chapter 3 was created as a tool to make sense of current theorising in an accessible, easy to follow, manner.

This volume has also considered the demographics of the cohort sampled and recognised there are similarities amongst the cohort of men; however the men are not a homogenous group. The demographic data of this cohort, nevertheless when considered in light of the reported demographic data of men who procure sexual services in existing studies such as Monto (2000), Sanders (2008a) and Milrod and Weitzer (2012), show similarities. Those who procure sexual services in NSW, Australia, share common features with other men who are procuring sexual services in different parts of the world such as in the United States of America and the United Kingdom. An interesting and important note to make here is how in the United States of America and the United Kingdom, the procurement of sexual services is criminalised. As noted above, the reasons men offer in explanation of why they purchase sexual services in this study have reflected not only physical reasons for procuring such services, but more expressive reasons as well. Research into sex worker clients has only recently begun to report on expressive reasons for procuring sex, as evidenced in the work of Sanders (2008a, 2008b) and Milrod and Weitzer (2012). This volume adds to this work and contributes evidence that supports the expressive reasons men purchase sex.

By addressing the aims and research questions outlined in the introduction of Part I, this volume has contributed a number of significant developments to the research of sex worker clients. First, the current binary, single factorial theorising for understanding men's procurement of sexual services has been challenged. Men purchase sex for a number of reasons, and there is an interplay of reasons that reflect physical, psychological and social factors. Therefore, binary typologies such as Monto and McRee's everyman/peculiar man perspectives should be rejected. Understanding this social practice through a single factorial prism is inaccurate and misleading and caution should be used when applying them to the social practice of procuring sex. This rejection of binary typologies and caution of using single factorial theories for making sense of men's procurement of sexual services is reflected in the MAPSS model presented in Chapter 7. Second, and in conjunction with the first development outlined above, this volume has specifically rejected employing the deviancy framework for understanding the procurement of sexual services. Not only has this book problematised the concept of deviance (see Chapters 2 and 7), but also understanding the procurement of sexual services through this theoretical framework fails to recognise the expressive reasons for purchasing sex. The results of the empirical component of this volume have offered evidence to support that the expressive reasons for purchasing sex are prominent reasons for engaging in this social practice, deviance theories that feature in the work of scholars such as Winick (1962) fail to recognise this. As a result of this shortfall, an inaccurate understanding of procurement is presented through work that relies on deviance theories to support their claims. The '5WH' mnemonic is the third significant development this current study has contributed to this area of research. The mnemonic has been devised to reflect five key questions that support an empirically robust platform for future sex worker client research to be conducted from. The five questions uncover information based on the context, setting and rationale for procuring sexual services and has the scope to be applied to future procurement research, in particular with other groups such as women purchasers.

A fourth significant development in this volume has been the differentiation of the reasons that men purchase sexual services for the first time, and those for why men continue to purchase. This has been an important development in the study as it has explicitly demonstrated a difference between physical reasons for procuring sexual services and more expressive reasons. It is common for men to purchase sex for the first time for reasons that centre on the physical act of sex, while further involvement in purchasing sex is centred more on expressive (emotions and intimacy based) reasons. The distinction of reasons for procuring sexual services in this way has afforded two major contributions to the research on the procurement of sexual services: the re-theorising of this social practice and the development of the MAPSS model presented in Chapter 7. In relation to the re-theorising aspect of this book and through the recognition of expressive reasons for purchasing sex, the fifth development within this volume has occurred – the application of a theory of well being, with the framework of positive psychology, being applied to sex worker clients. The application of well being as a theoretical framework applied to men who procure sexual services recognises the multi-factorial nature for engaging in this social practice. A theory of well being allows for the psycho-social well being of men to be recognised in the act of procurement, with the act allowing men to achieve a healthy sense of self. In recognising that well being can be applied to a range of behaviours, including the procurement of sexual services, a sixth development was made: a definition of well being as applied to the procurement of sexual services. This definition supports not only the multi-factorial nature of purchasing sex, but also recognises this act as a sexual right between consenting adults. Finally, the reconsideration of the SAPSS model in light of the full dataset lent itself to the redevelopment of the model and the presentation of the MAPSS model in the previous chapter. The MAPSS model not only encompasses the different reasons men have for procuring sexual services and the influences of these, but is a model that reflects why men procure sexual services for the first time and subsequently. As Milrod and Weitzer (2012) have noted, there is a small but growing body of research emerging on sex worker clients. The work presented in this volume has contributed to this body of knowledge and has provided a number of resources to support future research. Nevertheless, this research has its limitations like any empirical work, and these issues are addressed in the final section of this chapter, along with future directions in sex worker client research.

Limitations of the study and implications for further study

As with most studies, there have been limitations within the current study. First, the study has utilised a cohort of men in the state of NSW, Australia, so it is limited by its geographical focus. The state of NSW, Australia is unique due to the decriminalisation of sex work and its regulation. This makes it an appropriate focus for research. As a result of the state of NSW being the focus for this research, the consideration of procurers of sexual services in a legalised setting was sought and consideration given to whether they differed from men in previous research in non-decriminalised locations. Another limitation of the study was its focus on male purchasers of female sexual service to the exclusion of homosexual men and women, both heterosexual and homosexual or the trans-gender community. This limits the applicability of the study, yet offers an opportunity to use the tools developed in this study in relation to these groups in future research.

Whilst it could also be suggested that the self-selection by participants to take part in the study has skewed the findings, this latter point can also be challenged. The demographic constitution of the sample reflects existing studies that have been conducted in this area around the world to date, which allows for a comparison of findings between studies to take place. Furthermore, it must be recognised that the stigma that surrounds the procurement of sexual services and the wider sex work industry impacts on and limits the use of alternative sampling techniques that aim to attract random samples. Finally, it is important to acknowledge again that the work presented in this volume has focused on non-coercive sex work, it has not considered those who are involved in illegal activities associated with the sex work industry such as child prostitution and trafficking. These issues should be considered separately to those who engage in sex work in a voluntary capacity. The work and tools evidenced and developed in this study should not be viewed as tools that are applicable to investigating and examining illegal activities.

Reflecting on these limitations, the study provides an opportunity to consider further research in this area. For example, the model, mnemonic and theory/definition of well being as applied to the procurement of sexual services is now in a position to be applied to other states in Australia, as well other countries around the world. This type of research would also provide the scope to consider indigenous cultures and non-Western cultures, for example of Asia and Africa. The opportunity to extend this study and invite women (of different sexual orientations) who procure sexual services and men who procure sex from men for example, in order to examine the applicability of the developments made in this research is also available. By doing so this line of enquiry could examine how feminist theorising might contribute to understanding these forms of sex work, a limitation of this theoretical framework as noted in Chapter 7. The use of positive psychology and a theory of well being also provides an opportunity to examine the health benefits the procurement of sexual services may have in the lives of those who procure. For example, do people who do not have but wish to have sexual and intimate relations, but who do not have the opportunity to do so in a conventional marriage or partnership, experience more stress-related symptoms, and are such people more likely to develop illness, have slower recovery from illness and have a high probability of relapse and/or recurrence or illness? Does the procurement of sexual services mitigate such health risks? It has been demonstrated in health research that people who are not in an intimate relationship have higher mortality and accident rates, show depressed immunological functioning, and are more at risk of depression (Hook *et al.*, 2003: 463). The health implications on the lives of those who procure sexual services are a pertinent extension to the consideration of well being and worthy of attention in future research.

The empirical findings presented in this volume provide a new platform for the extension of the small but growing body of research into the procurement of sexual services to be conducted. This current study also identifies different groups to which this work can be extended, e.g. women procurers, as well as signalling potential relationships that need investigating, in particular the health benefits of procurement.

Final reflections

This volume began by recognising that sex work has been a contentious issue throughout history. While consideration has been given to why this has happened, for example the influence of the Church, the overarching position of the current study seeks to end this. This book has achieved its aim of making sense of men's procurement of sexual services by claiming that sex work, and in particular the procurement of this social practice, has been misunderstood over time. The procurement of sexual services has been inadequately analysed and addressed. In part this is a reflection of groups who have had a particular interest and influence over the area of sex work over time, such as radical feminists, yet who have not always fully recognised and understood the social practice. The empirical research found within this volume has revealed that men who purchase sexual services share common demographics such as age and length of time of procurement; however, the reasons men procure sexual services are multifactorial, and in most part, positive. By recognising this, a re-theorising of why men procure sexual services is engendered within this book. In order to make sense of why men engage in this behaviour in a contemporary context, in a more accurate way, recognition of the multifactorial nature of procurement, as well as a recognition of well being, should be applied to this social practice. This in conjunction with a rejection of demonising the social practice of procuring sexual services now needs to take place. This produces a more accurate and realistic contemporary understanding of why men purchase sex in the twenty-first century.

References

Alexander, P. and Delacoste, F. (1987) *Sex Work: Writings by Women in the Sex Industry.* Pittsburgh, PA: Cleis.

Allwood, G. (1998) *French Feminisms: Gender and Violence in Contemporary Theory.* London: UCL Press.

Anderson, B. and O'Connell Davidson, J. (2002) *Trafficking – a Demand Led Problem? A Multi-Country Pilot Study.* London: Save the Children.

Atchinson, C., Fraser, L. and Lowman, J. (1998) Men who buy sex: preliminary findings of an exploratory study. In J.E. Elias, V.L. Bullough, V. Elias and G. Brewer (eds.) *Prostitution: On Whores, Hustlers and Johns.* New York: Prometheus Books.

Australasian Legal Information Institute website, online, available at: www.austlii.edu.au.

Australian Bureau of Crime Statistics (2011) Australian and New Zealand Standard Offence Classification (ANZSOC), 2011. Online, available at: www.abs.gov.au/ausstats/abs@.nsf/mf/1234.0. Viewed 10 January 2013.

Australian Bureau of Crime Statistics (2012) Cultural Diversity on Australia: Reflecting a Nation: Stories from the 2011 Census. Online, available at: www.abs.gov.au/ausstats/abs@.nsf/Lookup/2071.0main+features902012-2013. Viewed 21 May 2013.

Bandes, S.A. (2009) Victims, 'closure' and the sociology of emotion. *Law and Contemporary Problems*, vol. 72, no. 1. Online, available at: http://heinonline.org/HOL/LandingPage?collection=journals&handle=hein.journals/lcp72&div=18&id=&page=. Viewed 21 March 2010.

Barry, K. (1995) *The Prostitution of Sexuality: The Global Exploitation of Women.* New York: New York University Press.

Baumeister, R.F. and Vohs, K.D. (2004) Sexual economics: sex as female resource for social exchange in heterosexual interactions. *Personality and Social Psychology Review*, vol. 8, no. 4, pp. 339–363.

Becker, H. (1963) *Outsiders: Studies in the Sociology of Deviance.* New York: New York University Press.

Bernstein, E. (2001) The meaning of the purchase: desire, demand, and the commerce of sex. *Ethnography*, vol. 2, no. 3, pp. 389–420.

Bindman, J. and Doezema, J. (1997) *Redefining Prostitution as Sex Work on the International Agenda.* London: Anti-Slavery International and Network of Sex Projects.

Blanchard, K. (1994) Young Johns. *Mademoiselle*, vol. 100, no. 5, pp. 130–133.

Bottomley, S. and Parker, S. (1997) *Law in Context* (2nd Edition). Sydney: Federation Press.

Braun-Harvey, D. (2011) *Sexual Health in Recovery: A Professional Counselor's Manual.* New York, NY: Springer.

Brooks Gordon, B. (2006) *The Price of Sex: Prostitution, Policy and Society.* Cullompton: Willan Publishing.

Brooks Gordon, B. and Gelsthorpe, L. (2003a) Prostitutes' clients, Ken Livingstone and a new Trojan Horse. *Howard Journal of Criminal Justice*, vol. 42, no. 5, pp. 437–451.

Brooks Gordon, B. and Gelsthorpe, L. (2003b) What men say when apprehended for kerb crawling: a model of prostitutes' clients' talk. *Psychology, Crime and Law*, vol. 9, no. 2, pp. 145–171.

Busch, N.B., Bell, H., Hotaling, N. and Monto, M. (2002) Male customers of prostituted women: exploring perceptions of entitlement to power and control and implications for violent behavior toward women. *Violence Against Women*, vol. 8, no. 9, pp. 1093–1112.

Buss, D.M. and Schmitt, D.P. (1993) Sexual strategies theory: an evolutionary perspective on human mattering. *Psychological Review*, vol. 100, no. 2, April 1993, pp. 204–232.

Caldwell, J. (2012) Mining wages. Online, available at: http://technology.infomine.com/reviews/MiningSalaries/welcome.asp?view=full. Viewed 17 October 2012.

Califia, P. (1994.) *Public Sex: The Culture of Radical Sex.* Pittsburgh: Cleis Press.

Campbell, J.L. and Snow, B.M. (1992) Gender role conflict and family environment as predictors of men's marital satisfaction. *Journal of Family Psychology*, vol. 6, no. 1, p. 84.

Campbell, R. and O'Neill, M. (eds) (2006) *Sex Work Now.* Cullompton: Willan Publishing.

Cao, L. and Maguire, E.R. (2013) A test of the temperance hypothesis: class, religiosity, and tolerance of prostitution. *Social Problems*, vol. 60, no. 2 (May 2013), pp. 188–205.

Chapkis, W. (1997) *Live Sex Acts: Women Performing Erotic Labour.* London: Cassell.

Chodorow, N.J. (2000) Reflections on the reproduction of mothering - twenty years later. *Studies in Gender and Sexuality.* vol. 1. no. 4, pp. 337–348.

Collins, N.L. and Feeny, B.C. (2004) An attachment theory perspective on closeness and intimacy. In D.J. Mashek and A. Aron (eds) *Handbook of Closeness and Intimacy.* New Jersey: Lawrence Erlbaum Associates.

Connell, R.W. (1995) *Masculinities.* Cambridge: Polity Press.

Connell, R.W. (2005) *Masculinities.* California: University of California Press.

Courtenay, W.H. (2000) Constructions of masculinity and their influence on men's well-being: a theory of gender and health. *Social Science and Medicine*, vol. 50, no. 10, pp. 1385–1401.

Coy, M.H., Horvath, M. and Kelly, L. (2007) *It's Just Like Going to the Supermarket: Men Buying Sex in East London.* London: Child and Woman Abuse Studies Unit, London Metropolitan University.

Criminal Law Consolidation Act 135 1976 (South Australian Consolidated Acts), online, available at: www.austlii.edu.au. Viewed 16 August 2010.

Dartnall, E. and Jewkes, R. (2002) Sexual violence against women: the scope of the problem. *Best Practice and Research Clinical Obstetrics and Gynaecology*, vol. 27, no. 1, February 2013, pp. 3–13.

Day, S., Ward, H. and Perrotta, L. (1993) Prostitution and risk of HIV: Male partners of female prostitutes'. *British Medical Journal*, vol. 307, no. 6900, pp. 359–361.

Demir, A.M. (2012) The development of normative sexuality. Online, available at: www.academia.edu/4054500/The_Development_of_Normative_Sexuality. Viewed 14 October 2012.

Diener, E. (2009) Subjective well being. In E. Diener (eds) *The Science of Well Being.* New York: Spring.

Diener, E. and Suh, E. (1997) Measuring quality of life: Economic, social and subjective indicators. *Social Indicators*, vol. 40, no. 1–2, pp. 189–216.

Diener, E., Suh, E., Lucas, R.E. and Smith, H.E. (1999) Subjective well being: three decades of progress. *Psychological Bulletin*, vol. 125, vol. 6, no. 4, pp. 305–314.

Disorderly Houses Amendment Act 1995, online, available at: www.austlii.edu.au. Viewed 16 August 2010.

Ditmore M. (2006) *Encyclopedia of Prostitution and Sex Work*. Westport: Greenwood Press.

Dodge, R., Daly, A.P., Huyton, J. and Sanders, L.D. (2012) The challenge of defining well being. *International Journal of Wellbeing*, vol. 2, no. 3, pp. 222–235.

Douglas, A. (1977) *The Feminization of American Culture*. New York: Macmillan.

Duckwork, A.L., Steen, T.A. and Seligman, M.E.P. (2005) Positive psychology in clinic practice. *Annual Review of Clinical Psychology*, pp. 629–651.

Earle, S. and Sharp, K. (2007) *Sex In Cyberspace: Men Who Pay For Sex*. Aldershot: Ashgate.

Earle, S. and Sharp, K (2008) Intimacy, pleasure and the men who pay for sex. In G. Letherby, K. Williams, P. Birch and M. Cain (eds) *Sex as Crime?* Cullompton: Willan Publishing.

Egger, S. and Harcourt, C. (1993) Prostitution in NSW: the impact of deregulation. In P. Easteal and S. McKillop (eds), *Women and the Law: Proceedings of a Conference Held 24–26 September 1991*. Canberra: Australian Institute of Criminology.

Elliott, K.E.H. and McGaw, J. (2002) *Kerb Crawling in Middlesbrough*. Middlesbrough: Safer Middlesbrough Partnership: Prostitution Task Group.

Ellsworth P.C.; Smith, C.A. (1988). Shades of joy: Patterns of appraisal differentiating pleasant emotions. *Cognition and Emotion*, vol. 2, pp. 301–331.

Ewasiw, J.F., Klein, C., Kennedy, M.A., Gorzalka, B.B. and Yuille, J.C. (2006) Characteristics of customers of street prostitutes. *Annual Meeting of the Canadian Psychological Association*. Calgary, Alberta.

Farley, M., Baral, I., Kiremire, M. and Sezgin, U. (1998) Prostitution in five countries: violence and post-traumatic stress disorder (South Africa, Thailand, Turkey, USA, Zambia). *Feminism and Psychology*, vol. 8, no. 4, pp. 405–426.

Faugier, J. and Cranfield, S. (1995) Reaching male clients of female prostitutes: the challenge for HIV prevention. *AIDS Care*, no. 7, pp. S21–S32.

Finstad, L. and Hoigard, C. (1992) *Backstreets: Prostitution, Money and Love. Cambridge*: Polity Press & Blackwell Publishers.

Fiske, S.T. and Taylor, S.E. (1991) *Social Cognition* (2nd Edition). New York: McGraw Hill.

Fox, J., Tideman, R.L., Gilmour, S., Marks, C., Beek, I. and van and Mindel, A. (2006) Sex work practices and condom use in female sex workers in Sydney. *International Journal of STD and AIDS*, 17, pp. 319–323.

Francis G. (2001) *Introduction to SPSS for Windows* (3rd Edition). Sydney: Pearson Education.

Fredrickson, B.L. (2001) The role of positive emotions in positive psychology: the broaden-and-build theory of positive emotions. *American Psychologist*, vol. 56, no. 3, p. 218.

Freud, S. (1923) *The Ego and the Id*. Vienna: W.W. Norton and Company.

Freud, S. (1962) *Three Essays on the Theory of Sexuality*, translated by J.E. Strachey. New York: Basic Books.

Freund, M., Lee, N. and Leonard, T. (1991) Sexual behavior of clients with street prostitutes in Camden, NJ. *Journal of Sex Research*, vol. 28, no. 4, pp. 579–591.

Gable, S. and Haidt, J. (2005) What (and why) is positive psychology? *Review of General Psychology*, vol. 9, pp. 103–110.

Gagnon, J.H. and Simon, W. (1970) Prospects for change in American sexual patterns. *Medical Aspects of Human Sexuality*, vol. 4, pp. 100–117.

Gaia, A.C. (2002) Understanding emotional intimacy: a review of conceptualization, assessment and the role of gender. *International Social Science Review - Kansas*, vol. 77, no. 3/4, pp. 151–170.

Garcia, S.G., Yam, E.A. and Firestone, M. (2006) 'No party hat, no party': successful condom use in sex work in Mexico and the Dominican Republic, *Reproductive Health Matters*, vol. 14, no. 28, pp. 53–62.

Garcia-Rodrigo, C. (2009) An analysis of an alternative to the radical feminist position on the institution of marriage. *Journal of Law and Family Studies*, vol. 11, no. 1. Online, available at: http://papers.ssrn.com/sol3/papers.cfm?abstract_id=1306642. Viewed 3 January 2011.

Garza-Mercer, F. de la, Christensen, A. and Doss, B. (2006) Sex and affection in hetero-sexual and homosexual couples: an evolutionary perspective. *Journal of Human Sexuality*, vol. 9 (Annual 2006).

Gecas, V. and Libby, R. (1976) Sexual behavior as symbolic interaction. *Journal of Sex Research*, vol. 12, no. 1, pp. 33–49.

Gergen, K.S., Greenberg, M.S. and Willis, R.H. (eds) (1980) *Social Exchange: Advances in Theory and Research*. New York: Plenum Press.

Giddens, A. (2005) *Sociology* (5th Edition). Cambridge: Polity Press.

Global Alliance Against Trafficked Women (2001) *Human Rights and Trafficking in Persons: a Handbook*. Bangkok: GAATW.

Good, G.E., Borst, T.S. and Wallace, D.L. (1994) Masculinity research: a review and cri-tique. *Applied and Preventive Psychology*, vol. 3, pp. 3–14.

Graaf, H. de and Rademakers, J. (2006) Sexual development of prepubertal children. *Journal of Psychology and Human Sexuality*, vol. 18, no. 1, pp. 1–21.

Graaf, R. de, van Zessen, G., Vanwesenbeeck, I., Straver, C.J. and Visser, J.H. (1997) Condom use by Dutch men with commercial heterosexual contacts: determinants and considerations. *AIDS Education Preview*, vol. 9, no. 5, pp. 411–423.

Groom, T.M. and Nandwani, R. (2006) Characteristics of men who pay for sex: a UK sexual health clinic survey. *Sexually Transmitted Infections*, vol. 82, pp. 364–367.

Grubman Black, S. (2003) Deconstructing John. *Paper presented at Dynamics: the forces of demand in Global Sex Trafficking: Conference Report*. Conference held 17/18 October, DePaul University, Chicago, Illinois.

Harcourt, C., Egger, S. and Donovan, B. (2005) Sex work and the law. *Sexual Health*, vol. 2, no. 3, pp. 121–128.

Hearn, J. and Pringle, K. with members of Critical Research on Men in Europe (2006) *European Perspectives on Men and Masculinities: National and Transnational Approaches*. New York: Palgrave Macmillan.

Heidensohn, F. (1968) The deviance of women: a critique and an enquiry. *British Journal of Sociology*, vol. 19, no. 2, pp. 160–175.

Hill, C.A. and Preston, L.K. (1996) Individual differences in the experience of sexual motivation: theory and measurement of dispositional sexual motives. *Journal of Sex Research*, vol. 33, pp. 27–45.

Holt, T.J. and Blevins, K.R. (2007) Examining sex work from the client's perspective: assessing Johns using on-line data. *Deviant Behaviour*, vol. 28, no. 4, pp. 333–354.

Holter, Ø.G. (2000) A revolt for equality? On men, women and gender discrimination. Online, available at: http://scholar.google.com.au/scholar?hl=en&as_sdt=0,5&q=Holter+(2000)+prostitution. Viewed 13 September 2011.

Hook, M.K., Gerstein, L.H., Detterich, L. and Gridley, B. (2003) How close are we? Measuring intimacy and examining gender differences. *Journal of Counseling and Development*, vol. 81, no. 4, pp. 462–472.

Hubbard, P.J. and Prior, J. (2013) Out of sight, out of mind? Prostitution policy and the health, well-being and safety of home-based sex workers. *Critical Social Policy*, February 2013, vol. 33, no. 1, pp. 140–159.

Huesmann L.R. (1998) The role of social information processing and cognitive schema in the acquisition and maintenance of habitual aggressive behavior. *Journal of Personality and Social Psychology*, vol. 9, pp. 73–109.

Humphreys, J.A. (2006) *Deviant Behaviour*. London: Pearson.

Ireland, J.L. (2008) Conducting individualised theory-driven assessments of violent offenders. In Ireland, J.L., Ireland, C.A. and P. Birch (eds) (2008) *Violent and Sexual Offenders: Assessment Treatment and Management*. Cullompton: Willan Publishing.

Jackson, N. (2013) Exploring subjective well being and relationships to lifewide education, learning and personal development. Online, available at: www.lifewideebook.co.uk/uploads/1/0/8/4/10842717/chapter__a4_09_06_13.pdf. Viewed 28 August 2013.

Jamieson L. (1998) Intimacy transformed? A critical look at the 'pure relationship'. *Sociology*, vol. 33, no. 3, pp. 477–494.

Jeffreys, S. (1997) *The Idea of Prostitution*. Melbourne: Spinifex Press.

Jordan, J. (1997) User buys: why men buy sex, *Australian and New Zealand Journal of Criminology*, vol. 30, no. 1, pp. 55–71.

Jordan, J. (2005) *The Sex Industry in New Zealand: A Literature Review*. Wellington: Ministry of Justice.

Kauth, M.R. (2007) The evolution of human sexuality: an introduction. *Journal of Psychology and Human Sexuality*, vol. 18, no. 2–3, pp. 1–22.

Kempadoo, K. (1999) *Sun, Sex and Gold: Tourism and Sex Work in the Caribbean*. Maryland: Rowman and Littlefield.

Kennedy, M.A., Klein, C., Gorzalka, B.B. and Yuile, J.C. (2004) Attitude change following a diversion program for men who solicit sex. *Journal of Offender Rehabilitation*, vol. 40, pp. 41–60.

Kesler, K. (2002) Is a feminist stance in support of prostitution possible? An exploration of current trends. *Sexualities*, vol. 5, no. 2, pp. 219–235.

Kinsey, A.C., Pomeroy, W.B. and Martin, C.E. (1948) *Sexual Behavior in the Human Male*. Philadelphia: WB Saunders.

Kilvington, J., Day, S. and Ward, H. (2001) Prostitution policy in Europe. *Feminist Review*, no. 67, pp. 78–93.

Kimmel, M.S. (1994) Masculinity as homophobia: fear, shame and silence in the construction of gender identity. In H. Brod and M. Kaufman (eds) (1994) *Theorising Masculinities*. Thousand Oaks: Sage.

Kimmel, M.S. and Plante, R. (eds) (2004) Sexualities: identities, behaviour and society. New York: Oxford University Press.

Kinnell, H. (1989) Prostitutes, their clients and risks of HIV infection in Birmingham. *Occasional Paper for Department of Public Health Medicine*. Central Birmingham Health Authority, Edgbaston, Birmingham.

Kinnell, H. (2006) Clients of female sex workers: men or monsters? In R. Campbell and M. O'Neill (eds) (2006) *Sex Work Now*. Cullompton: Willan Publishing.

Kinnell, H. (2008) *Violence and Sex Work in Britain*. Cullompton: Willan Publishing.

La Placa, V., McNaught, A. and Knight, A. (2013) Discourse on wellbeing in research and practice. *International Journal of wellbeing*, vol. 3, no. 1, pp. 116–125.

Lau, K., Dang, T., Kennedy, M.A., Gorzalka, B.B. and Yuille, J.C. (2004). *Men's Motivations for Soliciting Prostituted Women*. Poster presented at Annual Meeting of Canadian Psychological Association, St John's, NL, Canada.

Lawler, E.J. and Thye, S.R. (1999) Bringing emotions into social exchange theory. *Annual Review of Sociology*, pp. 217–244.

Lee, W. and Ogozoglu, O. (2007) Well being and ill being: bivariate panel data analysis. Discussion paper - Institute for the Study of Labour. Bonn: IZA.

Leafgren, F. (1990) Men on a journey. In D. Moore and F. Leafgren (eds) (1990) *Problem Solving Strategies and Interventions for Men in Conflict*. New York: Basic Books.

Leigh, B.C. (1989) Reasons for having and avoiding sex: gender, sexual orientation, and relationship to sexual behavior. *Journal of Sex Research*, vol. 26, pp. 199–209.

Lemert, E.M. (1951) *Social Pathology: Systematic Approaches to the Study of Sociopathic Behavior*. New York: McGraw-Hill.

Levinger, G. and Huesmann, L.R. (1980) An 'incremental exchange' perspective on the pair relationship. In K. J. Gurgen, M. S. Greenberg and R. H. Willis (eds) (1980) *Social Exchange: Advances in Theory and Research*. New York: Plenum.

Liney, P.A. and Joseph, S. (eds) (2004) *Positive Psychology in Practice*. Hoboken, NJ: John Wiley and Sons Inc.

Lombroso, C. (2007) *Criminal Man*, translated by M. Gibson and H.N. Rafter. New York: Praeger.

Longmore, M.A. (1998) Symbolic interactionism and the study of sexuality. *Journal of Sex Research*, vol. 3, no. 5, pp. 44–57.

Lowman, J. and Atchinson, C. (2006) Men who buy sex: a survey in the Greater Vancouver Regional District. *Canadian Review of Sociology and Anthropology*, vol. 43, no. 3, pp. 281–296.

Lyubomirsky, S. and Lepper, H.S. (1999) A measure of subjective happiness: preliminary reliability and construct validation. *Social Indicators*, vol. 46, pp. 137–155.

McKeganey, N. (2006) Street prostitution in Scotland: the views of working women. *Drugs: Education, Prevention and Policy*, vol. 13, no. 2, pp. 151–166.

McKeganey, N. and Barnard, M. (1996) *Sex Work on the Streets: Prostitutes and their Clients*. Buckingham: Open University Press.

MacKinnon, C. (1990) Confronting the liberal lies about prostitution. In D. Leidholdt and J. Raymond (eds) (1990) *The Sexual Liberals and the Attack on Feminism*. New York: Elsevier Science.

McLeod, E. (1982) *Women Working: Prostitution Now*. London: Croom Helm.

Macleod, J., Anderson, L. and Golding, J. (2008) *Challenging Men's Demand for Prostitution in Scotland: A Research Report Based on Interviews with 110 Men who Bought Women In Prostitution*. Glasgow: Women's Support Project.

Malinowski C. (1979) Cheating as a function of moral judgement and selected personality and situation variables. *Dissertation Abstracts International*, no. 39, pp. 5143–5144.

Mansson, S.A. (2004) Men's practices in prostitution and their implications for social work. In S.A. Mansson and C. Proveyer (eds) (2004) *Social Work in Cuba and Sweden: Achievements and Prospects*. Göteborg/Havana: Department of Social Work/Department of Sociology.

Marcus, S. (1975) *Freud's Three Essays on the Theory of Sexuality*. New York: Partisan Review.

Marques, O. (2010) Choice-makers and risk-takers in neo-liberal liquid modernity: the contradiction of the 'entrepreneurial' sex worker. *International Journal of Criminology and Sociological Theory*, vol. 3, no. 1, pp. 314–332.

Marttila, A.M. (2003) Consuming sex: Finnish male clients and Russian and Baltic prostitution. *Presented at Gender and Power in the New Europe, the 5th European Feminist Research Conference*, Lund University.

Matthews, R. (2008) *Prostitution, Politics and Policy*. New York: Routledge-Cavendish.

Meston, C.M. and Buss, D.M. (2007) Why humans have sex. *Archives of Sexual Behavior*, vol. 36, no. 4, pp. 477–507.

Millett, K. (1970) *Sexual Politics*. Illinois: University of Illinois Press.

Milrod, C. and Weitzer, R. (2012) The intimacy prism: emotional management amongst the clients of escorts. *Men and Masculinities*, vol. 15, no. 5, pp. 447–467.

Monto, M.A. (2000) *Focusing on the Clients of Street Prostitutes: A Creative Approach to Reducing Violence Against Women*. Final Report submitted to the National Institute of Justice. Award Number: 97-IJ-CX-0033.

Monto, M.A. and McRee, J.N. (2005) A comparison of the male customers of female street prostitutes with national samples of men. *International Journal of Offender Therapy and Comparative Criminology*, vol. 49, no. 5, pp. 505–529.

Mosse, G. L. (1998) *The Image of Man: The Creation of Modern Masculinity*. Oxford: Oxford University Press.

National Wellness Institute of Australia (NWIA) (Unknown) *Defining Wellness*. Online, available at: http://nwia.idwellness.org/defining-wellness/. Viewed 10 November 2012.

O'Connell Davidson, J. (1998) *Prostitution, Power and Freedom*. Michigan, US: University of Michigan Press.

O'Neil, M. and Campbell, R. (2006) Street sex work and local communities: creating discursive spaces for genuine consultation and inclusion. In R. Campbell and M. O'Neill (eds) *Sex Work Now*. Cullompton: Willan Publishing.

Outshoorn, J. (2005) *The Politics of Prostitution: Women's Movements, Democratic States and the Globalisation of Sex Commerce*. Cambridge: Cambridge University Press.

Overall C. (1992) What's wrong with prostitution? Evaluating sex work. *Signs*, vol. 17, no. 4, pp. 705–724.

Pateman, C. (1988) *The Sexual Contract*. Cambridge: Polity.

Perkins, R. (1991) *Working Girls: Prostitutes, Their Life and Social Control*. Canberra: Australian Institute of Criminology.

Pfohl, S.J. (1994) *Images of Deviance and Social Control: A Sociological History*. New York: McGraw-Hill.

Phillips, J. and Parks, M. (2006) Measuring domestic violence and sexual assault against women: a review of the literature and statistics. Online, available at: www.aph.gov.au/About_Parliament/Parliamentary_Departments/Parliamentary_Library/Publications_Archive/archive/ViolenceAgainstWomen. Viewed 12 March 2010.

Phillips, T. and Smith, P. (2003) Everyday incivility: towards a benchmark. *Sociological Review*, vol. 51, no. 1, pp. 85–108.

Phoenix, J. (2000) Prostitute identities: men, money and violence. *British Journal of Criminology*, vol. 40, no. 1, pp. 37–55.

Pinker, S. and Bloom, P. (1992) Natural language and natural selection. In J.H. Barkow J.L. Cosmides and J. Tooby (eds), *The Adapted Mind*. New York: Oxford University Press.

Pinto, S., Scandia, A. and Wilson, P. (1990) *Prostitution Laws in Australia, Trends and Issues in Crime and Criminal Justice No. 22: Prostitution Laws in Australia*. Canberra: Australian Institute of Criminology.

Pleck, J.H., Sonenstein, F.L. and Ku, L.C. (1993) Masculinity ideology and its correlates.

In S. Oskamp and M. Costanzo (eds) (1993) *Gender Issues in Contemporary Society*. Newbury Park, CA: Sage.

Plumridge, E., Chetwynd, S., Reed, A. and Gifford, S. (1997) Discourses of emotionality in commercial sex: missing the client voice. *Feminism and Psychology*, vol. 7, no. 2, pp. 165–181.

Pollard, E. and Lee, P. (2003) Child well-being: a systematic review of the literature. *Social Indicators*, vol. 61, no. 1, pp. 9–78.

Prieur, A. and Taskdal, A. (1993) Clients of prostitutes: sick deviants or ordinary men? A discussion of the male role concept and cultural changes in masculinity. *Nordic Journal of Feminist and Gender Research*, vol. 1, no. 2, pp. 105–114.

ProCon (2009) 82 Countries and their prostitution policies. Online, available at: http://prostitution.procon.org/viewresource.asp?resourceID=000772. Viewed 4 February 2010.

Prostitution Act 2011 (Queensland Amended Act), online, available at: www.austlii.edu.au. Viewed 15 November 2012.

Prostitution Amendment Act 1992 (Australian Capital Territory Act), online, available at: www.austlii.edu.au. Viewed 15 August 2010.

Prostitution Bill 2011 (Western Australian Consolidated Acts), online, available at: www.austlii.edu.a. Viewed 15 November 2012.

Prostitution Control Act 1994 (Victorian Consolidated Acts), online, available at: www.austlii.edu.a. Viewed 15 August 2010.

Prostitution Regulation Act 2004 (Northern Territory consolidated acts), online, available at: www.austlii.edu.a. Viewed 15 August 2010.

Radin, M. (1987) Market-inalienability. *Harvard Law Review*, vol. 100, pp. 1849–1937.

Reeser, T.W. (2010) *Masculinities in Theory: An Introduction*. London: Wiley.

Ridgeway, C.L. and Bourge, C. (2004) Gender as status: an expectation states theory approach. In A.H. Eagly, A.E. Beall and R.J Sternberg (eds) (2004) *The Psychology of Gender* (2nd Edition). New York: Guilford Press.

Roach Anleu, S.L. (2006) *Deviance, Conformity and Control*. Australia: Pearson Education.

Rosenblum, K.E. (1975) Female deviance and the female sex role: a preliminary investigation. *British Journal of Sociology*, vol. 26, no. 2, pp. 169–185.

Sanders, T. (2005) *Sex Work: A Risky Business*. Cullompton: Willan Publishing.

Sanders, T. (2008a) Male sexual scripts: intimacy, sexuality and pleasure in the purchase of commercial sex. *Sociology*, vol. 42, no. 3, pp. 400–417.

Sanders T. (2008b) *Paying for Pleasure: Men who Buy Sex*. Cullompton: Willan Publishing.

Sanders, T. and Campbell, R. (2007) Designing out vulnerability, building in respect: violence, safety, and sex work policy. *British Journal of Sociology*, vol. 58, no. 1, pp. 1–19.

Sanders, T., O'Neill, M. and Pitcher, J. (2009) *Prostitution: Sex Work, Policy and Politics*. London: Sage.

Sawyer, S., Metz, M., Hinds, J. and Brucker, R. (2001) Attitudes towards prostitution among males: a 'consumers' report'. *Current Psychology*, vol. 20, no. 4, pp. 363–376.

Scarlet Alliance (2012) State by state laws in Australia. Online, available at: www.scarletalliance.org.au. Viewed 4 September 2012.

Scott, J. and Marshall, G. (2009) *A Dictionary of Sociology* (3rd Edition). Oxford: Oxford University Press.

Scott, J., Hunter, J., Hunter, V. and Ragusa, A. (2006) Sex and the city: sex work in rural and regional New South Wales. *Journal of Rural Society*, vol. 16, no. 2, pp. 151–168.

Seal, D.W. and Ehrhardt, A.A. (2003) Masculinity and urban men: perceived scripts for courtship, romantic, and sexual interactions with women. *Culture, Health and Sexuality*, vol. 5, no. 4, pp. 295–319.

Sefcek, J.A., Brumbach, B.H., Vasquez, G. and Miller, G.F. (2007) The evolutionary psychology of human mate choice: how ecology, genes, fertility, and fashion influence mating strategies. *Journal of Psychology and Human Sexuality*, vol. 18, nos 2–3, pp. 125–182.

Seidler, V.J. (1994) *Unreasonable Men: Masculinity and Social Theory*. New York: Routledge.

Seidler, V.J. (2007) Masculinities, bodies, and emotional life. *Men and Masculinities*, vol. 10, no. 1, pp. 9–21.

Seligman, M.E.P. (2011) *Flourish - A New Understanding of Happiness and Well Being and How to Achieve Them*. London: Nicholas Brealey Publishing.

Seligman, M.E. and Csikszentmihalyi, M. (2000) Positive psychology: an introduction. *American Psychologist*, vol. 55, no. 1, p. 5.

Sex Industry Offences Act 2005 (Tasmanian Consolidated Acts), online, available at: www.austlii.edu.au. Viewed 16 August 2010.

Sexual Offenders Act (UK) (2003) Prostitution, S.51. Online, available at: www.legislation.gov.uk/ukpga/2003/42/contents. Viewed 23 August 2011.

Sex Work Outreach Program (SWOP) (2007) *A Paper Outlining the Key Facts about the NSW Sex Work Industry.* Sydney: SWOP.

Shields, S.A. (2008) Gender: an intersectionality perspective. *Sex Roles*, vol. 59, nos 5–6, pp. 301–311.

Shields, S.A., Garner, D.N., Di Leone, B. and Hadley, A.M. (2006) Gender and emotion. In J.E. Stets and J. Turner (eds) (2006) *Handbook of the Sociology of Emotions*. New York, US: Springer.

Sheldon, W.H. (1947) *Varieties of Delinquent Youth: An Introduction to Constitutional Psychiatry*. New York: Harper Brothers.

Shepherd, E. (1991) Ethical interviewing. *Policing*, vol. 7, pp. 42–60.

Shepherd, L.J. (ed.) (2009) *Gender Matters in Global Politics: a Feminist Introduction to International Relations*. London: Routledge.

Singh, K. and Duggal Jha, S. (2008) Positive and negative affect, and grit as predictors of happiness and life satisfaction. *Journal of Indian Academy of Applied Psychology*, vol. 34, pp. 40–45.

Smith, M. (2002) *Social Science in Question*. Milton Keynes: Open University Press.

Solomon, R. (1978) Emotions and anthropology: the logic of emotional world views. *Inquiry*, vol. 21, pp. 181–199.

Sprecher, S. (1998) Social exchange theories and sexuality. *Journal of Sex Research*, vol. 35, no. 1, pp. 32–43.

St James, M. (1987) The reclamation of whores. In L. Bell (ed.) *Good Girls/Bad Girls.* Toronto: Seal Press.

Sternberg, R.J. (1997) Construct validation of a triangular love scale. *European Journal of Social Psychology*, vol. 27, no. 3, pp. 313–335.

Stets, J.E. and Asencio, E.K. (2008) Consistency and enhancement processes in understanding emotions. *Social Forces*, vol. 86, no. 3, pp. 1055–1078.

Stroller, R.J. (1975) *Perversion: The Erotic Form of Hatred*. New York: Pantheon.

Sullivan, B. (2001) 'It's all in the contract': Rethinking feminist critiques of contract. In T. Carney, G. Ramia and A. Yeatman (eds) *Contractualism and Citizenship: Law in Context*. Victoria: Bundoora.

Sullivan, E. and Simon, W. (1998) The client: a social, psychological, and behavioral look at the unseen patron of prostitution. In J.E. Elias, V.L. Bullough, V. Elias and G. Brewer (eds) *Prostitution: On Whores, Hustlers, and Johns*. Amherst, N.Y.: Prometheus Books.

Sullivan, H.S. (1953) *The Interpersonal Theory of Psychiatry*. New York: Norton.

Summary Offences Act 1953 (South Australian Consolidated Acts), online, available at: www.austlii.edu.au. Viewed 16 August 2010.

Summary Offences Act 1988 (Federal), online, available at: www.austlii.edu.au. Viewed 15 August 2010.

Sumner, C. (1994) *The Sociology of Deviance: An Obituary*. New York: Continuum.

Taylor, P., Richardson, J., Yeo, A., Marsh, I., Trobe, K. and Pilkington, A. (1996) *Sociology in Focus*. Ormskirk: Causeway Press.

Thériault, J. (1998) Assessing intimacy with the best friend and the sexual partner during adolescence: the PAIR-M inventory. *Journal of Psychology*, vol. 132, no. 5, pp. 493–506.

Thompson Jr, E.H., Grisanti, C. and Pleck, J.H. (1985) Attitudes toward the male role and their correlates. *Sex Roles*, vol. 13, nos 7–8, pp. 413–427.

Touching Base Inc. (2009) *Our Principles*. Touching Base Inc. Newtown. Online, available at: www.touchingbase.org/about.html. Viewed 15 August 2010.

Turner, J.H. and Stets, J.E. (2006) Sociological theories of human emotions. *Annual Review of Sociology*, pp. 25–52.

UN Special Rapporteur on Violence Against Women (1999, May 20) *Position Paper on the Draft Protocol to Prevent, Suppress and Punish Trafficking in Persons, Especially Women and Children*. Submitted to the 4th Session of the Ad hoc Committee on the Elaboration of a Convention Against Transnational Organized Crime (A/ac.254/CRP.13). United Nations, Vienna, Austria, pp. 1–35.

Vance, C.S. (1991) Anthropology rediscovers sexuality: a theoretical comment. *Social Science and Medicine*, vol. 33, no. 8, pp. 875–884.

Vanwesenbeeck, I. (2001) Another decade of social scientific work on sex work: a review of research, 1990–2000. *Annual Review of Sex Research*, vol. 12. pp. 242–289.

Ward, T. and Brown, M. (2004) The good lives model and conceptual issues in offender rehabilitation. *Psychology, Crime and Law*, vol. 10, no. 3, pp. 243–257.

Waskul, D. D. and Plante, R. F. (2010) Sex(ualities) and symbolic interaction. *Symbolic Interaction*, vol. 33, no. 2, pp. 148–162.

Waterman, A.S. (1993) Two conceptions of happiness: contrasts of personal expressiveness (eudaimonia) and hedonic enjoyment. *Journal of Personality and Social Psychology*, vol. 64, no. 4, pp. 678–691.

Weitzer, R. (1999) Prostitution control in America: rethinking public policy'. *Crime, Law and Social Change*, vol. 32, no. 1, pp. 83–102.

Weitzer, R. (2005) New directions in research on prostitution. *Crime, Law and Social Change*, vol. 43, pp. 211–235.

Weitzer, R. (2009) Sociology of sex work. *Annual Review of Sociology*, vol. 35, pp. 213–234.

West, C. and Zimmerman, D. H. (1987) Doing gender. *Gender and society*, vol. 1, no. 2, pp. 125–151.

White, F., Hayes, B. and Livesy, D. (2010) *Developmental Psychology*. Frenchs Forest, NSW: Pearson Australia.

Winick, C. (1962) Prostitutes' clients' perception of the prostitute and of themselves. *International Journal of Social Psychiatry*, vol. 8, no. 4, pp. 289–297.

Wilcox, A., Christmann, K., Rogerson, M. and Birch, P. (2009) Tackling the demand for prostitution: a rapid evidence assessment of the published research literature. Project Report. Home Office. Online, available at: http://eprints.hud.ac.uk/7178/1/Kris.pdf. Viewed 4 July 2011.

World Health Organisation (WHO) (2006) Defining sexual health. Online, available at: www.who.int/reproductivehealth/topics/sexual_health/sh_definitions/en/index.html. Viewed 19 October 2012.

Xantidis, L. and McCabe, M.P. (2001) Personality characteristics of male clients of female commercial sex workers in Australia. *Archives of Sexual Behaviour*, vol. 29, no. 2, pp. 165–176.

Zheng, W., Xudong, Z., Chi, Z., Wei, L., Lu, L. and Hesketh, T. (2011) Detraditionalisation and attitudes to sex outside marriage in China. *Culture, Health and Sexuality: An International Journal for Research, Intervention and Care*, vol. 13, no. 5, pp. 497–511.

Glossary of terms

This glossary has been devised to explain the terms used in this book. It has been informed by glossaries prepared by the following organisations/agencies, which work alongside the sex work industry:

- Sex worker awareness for everyone (Safe Collingwood): online, available at: http://safeincollingwood.ca/faq/glossary-of-terms/.
- ProCon: online, available at: http://prostitution.procon.org/view.resource. php?resourceID=000124.
- Sex work activists, allies and you (SWAAY): online, available at: www. swaay.org/glossary.html.
- United Nations: online, available at: www.un.org/en/pseataskforce/over-view.shtml and www.unodc.org/unodc/en/human-trafficking/smuggling-of-migrants.html.

(Viewed 15 January 2013)

Brothel   A house, apartment, or other property where 'sexual services' are sold.

Criminalisation   Also referred to as prohibition; criminalisation is a government's absolute ban on a given form of sex work, generally used when speaking of prostitution.

Decriminalisation   The removal of laws relating to offences in the criminal code concerning sex work.

Exiting   The process of transition the person undergoes as they distance themselves from work in the sex industry and/or sex trade.

Exploitation   Taking advantage of a person experiencing inequality (i.e. poverty, homelessness, etc.) using force, fraud, coercion, power, finances or exchange.

John, Trick, Date, Customer, Client   Someone who trades or buys sexual services.

Legalisation   Permitting prostitution under regulated conditions, for example, government control over the lives and businesses of those who work as sex workers.

Massage Parlour   An establishment where customers (men) can purchase a massage, at times this can include sexual services.

People Smuggling   A crime involving the procurement for financial or other material benefit of illegal entry of a person into a state of which that person is not a national or resident.

Provider   A term used by some sex workers to describe themselves. It is especially common with sex workers who offer new age, tantric, or 'spiritual sex' services.

Pimp   A person who manipulates and/or controls and uses power over a sex worker for profit.

Prohibition   A legal approach that, when applied to sex work, aims to eliminate all forms of paid sex through making prostitution or certain activities associated with prostitution illegal.

Prostitute   One who engages in sexual intercourse or performs sexual acts in exchange for payment.

Prostitution   The act of engaging in sexual intercourse or performing other sexual acts in exchange for payment.

Sex Industry   Encompassing all forms of sex work such as prostitution, web cam services, cyber sex, dancing, massage, S&M, pornography, etc.

Sex Work   Work specific to the sex trade and/or sex industry.

Sex Worker   A person, such as an escort/prostitute, porn star, stripper, dominatrix, phone sex operator, sensual masseuse, or web cam performer who exchanges their own sexual labour or sexual performance for compensation. Sex workers are part of the larger sex industry, which includes movie directors, club owners, webmasters, retail stores, and more, Sex workers are distinct because their job involves making money from their own sexual labour, not writing about, photographing, managing, or selling the sexual labour or performances of others. The term 'sex work' was coined in the early 1980s by Carol Leigh, and was popularised by a 1987 anthology of the same name. (Derogatory words and phrases of the past are: prostitute, hooker, whore, ho, scarlet, streetwalker).

Sexual Exploitation   Any actual or attempted abuse of a position of vulnerability, differential power, or trust, for sexual purposes, including, but not limited to, profiting monetarily, socially or politically from the sexual exploitation of another.

Trafficking   'Human trafficking' is illegal in most countries and is a complex issue of labour, class, choice, and migration, but it is most commonly associated with the sex work industry, even though most 'human trafficking' is within industries such as agriculture and domestic labour (e.g. fruit-pickers and nannies). Trafficking involving the sex work industry typically involves underage sex trafficking and slavery by groups whose actions bring into disrepute *consensual* sex work.

Index

Page numbers in *italics* denote tables, those in **bold** denote figures.